Beatniks

Toby Litt was born in 1968. He grew up in Ampthill, Bedfordshire. He was educated in Oxford and East Anglia. From 1990 to 1993 he lived in Prague. He is the author of *Adventures in Capitalism*. He lives in London.

Also by Toby Litt

Adventures in Capitalism

Beatniks

An English Road Movie

TOBY LITT

Secker & Warburg

LONDON

First published 1997

1 3 5 7 9 10 8 6 4 2

First published in the United Kingdom in 1997 by
Martin Secker & Warburg
Random House, 20 Vauxhall Bridge Road, London SW1V 2SA

Random House Australia (Pty) Limited
20 Alfred Street, Milsons Point, Sydney,
New South Wales 2061, Australia

072509981

Random House New Zealand Limited
18 Poland Road, Glenfield,
Auckland 10, New Zealand

Random House South Africa (Pty) Limited
Endulini, 5A Jubilee Road, Parktown 2193, South Africa

Random House UK Limited Reg. No. 954009

**A CIP catalogue record for this book
is available from the British Library**

Papers used by Random House UK Limited are natural,
recyclable products made from wood grown in sustainable forests.
The manufacturing processes conform to the environmental
regulations of the country of origin.

ISBN 0 436 20371 5

Printed and bound in Great Britain
by Mackays of Chatham PLC, Chatham, Kent

When was the last time you created a generation?

Seymour Krim

Prologue

Friday, 29th July, 1966

It is very early in the morning, perhaps.

Dylan has been up for three days straight, trying to come down from the high of his latest tour. He wants to persuade his wife, Sara, out of bed. The room is quite cold. He is already out of bed, standing by the window. He tells her – in the half-dark – he wants to ride his motorcycle to the repair shop, get the gears fixed. Something like that. It is just the latest of his whims.

Sara is a very weighty and very maternal young woman – heavy face, heavy limbs, heavy breasts. Dylan's type, it could be said. Her gaze is always judgement, and this Dylan enjoys – especially when, as now, it is a judgement he is outraging.

After groaning darkly, Sara gets up and starts to dress herself. She almost always obeys Bobby's whims. She loves him.

It is likely that Sara moves slowly. She is eight months pregnant with Jesse, their first child.

Dylan goes to sit in a chair in the corner in the half-light, watching. He is enjoying her annoyance almost as much as her compliance. He is aware that she is aware of this.

'I'll go get ready,' Dylan says. 'Yes?'

'Yeah,' says Sara.

Dylan walks through the house. His Cuban heels clang out upon the brick floor. He hums.

This may very well not have happened.

Dylan walks out into the dirt yard.

This latest version of Dylan is the most perfect yet. He is a very beautiful, very wasted young man. His face is an almost perfect hexagon. His Afroish hair, when tamed, transcribes three-quarters of a circle. It seems as if his appearance might be described by a very short, very simple, very beautiful mathematical equation.

Over the past couple of weeks, Dylan has been trying to take fewer of the amphetamines that have carried him this far. He is afraid that too much more of the stuff will turn his teeth to chalk and his mind to jelly. It has been alleged.

His friend, Bob Neuwirth, may be the one who drives the speed up from New York City. It comes in funny-coloured pills that people end up writing songs about: Purple Hearts, Blue Meanies, Yellow Submarines.

Sara doesn't like all of Dylan's friends equally. Some of them, she believes, are bad for Bobby. This is pure speculation.

'But,' Dylan might reason, 'are they bad in the right way? Does the bad have any issue? If it does, then it's acceptable.'

Some of Dylan's greatest songs – perhaps all of his greatest songs – are songs of pure hate: 'Positively 4th Street', 'Like a Rolling Stone', 'Ballad of a Thin Man'.

Bob Neuwirth always did bring out the kid in Bobby. Over the past week they've gone for whole days repeating the same infuriating phrase in reply to every question. ('You go where you get what's good, brother,' and 'But what it is

4

ain't nothing but which it was.') This they find endlessly amusing.

They spent the week before last believing – or pretending to believe – that the trees around the house were plotting to murder them.

'It's Birnam Wood,' Dylan may have muttered. 'And it's here already.'

But, still, Sara has been trying to remind Dylan of certain good things – eating properly, sleep, their marriage, their adopted child, their child-to-be.

Sara pulls her boots on and follows her husband out into the yard. She hopes she can get back before Anna (their adopted child) wakes up and does any damage to the house or to herself.

This, she thinks, is a stupid idea.

Dylan already has the bike running. He is listening to the engine, revving with his right hand, head cocked.

Half of him wishes he was enough of a mechanic to fix it himself; half doesn't give a shit – he's had other people to get things done for him for years.

Sara gets into the car, starts the engine. She puts the lights on, though it is already light.

But then again, perhaps not.

In the liner notes to his first album (*Bob Dylan*, Columbia, 1962), in reply to the self-posed question, 'If I had a lot of money what would I do?' Dylan definitely gave the answer, 'I would buy a couple of motorcycles,' to which he added, 'a few air conditioners and four or five couches.'

In the four years since, this is pretty much what he has done. His motorcycles, air conditioners and couches; wife, child and house; manager, entourage and legend are all gathered together in Woodstock, upstate New York.

There is a track on Dylan's fourth album, *Another Side of Bob Dylan*, entitled 'Motorpsycho Nightmare'.

On the cover of *Highway 61 Revisited*, his last-but-one album (*Blonde on Blonde* has just been released), Dylan – under his turquoise-and-pink silk shirt – is wearing a white T-shirt bearing the blue legend: Triumph Motorcycles.

It is the 1960s.

It is Friday, 29th July, 1966.

They are now out on the Striebel Road. Dylan ahead on the bike; Sara following in a car. The rattle may have been bothering him for the past couple of days. Or maybe it was the gears, after all.

Dylan is a young man for whom sounds are very important. He has just finished one of the most notorious tours in pop history – gunning his 'wild mercury sound' into viciously hostile audiences: American, English, French and Australian.

At the 1965 Newport Festival, the quiet messiah of acoustic folk had revealed himself to be an electrified disciple of Elvis. He had not been forgiven.

At one concert, in England, someone called him 'Judas'. At another concert, in Ireland, someone called him a 'stuffed Golliwog'. To the English heckler Dylan replied, 'I don't believe you – you're a liar.' He then turned to his Neanderthal drummer, Mickey Jones, and uttered the famous words, 'Play fucking loud.'

His reply to the Irish heckler is not recorded.

The Striebel Road is a lightly gritted but mostly

smoothed-off tarmac. A lot of logging trucks run up and down it.

Dylan has made a great deal of money from his sounds. His album sales are now close to 10,000,000. This is a fact.

Albert Grossman, Dylan's polar-bearish manager, will soon renegotiate his most lucrative client's contract at a double royalty rate. This happened.

Grossman has just set up another sixty-date tour for the fall. This would definitely have taken place.

Silver birch trees approach close to either side of the road. And Dylan is diversifying out of just music.

His speed-freaky first novel, *Tarantula*, is due from Macmillan.

The ABC TV network has paid $100,000, sight unseen, for the as-yet-uncompleted documentary of the '66 tour.

The Triumph's petrol tank, trilling away between Dylan's thighs, is the red of a cherry-flavoured boiled sweet.

But the documentary is in trouble: D. A. Pennebaker, who shot the footage, has quit – complaining about Dylan's amateurish intrusions.

This is on record, somewhere.

Dylan isn't wearing a helmet or gloves. He is a right-handed guitarist, so the fingernails of his right hand are longer and tougher than those on his left hand. His hair still hasn't been cut.

They've done this before – driven to the repair shop. Dylan rides the cycle there, Sara follows in the car and then drives Bobby home. It's an arrangement.

We don't know exactly what kind of car it was. It may possibly have been the red Ford station wagon mentioned in the sleeve notes to Richard and Mimi Farina's album *Reflections in a Crystal Wind*.

(Richard Farina, author of the cult novel *Been Down So Long It Looks Like Up to Me*, died, in early 1966, in a motorcycle accident. For definite.)

They round a corner and something happens, possibly.

Dylan is about to brake, stabbing his foot down too hard, grabbing too hard with his hand, panicked by something evil in his peripheral vision. Or, according to another version, he catches the sun full-on in his eyes and brakes without thinking. Or, Dylan once asserted, he hits an oil slick. Or, just maybe, some unreliable sources claim, there *was* no crash at all: Grossman faked it to get Dylan out of all the contracts he was in no state to fulfil and into a drug rehab centre. But say that we take version one: the Triumph's front wheel will zigzag wildly. The back wheel will skid round to the side, will pivot – Sara is watching – will lift, will flip Dylan over the handlebars. Sara is braking, hard. Dylan will land: half on his shoulder, half on his neck – according to this version. Sara is turning the steering wheel to the right, taking the car up onto the verge. The Triumph will make a few further flips, caroming down the road. Sara, though there is no evidence for this, is starting to call Bobby's name. Dylan will be lying there, without moving. He may or may not be conscious. He may or may not be alive. Sara is thinking about getting Bobby off the road before a car or a truck comes along. Dylan will have cracked a couple of vertebrae and there will be abrasions on his cheeks, hands and knees. He will spend a week in Middletown Hospital and will leave wearing a neck-brace. But not necessarily.

'Bobby!' Sara is or is not screaming, getting out of the car.

Fact: the sixty-date concert-tour will be cancelled.

Fact: *Tarantula* and *Eat the Document* will be put back.

Fact: neither Dylan nor the 1960s will ever be quite the same again.

Dylan is lying on the verge, looking up, seeing his wife's gaze turning, all at once, from judgement to forgiveness.

Maybe.

Part One

I

Saturday, 29th July, 1995

Bongos?

I was standing in front of a plain-looking door on the top landing of a strange house: *Neal's Room*, read a little porcelain lozenge with lilacs interweaving round the edge.

And an acoustic guitar?

Downstairs, I could hear the sounds of the party – the party I was trying to escape, the party I hadn't wanted to come to in the first place.

My temporary friend, Claire, had dragged me along –

('Boys,' she had said. 'Boys will be there.'

'You still call them *boys*?' I said.

'What do you call them?'

I couldn't think of an answer.)

– dragged me along and then dumped me the moment we got through the front door, walking off with a boy. Thanks.

And singing?

After taking a can of lager from the fridge in the kitchen, I'd started to explore the house. In the front room, a load of clubber-types were trying to have a rave; in the garden, some lads were doing their best to keep a football from touching the ground; in the basement, Goths and Gothgirls were silently backcombing each other's hair; in the upstairs living room, Crusties were taking hit after hit from a monster bong.

Claire was nowhere to be seen – so, no shared taxi home.

This was my first party since university, and it wasn't going very well. Neal's Room and the room next door – these were all that I had left. If nothing was going on here, I would leave.

I turned the doorhandle and walked in.

2

Neal's Room was very dark – lit only by some black candles and a bedside-lamp with a red lightbulb. I could still make things out, though.

There were three people in the room: two male, one female – all singing. One of the guys was strumming a battered Spanish guitar, the other was tapping on a set of homemade bongo drums. The bongoist had a goatee beard. The guitarist was wearing a black polo neck. All three of them had bare feet.

My first reaction was to laugh. Was this the fancy-dress floor? Why hadn't anyone told me?

I smiled, expecting them to stop singing.

When they didn't I was left feeling awkward and humiliated.

The air in Neal's Room was layered with incense.

I sat down in the armchair.

They sang a verse about Shakespeare.

It was a Bob Dylan song. As I later learnt, their singing was dogmatically faithful to the original: they followed Dylan's vocal line, his emphases and hesitations, his breathing. There was no harmonising; the three voices approached one.

The room was medium-sized. The two guys were side by side on the edge of the bed. The girl was sitting at their feet.

There was a dark velvet sofa (green, I later found out), covered with stacks of typewritten A4 paper.

The guy playing the bongos looked across at me. Before thinking too much about it, I smiled at him. He looked down to where his hands were hitting the off-yellow skins. The beat skipped for a moment. It was nothing. He was probably drunk, too.

I'd've liked to have thought the bongo guy was cute, but I didn't. It was the guitarist who interested me.

I took another sip of beer and looked down at the carpet.

What would be the best thing to say when they'd finished the song?

I didn't know how long it would go on for, so I didn't know how long I'd have to think.

As far as I could tell, the carpet was deep blue.

I took another sip of beer.

They sang a verse about a wedding.

The bongoist (Neal, if that was his name) looked about twenty. That made him a couple of years younger than I was. He was stocky and I thought (not having seen him stand up) probably a little shorter than me. His hair was gingery-blonde and slightly curly.

They sang a verse about a tea-preacher.

But my attention was focused more and more on the dark-haired guitarist. He was singing with his eyes closed – obviously the leader in the song. He might still be Neal, I guessed – though he didn't *look* like a Neal. He was tall, I could tell, and his fingers were almost too long to play the chords. He had the Dylan-look completely down: the sour cheekbones, the woe-weary eyes, the dangerous lips.

I suddenly became very glad I'd come to this particular party.

I tried to take a sip of beer, but discovered my can was empty.

The girl gave Neal a sympathetic look, and I guessed they were a couple. I hoped so.

I wondered where the guitarist's girlfriend was, and if he had one, and − if he didn't − was he gay?

He looked almost too beautiful to be anything but gay.

They sang a verse about people just getting uglier.

The girl was about eighteen, I thought − or maybe even a bit younger. She was wearing a Beatnik outfit: black polo neck, charcoal slacks. Her hair was long and naturally blonde, but done up in a sex-kittenish coiffure. Her make-up was far too dark and heavy for her complexion. On me it would have been alright, I thought − wishing I'd at least worn eyeliner. Her breasts were bigger than mine and her toenails were painted. Her lips, which I could see in profile, weren't so much beestung as hornet-humped.

Later on, when I got to know her, my private nickname for her would be Budget Bardot.

They sang a verse about a debutante.

How many bloody verses did this song have?

I looked round the room again.

There were lots more posters on the wall, mostly of the same people as on the landing. Neal's pantheon seemed rather limited, if not obsessive: Dylan, Kerouac, Ginsberg, Dean. It also seemed a little adolescent. I'd been into the Beats and all that, briefly, when I was about sixteen. But then I got into Rimbaud and Rilke, Dickinson and Brontë − the originals. Kerouac, I'd thought, was just boy's stuff; and Ginsberg, I'd soon realised, was sub-Blake, sub-Whitman. I liked the look − I still dressed a little Beat (the black, the sandals), but there were other, better things.

In this light, I couldn't make out the title of any of Neal's books – most of them were dark-spined paperbacks.

The song was slowing down. They were about to end. I got ready to say something.

The guitarist opened his eyes – they were green. I've always wanted green eyes.

He looked at me.

Lost and gone for ever.

I started clapping – remembering only halfway through how sarcastic solo applause always sounds.

Also, the applause has, at some point, to stop. So I began speaking before I stopped clapping:

'Bob Dylan, isn't it?' I said. 'He's great.'

'Dylan?' asked the guitarist, his voice rough and low. 'Do you like Dylan?'

'He's great.'

'Yeah,' he said, looking at the other two. Smiles were exchanged.

'Who else do you like?' the bongoist asked.

'Oh, lots of people.'

'Cool,' said the girl.

'You're Neal, right?' I said to the bongoist.

'Good guess.'

'I'm Mary. I saw your name on the door.'

'Dylan is God,' said the guitarist.

'Oh,' I said, about to try and be funny. 'I thought Clapton was God.'

(I'd had a boyfriend at university into all things rawk. He'd wanted to take me to one of God's gigs at the Royal Albert Hall. Luckily, we'd split up long before it came round.)

'He's the new guitarist with John Mayall's Bluesbreakers, isn't he?'

'What? No – Eric Clapton. You know, "Layla".'

'Layla?' said the girl. 'Is that a girl's name?'

'It sounds like it, I suppose,' said Neal.

'You haven't heard of "Layla"?' I asked.

'No,' said the guitarist. 'We haven't.'

'What about you?' I asked the girl.

'Is it a group or a singer?' she replied.

I turned to Neal. 'And you?'

There was a clear moment of hesitation. He frowned to try and cover it, only making it more obvious. The other two looked at him, viciously. He dropped his eyes to his drumskins.

'No,' he said. 'No, I haven't.'

Why are you lying? I thought.

'"Layla", it's an AOR classic.'

'Ay Oh Ah?' said the girl, looking puzzled.

'Adult-Oriented Radio,' I said.

'We don't dig the radio,' said the guitarist. 'It's all square out there. We don't dig square cats. The radio's all wrong.'

'And which *we* is that?' I was beginning to feel angry, frustrated at being out of the loop.

I was also aware that I'd done nothing but ask aggressive questions since we'd started talking.

'*We*,' said the guitarist. 'Neal and me and my chick.'

'Your *chick*! Are you his *chick*?'

'Yeah,' she said, reaching across for a cigarette. 'I'm Jack's chick.'

'Jack?' I said, looking at Jack.

Shit, he has a chick – I mean, he calls women chicks.

'Yes, Mary?' he said.

'What's your *chick's* name, Jack?'

'We call the chick "Maggie".'

'But is that your real name?' I asked.

'It is now.'

'What does that mean?'

'If Jack says so, I guess that's what it is. I can dig that.'

'You don't even decide your own name?'

'Things change. Names change. Keeping the same name is just too square, sister.'

'I'm quite happy with my name,' I said, primly – and I'm *never* prim.

'It's a hip name,' said Neal.

Something had been bothering me – I'd worked quite a lot out, but I wanted confirmation before I left.

'What's wrong with the radio?' I asked. 'Isn't God on it enough?'

'Oh, man,' said Jack. 'It would take too long to lay this jive on you.' He strummed a chord, then looked me up and down. 'And I don't think you'd get hip to it even then. Chicks don't usually get Dylan.'

'I'm *hip* to plenty – and I'm not a *chick* – and what exactly don't we get about Dylan?'

'Which *we* is that?' asked Neal, but then looked rather ashamed.

It seemed that he, at least, wasn't enjoying being nasty to me. He wasn't very good at it, either.

Maggie – or whatever she was called – was coolly adding to the smoke in the room. I noticed her brand: Chesterfields.

'Everything,' said Jack, after another chord. 'You chicks miss everything – you miss that Dylan is the last wild true bop poet of the pure fast Beat school, which is not a school, straight mantle-inheritor of the dharma of Ginsberg and Kerouac, Burroughs and Ferlinghetti – line traceable way back through Rimbaud/Verlaine, Whitman to Blake and other wild cats of the long-gone crazy past – masters of spontaneous bop prosody – with Dylan died Beat, for a long sad temporary time, and everything went wrong – including radio.'

'But Dylan's alive,' I said. 'It may be unfortunate at times, especially when he sings, but he is.'

'No,' said Neal. 'Dylan's dead.'

'So, when did he die?'

'He died on July 29th, 1966,' said Neal. 'We're having this party to celebrate the 29th anniversary of his death. Glad you could make it.'

'Well, then,' I said, standing up. 'I hope you enjoy it, because I'm going to beam back down to planet Earth.'

I looked at Jack.

What a waste.

'Bye-bye,' I said.

'I told you chicks don't get it with Dylan.'

I looked at Neal. He seemed about to say something to Jack, something like, *Shut up!* I waited, giving him the opportunity.

'Neal?' asked Jack.

Neal patted the higher-pitched bongo a couple of times and hummed.

'Nice party, Neal,' I said, 'especially the bit downstairs – where the normal people are.'

'Yeah,' said Jack, sneering. 'Go join the other squares!'

'Oh, stop pretending to be American,' I said.

I looked at Maggie.

'You're not a *chick*, okay?'

'The squares are waiting,' she said, cutting me.

'Better a *square* than a –'

'Oblong?' put in Jack.

'No,' I said. But I couldn't think of anything apart from *cunt*, and I hated saying that.

I stomped out the door and across the landing.

'Jack!' said Neal. 'Did you have to —?'

'Shh!' said Jack. He started playing a sequence of chords. 'Square chick is still tuned in,' he crooned.

It was true. I'd stopped at the top of the stairs.

I rarely stormed out of anywhere, and I was curious what effect my exit had had.

'So,' said Jack, 'as we've got an audience.'

He finished the intro and began singing 'Sad Eyed Lady of the Lowlands'.

There, on the landing floor, outside Neal's Room, I could see their shoes — all piled on top of each other.

I understood later on that, when I'd walked in on them, what they'd been doing was acting cool in order to test me — to see if I was hip or square.

Looking back, I could see that I really squared out. I'm surprised they ever wanted anything to do with me again.

Just before I left the room, I had sensed that Jack — even though he wasn't looking at me — was sending me a message: it was a sideways smile, conveyed only by understood attitude. He knew I'd feel it, if he sent it — and I did.

But what the smile said, I didn't yet understand.

In Dylan's version 'Sad Eyed Lady of the Lowlands' takes up the whole of the fourth side of *Blonde on Blonde* and, according to the timings given on the record label, lasts exactly eleven minutes twenty-three seconds.

I don't know how long Maggie and Jack and Neal took to sing it, but I must have been out of the house long before they reached the final verse.

As I walked to the bus station, I was embarrassed to find myself remembering the way Jack had looked at me, in between insults – remembering, that is, with pleasure.

I wondered if Maggie had noticed.

He had very pale skin, dimples, stained teeth.

(Why is it, I wonder, that I've always been attracted to people with bad teeth? Not bad as in rotten, but bad as in badly arranged, too close together, overlapping.)

Thinking about Jack's teeth was dangerous – I was almost admitting to myself that I found someone who called me a *chick* sexually attractive.

'He's a prick,' I kept saying to myself.

By the time I got home and snuggled down into my bed, fairly sobered up, I was on to thoughts of Maggie – jealous thoughts – thoughts of what she might, just conceivably be doing at that exact moment: what? and where? and for how long? and how well?

She was two or three years younger than me and, I was sure, now that I thought about it, quite a bit less attractive. Certainly not Jack's type, really.

I did wish I was just that little bit smaller, that my lips were just that little bit fuller; and, of course, I wished I weighed less. But, even given the choice, I'd rather have looked like me than Maggie.

Given the choice, I was pretty sure Jack would choose me over Maggie, as well.

Yes, but that was the problem.
Given the choice.
Given the choice.

3

The first things I saw when I opened my eyes the following morning were the glass of stale water and the giant spider plant on my bedside table.

For no particular reason, I began to count the leaves on the plant. First I counted those I could see from where I lay, without moving my head.

Twenty-three. My age.

Next, I got up on one elbow and counted every single leaf, including the baby ones. It took three goes, one to check. Sixty-six. The year Dylan died.

My arm was getting stiff. I fell back on the pillow, my eyes closed. I gave myself ten counted seconds to think of three good reasons for not going back to sleep.

I could only think of two:

– that I was hungry

– that I didn't want my dad to call me a lazy layabed lummox ever again.

But I got up anyway and put on my ultra-sloppies: an old grey sweatshirt, some leggings, wool socks, Adidas trainers.

Checking in on the bathroom mirror, on the way downstairs, I saw the sort of face usually pictured above the caption: 'Found in woods nearby her home'.

O

My mum was in the kitchen when I slunk in.

Groan.

'You know what your father would call you,' she said.

'A lazy layabed lummox,' I said, without missing a beat.

'He would,' she said, genuinely surprised that I'd known.

'Which is exactly why you should divorce him.'

'I beg your pardon.'

Neither of my parents appreciate this sort of humour – my sort of humour. To be honest, they find slapstick a little highbrow. What really tickles them is dog-exploits and poo-jokes. (If your joke manages to involve a dog-poo-exploit, the sofa will rock.)

'Sorry, Mum, I expect it's why you married him.'

'You're in a strange mood today, I can tell.'

What is it with mothers? How do they always end up hitting on the right solution after closely examining all the wrong clues?

'Was it a nice party?'

I went to the fridge – bad move.

Just opening the door was enough to put me off solids for the rest of the day. It wasn't dirty or smelly or anything, it was just that it contained butter, full-fat milk, cream, bacon, cheese, suet, lard.

Well, not quite *lard* – but almost. Suet is just lard in disguise, isn't it?

I could have extracted my soya marg and soya milk from deep in the calorific depths, but I decided to stick to the Tesco's Own Brand orange juice.

'Was it a nice party?'

'Sorry, Mum, yes.'

'Well, you seem to have enjoyed it.'

After pouring out a large glass of orange juice, I decided

against it. It was just too orange – so orange, it hurt. I would have dry toast, instead – and black coffee.

'Do we have any other bread?'

'Did you meet anyone nice?'

I was now beside the bread-bin.

'Oh, there were some people, you know.'

'The brown's in the freezer, if you want to toast it.'

'Right,' I said.

'There usually are.'

I bent down and opened the freezer compartment. Did I *really* want toast?

'What, Mum?'

'There usually are people at parties. That's what parties are for, unless I'm mistaken.'

I opened the fridge door again.

'Do we have any grapefruit juice?'

'It's alright if it's classified. But just tell me if it's classified.'

'No, Mum. I'm just trying to get my shit together.'

She hates it when I say *shit*.

'The grapefruit juice is in the cupboard on the left.'

'But it won't be cold.'

'We'll see you when we get back from the park.'

That sounded interesting. My parents never usually *saw* me.

Mum went and fetched Dad from the living room, where he was working on his computer.

My place in the family, when I left for university, had been taken by a small, combative Jack Russell: Rufus.

It was Rufus that my parents were taking to the park, probably for the second time that day.

'You're a lazy layabed lummox,' my dad said, as he walked past the kitchen door.

Rufus started barking when he saw Dad sitting down and taking his slippers off.

There was no escape: these were and would always be *My Parents*.

I sat down at the dining table with my breakfast in my hand: a glass of lukewarm Tesco's Own Brand grapefruit juice.

Groan.

My parents went off down the garden path.

Had I met any nice people? I really wasn't sure any more.

My dad is a mathematician. I don't really understand the kind of maths he does – only that it is applied, not pure. (He has a joke about this which it would literally *kill* me to tell you.) For most of his working life he has been involved with computers. This began back in the days when they were the kind of thing you'd see in Cold War spy movies: a huge room full of American-sized fridge-freezers, each with two reels of tape twitching back and forth on its forehead. He had to put on a white boiler suit, a hair net, and spend all day working in a dust-free environment.

He had come to Ampthill – a sleepy town in Bedfordshire – to work for Hunting Engineering, an MOD subcontractor. He'd been married to Mum for five years by then, living in Portsmouth. I was on the way.

When I used to ask him about what he did, he'd reply – all serious and everything – 'I'm afraid I can't tell you. That's classified information.' If ever my parents asked me anything I didn't want to tell them, I just said *Classified*.

When the other kids at Russell Primary School asked me what my dad did, I told them he was an astronaut. What he *actually* did was something to do with guidance systems for Intercontinental Ballistic Missiles.

However, my dad had given up being a full-time Destroyer-of-Worlds the previous summer. His mega-pension had started to kick in, but Huntings kept him on in 'a consultative capacity'. This meant he spent a lot of time e-mailing replies to technical queries.

My mum has also spent most of her life working in a dust-free environment – only that dust-free environment happens to be our house, and her work mostly involves keeping it that way.

My mum is very loving, but has always been very strict.

She's relaxed a bit in recent years, but once upon a time there were hundreds of things that she – implicitly – considered to be works of the devil. Among these were: Smash Instant Mashed Potato, bubblegum, banana milkshakes, Mike Read's *Breakfast Show* on Radio 1, boys who wore slip-on shoes, girls below the age of consent with pierced ears, anyone at all who held their knife like a pen, Pot Noodles, microwave ovens, John Travolta and Olivia Newton John, hair dye, dirty fingernails, Space Dust, Sodastreams and Breville Snack-and-Sandwichmakers, Labour MPs, skateboards and BMX bikes (especially on the pavement), Boy George (especially on *Top of the Pops*), answerphones, hot-air balloons, Frosties, Children's ITV, diets, taxis.

But it wasn't like she was mad or anything.

As it turned out, my parents didn't want to *see* me in any major way. We sat down at the dining table a little more formally than usual – and they had tea and biscuits, so I knew I wouldn't be able to get away for at least a quarter of an hour – but all they wanted to say was:

'We're worried about you.'

'It's good you've started going out again.'

'We're not putting any pressure on you.'

'It's nothing like an ultimatum.'

'We're very interested in your progress.'

'It's a good time to start thinking about what you want to do in life.'

'We're not going to throw you out on to the streets.'

'It's alright.'

'We're happy if you're happy.'

'It's *The Archers* on in a minute.'

Afterwards, I went up to my bedroom and cried for half an hour. Then I sat down and rewrote my CV.

Monday, I decided, would be a brand-new start: I would go into town and buy myself the perfect summer dress; I would take all my unread books back to Bedford Library; I would maybe, perhaps, completely by accident, bump into Jack.

4

I took the 142 bus into Bedford, sitting on my own, upstairs, a bag of books between my feet.

My dad had wanted the car for shopping, so I hadn't been able to borrow it.

I have always enjoyed leaving Ampthill.

The 142 drove up Greensand Ridge. When it reached the top, I looked out over the view. Down in the middle-distance were the London Brick Company chimneys – not as many as there used to be. The train line to London and Brighton ran along the far left of my vision.

Yes, I wanted a magic summer dress – something that would make my breasts look bigger and my waist slimmer, something that would make gorgeous young men fall in love with me.

The bus swooped down through some scraggy trees. In a moment, Houghton House would be visible – pink, ghostly, derelict, a hide-and-seek Mecca.

Hunting Engineering would go by on our right.

Bedford was twenty minutes away.

I thought I'd have a fairly good chance of seeing Jack if I checked out the record shops, the bookshops, the charity shops and looked into a couple of pubs. He might even be in the library.

I got out one of the books and started browsing it.

Perhaps I'd renew this one, after all.

The bus station was crowded. Prams were being offloaded from double-deckers. Boys in tracksuits were throwing chips at each other and fizzing cans of Coke onto the floor. A bunch of oldsters with their brown tartan wheelies were sitting beside the Photo-Me Booth.

I walked across the pigeon-haunted Church Square, then down the alley between BHS and Woolies. It brought me out, as I'd intended, almost opposite Our Price.

Jack wasn't in there, nor in Smiths.

I came out the front of the Harpur Centre. There was Bedford Central Lending Library: tall and lumpy, concrete and glass. I went in and up the escalator.

The library was okay by me: I liked the filter coffees that they served in the snack bar upstairs; I liked to hang out among the stacks, eavesdropping and people-watching.

Boldly, I returned all my books. I could survive without them, I knew I could.

New start. New start.

I realised – if I was to hold true to my pretence – I should really start looking for the magic summer dress.

Walking down Silver Street, I stopped outside a couple of clothes shops but found I couldn't make myself go in. There were *people* inside them – people buying clothes, people who worked there, people who weren't Jack.

I waited at the traffic lights, crossed.

Jack wasn't in Pemberton's either. I looked at a copy of the *Penguin Book of the Beats*, but didn't buy it.

I felt very thirsty and a little faint. I needed a sit-down. I decided to walk round to Alfonse, my favourite café.

○

I was thinking of what to have with my cappuccino when I noticed that Neal was one of the three people serving behind the counter. I've been going into Alfonse for as long as I've been drinking coffee – I might even have had my first coffee there. (My parents are tea people.) This, though, was the first time I'd ever known anybody who worked there.

Neal was spreading something into a white bread sandwich. I glanced at him between the cans of drink on the display shelf. He'd shaved his goatee off since the party and looked better for it.

Pretending I hadn't decided what I was going to order, I stepped aside to let a couple of people go ahead of me. I wanted to make certain that I would be served by Neal.

I wasn't quite sure what I was going to do, but, whatever it was, it was aimed at Jack and not Neal.

He was now taking the money for the sandwich.

I was next in line.

A paperback copy of *On the Road* lay, face down, beside the chopping board.

Neal stepped back from the till.

'Can I help?' he asked, automatically.

'Hello, Neal,' I said.

'Neal?' exclaimed one of the other people behind the counter. It was a fifteen- or sixteen-year-old girl. She looked at him, amused. 'Can I help?' she said to the person behind me.

'What would you like?' asked Neal, inspecting the spatula in his hand.

'Just a cappuccino.'

'Upstairs?'

I usually sat on one of the high stools round the narrow counter in the downstairs room. Non-smoking.

'Okay.'

'I'll bring it up to you,' Neal said.

I started up the stairs, past the sign reading *Heads Must Be Carried Separately*. At the top of the stairs was another sign reading *Duck or Grouse*.

'I'm on break, okay?' I heard Neal say.

'Okay, Matthew. Fifteen minutes, remember.'

Upstairs was a very pale green, washed-out place. As I waited for Neal, I counted the things in the room. There were three tables, eight chairs, one poster reading 'Make It a Milkshake', two spider plants. A single square window looked down into the alley through the leaves of a tree. The floor was a sparkly slime-green. The other tables were covered with empty cups and full ashtrays. I remembered when I used to meet boyfriends here, during lunchbreak and after school.

Neal carried up two cappuccinos, one of them resting on the cover of his copy of *On the Road*.

He put one down on the table in front of me, then sat down with the other – at another table.

I watched as he carefully pulled out his bookmark – a postcard of the two distinctively-shaped airship hangars in Cardington.

Obviously, I was going to have to be the one to speak.

'I was thinking of reading that again.'

Neal looked up.

'I'm not reading it,' he said. 'I'm learning it.'

'By heart?'

'Yes. I'm on page 12.'

'Aren't you going to sit at my table?'

Neal's cup tap-danced round the saucer as he carried it over.

'Sorry I called you Neal.'

'That's okay. You weren't to know.'

'What's your real name?'

He took a moment before saying:

'Matthew.'

I concentrated on sipping my cappuccino. Neal had covered the foam and most of the saucer with a thick layer of powdered chocolate. It was *definitely* the best I'd ever had in Alfonse.

'And what's Jack's real name?'

'I can't tell you that.' He actually looked *scared*.

'Has he threatened you?'

'No. I just don't know. I think it may even be his real name.'

'But it might *not* be?'

Neal took a sip and looked out the window.

'Hmm.'

'What about Maggie?'

Neal hesitated, balancing his spoon on the fluff of his cappuccino.

'Um, Kate – but don't tell her I told you.'

'Am I likely to see her again?'

Neal looked at me directly for the first time. His gaze asked me for help.

'Um, you will if you come along on Friday. We're having a reading.'

'Is that an invitation?'

'Yes,' said Neal. 'It is.'

'That would be great.'

'I'm sorry about Jack,' he said. 'At the party. He gets like that with people sometimes.'

'I understand.'

'He gets like that with me as well. Everyone.'

'Why's that?'

He sat there for a long moment, looking out the window into the leaves of the tree.

'He's a great man – great men are like that. They're under great strain.'

'Did he introduce you to the works of Jack Kerouac?'

I nodded towards Neal's copy of *On the Road*. It was a mushy, fall-apart paperback – held together by nothing but love and history. On the cover was that famous photograph of Jack Kerouac and Neal Cassady, leaning up against a barn door, squinting into the light, somewhere in 1940s America.

'Jack introduced me to everything.'

'Not to any girls, though?'

'Jack has no problem with chicks. They love him.'

'You're not answering my question.'

'I have to get back downstairs. Can you find your way back to my house?'

It hadn't been anything *like* fifteen minutes.

'I think I could.'

'I'll write you the address down if –'

'Neal, I *can*.'

'We'll meet up there at five, before we go down to the reading.'

'Are you reading anything?'

Neal nodded. 'But Jack mainly.'

'Poetry?'

'Mine's mostly poetry. Jack's written down some of his dreams, as well. He might read those. Jack has great dreams.'

'Don't we all?'

Neal stood up.

'Stay as long as you like,' he said. 'I'll bring you up another, if you want.' He gestured towards my empty coffee cup. 'You won't have to pay.'

'That's very kind of you, Neal. But I think I'll leave it for now. Maybe another time.'

I stood up. Neal picked up my cup.

'Any time,' he said, tracing the edge of the saucer with his thumb.

He let me go down the stairs in front of him.

'See you Friday, Matthew,' I said.

'Yeah,' he said.

'Who's she?' asked the girl who'd laughed.

I'm not really used to things going *just* the way I want them. When they do, I get high on it. Things start to appear in front of me that I wouldn't otherwise have seen.

The day had become a very lovely early summer day. The skies were taller. People moved more sexily down the streets, freer within their own limbs, as if they could afford to be more generous with the world, and it with them.

My sense of balance felt unusually acute.

There, in the window of Next, was the summer dress – but I didn't want it any more: I was going to wear black and smoke pot; I was going to attend poetry readings; I was going to become a Beatnik.

Something about that whole lifestyle suddenly appealed to me. I felt like being an adolescent again, even if only nostalgically, ironically, temporarily.

On the way to the bus station, I stopped in at Andy's Records and bought a tape of *Blonde on Blonde* – the album with the songs they'd been singing at the party.

The summer had found its soundtrack and its style.

When I got home, I would get my copy of *On the Road* down from the attic.

I might even write a poem or two – though I doubted that Jack would let a mere *chick* perform at his reading.

5

In fact, I lived in such abject sloth during the week leading up to the reading that I wrote nothing, not even my diary. I ate a lot of fresh fruit, though – and tried to drink lots of chilled water. And I did manage to get through *On the Road*, though I skipped quite a bit towards the end.

The night before the reading, Thursday, I had one of my epic Indulgence Baths.

I laid six of my mum's powercut candles along the avocado edge of the tub, next to the avocado wall tiles.

Marie Claire and *Cosmopolitan* lay on the non-fluffy avocado bathmat, beside the large plate of soggy toast and Marmite.

I brought my portable tape-player through from the bedroom – Miles Davis, *A Kind of Blue*. (The only jazz album I had.)

A bottle of chilled white Burgundy and a glass waited, behind the taps.

There was Body Shop lavender oil in the water, making slidy little slicks round the plug chain.

Last thing, I emptied a just-boiled kettle into the water – to make it even more sinfully move-and-you're-scorched hot.

And for an hour at least of lovely luck, neither my mum nor my dad knocked on the door.

I had a little underwater wank, shaved my legs, finished the wine and felt incredibly sophisticated for the rest of the evening.

My dad's car was a silver P-reg Vauxhall Chevette L 4-door, absolutely pristine. Its brown plaid seat covers were unworn and the ashtray had never seen a cigarette. A pine-fragrance Magic Tree always swung from the rear-view mirror. It had just passed its nth MOT.

I parked opposite Neal's house and sat for a moment, getting it together.

One final time, I checked myself in the rear-view mirror: I'd put on much more eyeliner than usual, and had experimented with mascara. I thought I looked witchy and sexy.

My clothes, I hoped, were the kind that Jack would approve of: leather sandals, black jeans, Breton long-sleeve T-shirt.

I'd held back at the beret, though I did own one.

As I crossed the road in front of Neal's house, I could see a piece of A4 paper stuck up in the living-room window.

It turned out to be a carbon copy of the invitation, typed out on an old-fashioned mechanical typewriter:

```
Neal reading manuscript of late great Otto Lang &
own poems -- Jack, own poems only -- other from
the floor and (perhaps) ceiling -- all sharp new
straightforward writing -- remarkable pair of
angelheaded hipsters on one stage reading their
poetry -- no charge, small collection for wine --
witness Bedford's own renaissance. Be there or be
square, cats. Charming Event II.

     8pm Friday Night  August 4th 1995
   Lecture Room, Bedford Library, Harpur Street
```

Written at the bottom, in Neal's handwriting, or so I guessed, were the words: 'Ask inside for further details.'

There were plaster faces set into the lintels above the semi's two front doors. They were human, male, but lionish.

My delaying tactics all used up, I knocked on the door and waited.

It was Neal's mother who answered. She was a frazzled-looking woman, about fifty, with something gypsyish in her colouring. Her eyeliner had begun to seep out along her crow's-feet. Between her brown fingers was a very tight roll-up.

'Mary!' she said, as if I was a cousin. Then, looking over what I was wearing: 'Very period. Very *then*.'

Her lips pursed as she spoke, as if her words or her teeth tasted sour.

I was glad she didn't embrace me: her perfume would have effaced mine for the rest of the evening.

When she turned round, to walk away from me, I saw that the black dress she was wearing was backless – her figure was good, even down to the Marilyn Monroe bum and belly. I also saw that her dry black hair was held off her face by a large butterfly clip.

Halfway down the hall, she said:

'You don't want to meet my husband, do you? I wouldn't if I were you – it would probably put you off Neal forever.'

She turned to face me.

'Unfortunately, I have to assure you that he *is* the father – much to my shame.'

When she wasn't speaking, she looked at a point about six inches above your head. For a moment, I wondered whether I was developing an undeserved halo – then I realised it was an anti-double-chin measure.

I thought she'd finished with me.

She went through the doorway to the kitchen, holding the roll-up between forefinger and thumb. When she came back, it was gone.

'Don't worry, Mary, Neal's told me everything. He's upstairs, squatting in his *estaminet* – his room at the top. Jack and Maggie are there – probably spliffed out of their little heads. I should have offered you some, I know – a little tokey-wokey for our guest – but it would have had middle-aged slobber all over it. Jack's spliffy is always much better quality than mine. Go on up, then. They're waiting for you.' I started up the stairs. 'Quietly,' she added, as an afterthought.

'Who was it?' a low male voice asked from the kitchen.

'It's Mary . . .'

I hurried discreetly out of earshot, not wanting to hear Neal's mother's verdict – though I thought it would probably be positive.

On Neal's landing, I took my sandals off and placed them with the other shoes outside his door.

I passed a fluttery hand over my hair to smooth it out; then, deciding this wasn't desirable, I ran my fingers through it a couple of times – as if scrunch-drying.

Then I knocked, fingers crossed.

No answer. Another knock. No answer. Another two louder knocks.

'Hello?' I said, opening the door just enough to see in.

Neal's room was empty, but someone had been around quite recently. Cigarette smoke was hanging in the air and a stick of incense was still burning.

Something moved on the sofa, coming towards me. It was a black cat.

I picked it up – which it seemed to like – and began to look round the room.

As always, I started with the bookcase. Neal's library was pretty predictable, given his posters: Kerouac, Burroughs, Ginsberg, Corso, Dostoyevsky, Sartre. Books on jazz. Dylan songbooks. Jackson Pollock. Munch. Some weird-looking books by a Lobsang T. Rampa. Also, unexpectedly, some thrillers by Len Deighton and John le Carré.

Then I looked along the spines of his records. There were all the early Dylan albums, but none of the later stuff. No *Blood on the Tracks*, no *Infidels*. Hard to write songs, I guess, when you're dead. There was a huge amount of jazz: Charlie Parker, Miles Davis, Billie Holiday, Dizzy Gillespie. But something about the whole collection was a little odd. Then I realised: there wasn't a single record from when Neal would have been growing up. No *Grease*, no *Kids from Fame*. Nothing with a high embarrassment or nostalgia quotient. Nothing later than, when? – I wasn't too sure of the dates – the end of the 1960s, maybe.

Neal's desk looked one of the two ways I imagined the desk of a writer to look – either very tidy or very messy. Neal's was very, very tidy: Underwood typewriter, anglepoise, shiny leather satchel, copy of *Howl*.

After five minutes or so, I decided to try the other room.

I carried the cat onto the landing, feeling like Holly Golightly, shifted it onto one arm and knocked on the door.

Again there was no reply.

Perhaps I had better go downstairs and encounter the mother again.

This was a door I was far less certain I should open – but I did, anyway.

O

Yes, there they were. But I noticed them only peripherally. The room was very pale. The walls were cornflower blue. The ceiling was white. The floor was covered by a white sheet, held taut by white-painted bricks lining the wainscot. I feigned a squint, unseen, for my own pleasure, as I walked in.

Jack, Neal and Maggie were sitting, cross-legged, in a line – facing away from me and towards an empty white plinth. On the floor, before this homemade altar, were three little dots of colour – an apple, an orange, a lemon. Behind the plinth, tacked to the wall, was a pencil drawing of the Buddha, jolly and fat, with huge earlobes.

The cat flipped itself over backwards, out of my arms. It landed almost silently, then padded over to Neal.

His hands were held out on either side of him, thumb and forefinger touching, other fingers stretched out. Some kind of secret-meaning meditation thing, I thought.

The cat went up to him and rubbed its eyelids against his fingers. Neal's head twitched – shocked by the sudden slink of the cat's fur

He took a deep calm-down breath, then spoke:

'Mary? Could you take Koko out on the landing and close the door?'

'Okay,' I said, immediately realising speech was the wrong thing.

As I went to pick Koko up from Neal's side, careful not to touch him, I glanced along the line of them – profile behind profile behind profile, eyes all closed.

Jack didn't seem to have shaved. Maggie, I was glad to see, was again wearing make-up as stagey as my own. Neal's eyelids flicked, sensing I was looking at them all – disturbing their meditation.

Koko didn't want to move; her front claws held on to the sheet. I could feel her muscles hardening, sliding shinily beneath her pelt. Kneeling down, I started to unhook them one by one.

I watched as, eyes closed, Neal reached out to stroke Koko, calm her down. But he aimed too far back and ended up stroking my knee.

At this, his eyes opened. He looked up at me, realising what he'd done. Koko's last claw came loose.

I lifted her up to my chest, standing up. Neal closed his eyes and turned his head forward again. I could see from his ears that he was blushing.

Even from several steps away, black cat hairs were visible on the white of the sheet.

Out on the landing, the door safely closed behind me, I put Koko down again.

Should I go back in and join them? Had I been wrong to go in in the first place, cat or no cat?

I decided that, as I wouldn't even be sure what to do if I *did* join them, I was better off finding myself a book back in Neal's room.

The book I chose was Allen Ginsberg's *Howl and Other Poems* – the worn-out round-edged copy that had been lying on the desk.

I sat down on the sofa. On the coffee table in front of me was a two-litre carton of full-fat milk. I picked it up. It was empty. There was a blue and white circled bowl on the floor. Koko joined me almost immediately, colonising my lap.

Neal came through just as I'd finished the poem's hysterical first section.

'I'm sorry about –'

'Sorry. I should have left a note out, or on the door, or told my mother, or something.'

'I hope I didn't mess it up too much.'

'No. I needed to replace the sheet anyway.'

'I meant the meditating, whatever.'

'Hey, Mary,' said Jack, coming through the door. 'Who hipped you to the groovy threads?'

Luckily, he nodded at my clothes.

'I wanted to wear something appropriate.'

'Mmm,' he said, looking at my bare feet. 'Maybe they are, maybe they aren't. We'll have to take a rain check about that.'

I tried to stop myself glowing too obviously at his near-approval.

'Hi, Mary,' said Maggie, out from behind him.

They were holding hands. I noticed that they had put their shoes on already.

'Take a pew,' Neal said.

'Thanks,' I said, sitting down again on the sofa. He sat down on the bed.

'Let's cut out of here, brother,' said Jack. 'History awaiteth us in Harpur Street.'

I didn't laugh. (I had already realised that, if I was going to spend any time around Jack, I'd have to do quite a lot of not-laughing.) I got the feeling Jack was sending himself up, a bit, probably. But to show any understanding of this would definitely have been uncool.

It was half past seven. Neal stood up again. I moved to follow him. Jack and Maggie were already out on the landing.

'Are you okay?' asked Neal, quietly. 'I'm glad you could –'

'Neal, come on! We gotta go, go, go!' shouted Jack, from the stairs.

'Go! Go! Go!' echoed Maggie.

We put our shoes on and went, went, went.

Out, out, out of the house without even saying goodbye to Neal's parents. As we came onto the ground floor, I heard music playing in the kitchen: Jimi Hendrix. Up ahead, Jack was walking quickly out the front door, fingers in his ears, humming something jazz. Maggie was doing exactly the same. I looked at Neal, who had cupped his hands over his ears on the first-floor landing – just before the music became audible. I laughed and sang along for a line (it was 'All Along the Watchtower'). I'm sure Neal heard me.

When we joined them out on the street, Maggie and Jack had put on dark glasses. They were walking fast, heads down, like film stars into a courthouse. Neal brought two further pairs out of his shiny leather satchel.

'I thought you might not have any.'

'What are they for?' I asked. 'It's not exactly dazzling.'

'If you'll put them on, I'll tell you.'

'Come on!' Jack shouted back at us.

'Yeah, come on!'

I put them on.

The lenses were very dark indeed – when I looked through them, the silver birches became blank vertical lines, makes of car became almost indistinguishable. I had trouble picking the Vauxhall out.

By this time, I was beginning to understand what was going on with their little gang.

'So,' I said to Neal, before he started explaining. 'It's a case of the three monkeys, is it?'

'What?' he replied, still trying to think of the best way to begin.

'See no evil. Hear no evil.'

'Yes! Yes, it is!' he said. 'Exactly. There are evil things around. We wouldn't call them evil. We'd call them unhip or uncool or wrong. We try to avoid unhip things.'

We were now only about ten paces behind the other two. They weren't holding hands any longer.

'What's with you two?' Jack said, back over his shoulder.

'Yeah, what?' echoed Maggie.

'You're walking too fast,' said Neal.

'No one walks too quick,' said Jack.

'Never can be, Neal,' said Maggie. 'No, it never can.'

Jack put his arm approvingly round Maggie.

'You must be very intelligent,' said Neal. 'You seem to understand everything already.'

'Don't you mean, I'm *hip* to it?'

He gave me his best scared-marsupial-peering-out-of-its-burrow eyes.

'Of course,' he said, then hurried to catch the others up.

I didn't immediately follow him. I was thinking about whether I should just slowly drop back, turn off, run away.

For about five seconds, they were out of sight. The Forester's Arms stood opposite, an inside of normality. (Or so I assumed; I'd never actually *been* inside it.)

Perhaps, in their sunglassed state, I could make it in there before they missed me. Perhaps The Forester's Arms was the sort of place, for reasons I was beginning to understand, they would avoid entering. It was, by any measure, *unhip*.

But as I *did* follow them round the corner, *did* catch up, *did* go to the reading, it wasn't actually 'them' I was following.

From the moment I turned that corner, 'them' became 'us' and 'they' became 'we'.

Jack was whispering things to Maggie, things that made her laugh and me jealous. Neal was still embarrassed. It was obvious that I would have to find something to be nice to him about before he would speak to me again. I didn't really feel I had the material to say anything original. To say too much about *him* would be lying: I hadn't yet found him witty or intelligent or cute. (And I was still to notice how kind he was.) In the end I chose the most obvious thing to say:

'Tell me about Koko. She's a beautiful cat.'

He looked at me, thankful. I was glad I knew people – pet-owners – well enough to, now and again, hit the right note. (Don't call it 'your cat' and don't call it 'it'; call it by its name.)

'She's named after a Bird song – I mean, a song written by Bird – Charlie Parker – the jazz musician. Do you know who he is?'

'Modern jazz,' I said.

'Re-bop or bebop. I think Jack would want you to say Re-bop. It's a little more hip. That's what they called it at the time, anyway. Dizzy Gillespie's Re-boppers. Do you dig jazz?'

I smiled down at the pavement, glad to have lost a point to Neal: it was something I saw, even then, that I would have to do a lot of. With Neal, I would have to act dumber, more clumsy – if I didn't, he'd never develop; and already I was beginning to take responsibility for ensuring that he did. I wanted to develop him away from Jack. (I wanted to develop everyone away from Jack – everyone except me.)

'Koko the Re-bop cat,' I said.

'A very hep cat,' said Neal.

'So why don't you let her into the blue room?'

'She gets hairs all over the place – and she won't leave me alone when I'm trying to meditate.'

We were now crossing the road at the lights, turning onto Bromham Road. There was an empty redbrick building, advertising thousands of square feet of office space.

Jack said something that sounded very like rhubarb-rhubarb-*she*-rhubarb. Maggie leaned on him for support against her laughter. I was sure he'd said something about me, though neither of them looked back.

'I thought about bringing her into the Temple in her travel basket, but she hates getting inside it. She associates it with going to the vet's and anaesthetic and being barked at by dogs. She hates it.'

'How long have you had her?'

'Eight years. She hasn't always been called Koko. We changed her name about a year ago – when she became one of us. We had a ceremony and everything. She loves listening to Charlie Parker, you see. She was called Godot before. My mother called her that.'

'Oh,' I said, wondering if my favourable impression of Neal's mother had been correct.

Jack and Maggie had paused for a couple of seconds, moving to one side. When we reached them, they started walking again.

Then, all of a sudden, Jack put his arm round Neal and started speaking incredibly fast:

'Aren't you buzzing? – Can't you feel the excitement? – It's coming up off the streets – This is just going to be the *swingingest* thing that ever hit – This is what Bedford's been a long time waiting for – The whole thing is about to happen, explode – I'm wired for it – It's going to go and we're going to hit it – We'll be high and joyous and swinging – Everything is going to change, you'll see – This whole

dead town, it will awake – The dead will arise – Hallelujah
– The revolution and the renaissance are at hand – Yes! –
And you and I, Neal, we are going to make it go – We're
taking it there *now*, this very evening – Tonight of all nights,
that we have chosen or been chosen by – The streets of
Bedford, the alleys and yards, the sidewalks and through-
roads – We will transform them with holy singing vision –
The pubs and churches, offices and shops – The river, our
great Ouse – The Bridge – The bridges – The statues –
We're going to create it, spontaneously, as if it wasn't even
there before – Brave connections are going to be mightily
made – Blakean fires of horrible holy burning soulness will
be ignited – People will talk, rave, resonating with our
vibrations, for years into the future – Into America – We,
Neal, *we*!'

This was the first time I'd heard Jack speak like this.

After he'd finished, he put his arm round Maggie and
began walking even faster. His energy made me wonder
whether he wouldn't after all make some converts that
evening.

Maggie and Jack crossed over, not at the lights. They
strode along the start of Allhallows, ignoring the long row
of estate agents. When we turned on to Harpur Street
opposite Save the Children, Neal and I were only a couple
of feet behind them.

A group of ordinary-looking young women, about my
age, were standing outside the pub.

I was suddenly aware of how we must appear to other
people – and was glad of the dark glasses, just as they became
the major point of embarrassment. We were a gang, a real
gang – so fucking cool and odd-looking – with a style all
our own. I knew that if I hadn't been one of us already,
I'd've wanted to be.

Yes, I'd've wanted to be the one up front, the blonde, the one arm-in-arm with the really cool-looking guy.

We passed Our Price on our left and Mothercare on our right.

Bedford Central Lending Library was up ahead.

I thought I might tell the others that the first time I'd read *On the Road* the copy had belonged to Bedford Library. (I had bought my own copy afterwards, of course.) I wondered what discoveries *they* had all made there.

'Are you feeling nervous?' I asked Neal.

'I wasn't,' he said.

For some reason, I reached out for his hand and gave it a squeeze. I let go almost immediately, realising my mistake.

'Oh, God,' said Neal. 'Now I'm really shitting myself.'

A young woman was standing inside the glass doors.

'Hi, Jack,' she said, as we walked in. 'Maggie, Neal.'

She was a slim, pale girl whose blonde hair was done in a ponytail. Jack's type, I guessed – and he was obviously hers: obviously from her lit-up smile.

Shit! Another one!

She was wearing a peony-patterned summer dress, black cotton stockings and black-ribboned ballet shoes. (She *did* look dancerish – a little overpoised and bodily smug.)

I looked at the way she and Jack stood in relation to each other, trying to figure out if they'd ever had sex.

It seemed likely – they were standing very close.

'Big turnout?' Jack asked.

'I'm Mary, by the way,' I said.

'Jane,' she said, looking from me to Neal, assuming things. 'Yes. No. There are some people here.'

It was seven forty-five.

'How many?' asked Maggie.

'I haven't really counted.'

'A hundred?' asked Jack.

'Um, more like ten.'

'Less than ten?' asked Neal.

'Definitely more than five,' said Jane, laughing.

'Man, don't mind that. They're just balling in the pub,' said Jack. 'Soaking up the rotgut. That's where I'd be, anyway. It's unhip to be here punctual-like.'

He betrayed no doubts whatsoever, unless holding Jane's hand as well as Maggie's meant anything.

'Let's go upstairs, hang out in the green room,' Jack said. 'We can wait there for the flood to arrive.'

'Um,' said Jane, 'Actually –' But Jack wasn't listening.

He walked up the escalator.

As we stepped onto it, Neal took my hand – and I didn't have the heart to take it away.

At the top of the escalator, we turned left through some fire doors. This was the main room of the library. The fiction shelves stood dead ahead, behind the renewals and returns desk.

We turned left again, went through some more fire doors and all the way up the stairs.

Neal held my hand the whole time. It was getting clammy.

Finally, I managed to escape into the women's loos – nipping in just behind Maggie. As the door swung itself shut behind us, I realised that this was the first time she and I had been alone together. She went into the far cubicle, I went into the near. I thought about speaking, but didn't.

Maggie was younger than I was. This had begun to worry me – or it was, at least, becoming something I thought about. If she was my rival, I had to assess her advantages. What did Jack find attractive about her? She was still practically a schoolgirl. Her teeth were good, but she never smiled. I suspected she'd spent most of her adolescence imprisoned by braces. Neal had the look of a pretty girl's first post-braces boyfriend; Jack of the second. But how had it happened? How did Jack and her get it together? How did Neal feel about them? I had more questions for my rival than was really decent.

I timed my exit from the cubicle to match hers – joining her at the sinks, the mirror.

We both took off our shades and put them down.

'We haven't spoken much, have we?' I began. 'I hope we can be friends.'

The look I got was hydrochloric.

Maggie went back to concentrating on her make-up.

I tried again:

'I hope the reading goes well.'

Maggie spoke slowly, as if she'd been saving this up.

'Why bother with hoping? It's all happened before, if only you'd read enough. This isn't really happening here – this is years and years ago. This is in San Francisco. You and me, we're thousands of miles apart. There are decades between us. I can't see you. Shout and I won't hear you. I don't want to hear you. I'm dead, already, by the time you've learnt to talk. You can't even telephone me. This isn't long-distance, Mary – this is a seance. You're knocking on the tabletop; I'm knocking on the underneath. You can't see me. I'm a ghost. Do you want to be a ghost?'

Maggie looked at me in the mirror, even more intensely than I'd been expecting.

'You don't know what's going on at all, do you? Why don't you just leave us alone? We have our own scene going, and you're not part of it. You wouldn't want to be. Not if you truly dug what was going down. You can leave any time you want. We're stuck. Here. Bedford. This is us for ever, and you can't pretend your way into it. We can't pretend our way out. This isn't just a style. This is us trying to survive. We're not wearing fancy dress.'

'I didn't say you were.'

She started for the door.

'Maggie,' I said, after her, 'could we meet up some time and talk about it? I'd like to be friends with you. I mean, you on your own, not with Jack or Neal.'

'You're not interested in me at all. You don't want to know me on my own. There isn't a me-on-my-own, anyway. You're just interested in him. Don't think I can't see that.'

I began to say something else, but –

'Leave us alone. We don't want you.'

'Neal seems to.'

'Neal does what Jack says. Jack listens to me. I'm going to speak to Jack.'

The door closed behind her.

Maggie was one very scared, very scary chick.

6

There was, as Jane had finally managed to tell Jack, no green room.

When I came out of the loos, Neal was suggesting we go to the pub. Maggie was standing behind Jack, clutching his arm, looking into his face, waiting for him to speak.

Jack said it would be better if they went and waited onstage. Neal said that was a cool idea.

We walked into the lecture room, Jack and Maggie leading the way. Unavoidably, Neal took my hand and gave it a pleaful squeeze. I repaid him with the best smile my face would allow.

The lecture room, with its scuffed blue carpet and stained white ceiling, was as unatmospheric as a place can be. Full, it would have seated around forty. But it wasn't full. I counted the audience. Thirteen, including Neal, Jack, Maggie, Jane and me.

Jack and Neal went up onto the stage. It was a raised lino platform in front of a white board. There was a table with two black vinyl chairs behind it. Jane had obviously been briefed.

For a moment, I thought Maggie was going to sit on the opposite side of the room to me – but that would have been too obvious; that would have told Jack, and Neal, too much. So, Maggie and I ended up sitting side-by-side in the middle of the front row – where the two handwritten RESERVED signs were.

I didn't feel any more comfortable, knowing that Maggie wasn't going to disown me in public. At least that would have forced Jack to decide whether I was worth the effort of keeping. Neal, I was sure, wanted me very badly to stick around – but he had no power over Maggie. Except whatever small influence he had over Jack. This, I had yet to work out. I'm not sure I ever really did.

'Have you read any of the poems before?'

Maggie turned to look at me.

'Of course I have – all of them,' she replied. 'I typed most of them out. I was in the room when some of them were being composed – and loads of them are about me, as well. I'm their muse.'

She turned away from me again, victorious.

'Wow,' I said, half-sarcastic.

'They're going to dedicate the first issue of the magazine to me.'

'The magazine?'

'They're going to announce it. Wait and see.'

I didn't have time to ask any more – and I doubt if she'd have told me anyway (having neatly proven by just how much she was 'in' and by how far I was 'out'.)

Jack stood up. He'd obviously realised that this – this thirteen – was all the audience he was going to get.

'Welcome to the beginning and the rebeginning,' said Jack. 'You, here, tonight, are about to witness the birth and the rebirth of cool. So, welcome to the renaissance. What we're trying for in our poetry is to get back to some of the purity and energy of our sources and inspirations. A load of other stuff has gone by since, none of it worth diddley. I hope, by the end of the evening, you will agree that this has been a charming event.'

Despite his best attempts, Jack could never have passed for anything other than English. In his mouth, the words 'charming event' suggested a tea dance or a croquet match.

'First, we're going to hear Neal reading some poems by our chief and most direct inspiration, Otto Lang. We didn't know Otto very long, only about six months. In fact, it was Otto who introduced us to each other. But during that short time he had a total effect on us both. It was Otto that got us into Charlie 'Yardbird' Parker and Dizzy Gillespie; Otto who turned us on to Jack Kerouac and Allen Ginsberg. Otto Lang was a great man and a great poet. He would have become an even greater one but, as some of you already know, he took his own life early last year – by drowning himself in the great River Ouse. In actual fact, he ended up dying of hypothermia – just like Neal Cassady – on January 25th, 1994, in Bedford Hospital. Since then, we have carried on in his name. With his pure death began the rebirth, sadly and with much grief. Later, we'll have an announcement about something exciting that's coming up. First, though, Neal's going lay a few of Otto's poems on you. I'm sure you'll dig them.'

Jack sat down. The audience clapped. Neal stood up. The audience hushed.

'Thank you,' said Neal. 'I'm going to start with something Otto wrote right at the end of his life – maybe only a couple of days before he died. I copied it out from his notebook, which his mother kindly let us borrow.' Neal smiled shyly towards someone a few rows behind me. I heard a cough and a nose being blown. 'The poem is called – well, it's untitled, but we titled it – I think you'll see why – "Orgy of Roses".'

Orgy of roses –
   welcome, thou, my love, touch-torched, into the
deep garden of Blakean benevolence, fragility & pure going
nakedness of form

Orgy of blood –
   O recline, beloved, lily upon lily, hair over grass,
roses bloom-blown, flesh into earth, going, slow, no, O

Orgy of light –
   see, spirit-maiden, where Being bodies itself forth
in all its overt utterness, flower-embraced & solemn,
throughout the whole non-space of Voidness, now, forever

Orgy of nothing –
   depart, thou, my love, tickle-torn, from the deep
garden of Blakean benevolence, fragility & pure going
nakedness of form

The audience clapped appreciatively, and Neal's voice
stopped shaking quite so much.

He read another poem, then another longer one, then
Otto's final fragment – 'Ouse':

You, Ouse,
   tulips, two lips –
schizophrenic river, arriver & departer, great & green –
   the faithful leaps
of your frigid bridges
   bowing to the terrible unseen –
unhaunted by ships
   what is it that you mean?
with your slow & sorry slip

       seawards
     no words
       can grace the

And there it ended, and so did Neal.

As he sat down, he glanced at me, looking for approval, looking for a smile.

The audience paused for a moment before starting to clap. It seemed only tasteful.

Before we had finished applauding, Jack was on his feet. His gaze tickled over us, teasing everyone with the possibility of eye contact. But he was too clever for that. He picked up his lever-arch file from the table. Already we were anticipating something special.

'I wanted to kick off by blowing a few choruses on the subject of our beliefs – beliefs as far as art goes, that is. This isn't the place or time to say what we reckon to the whole complexity and confusion and bigness that is life.'

Jack waited as his audience switched from their poetry-listening poses (heads down, chins on knuckles) to their prose-listening poses (shoulders back, fingers interlaced).

From the corner of my eye, I saw Maggie's cheek bulge – she was smiling encouragingly, intimately, at Jack.

'All of this – our poetry – began back in the Six Gallery in San Francisco in 1955. That was when Allen Ginsberg, the great American Jew and poet, stood up, a little drunk, shaking at the knees, to read out part of his great poem, 'Howl for Carl Solomon'. American literature – strike that – WORLD literature was never to be the same again. It was the greatest ever thing to hit. There were five other poets at the reading: Gary Snyder, Philip Whalen, Philip Lamantia,

Michael McClure, Kenneth Rexroth. Jack Kerouac, who I'm named after, and Neal Cassady, who Neal took his name from – they were both also there. This was the moment when poetry and word and voice and breath got their freedom. Since then, there's been lots of attempts to imprison them. These attempts have been successful. That's why everything's so unhip and uncool, you see. But, tonight, we're trying to set everything free again.'

Then he opened his lever-arch file and read his first poem – and it was awful. It was called 'Legends of the Midnight Oil'.

The first stanza went:

> Her hair cut madly during thunderstorms
> Confirms her self-assurance and her coil
> She bruised my neck with kisses
> As a shadow darkens even graveyard soil
> And as the night was just about to overboil
> She and I became legends of the midnight oil.

About fifteen more Dylanesque stanzas followed, before the final one:

> Her fingers they were badly bleeding
> By the time the wind of circumstance had blown
> And I was borne out into the street
> Where the air felt better mixed with no breath
>   of her own
> And as the house was just about overgrown
> She and I became legends of the silent phone.

His next poem was worse. The third was merely dire. But the fourth redefined the word crummy. And the fifth went on for so long even Maggie started to fidget.

I was shocked. Derivative, I'd been expecting; embarrassing was understandable; but *this*?

I couldn't help glancing at oh-so-proud Maggie. She was right – she had been the muse. One of the poems mentioned her 'milk-flowing silk-showing skin' – or was it 'bosom'?; another, her 'eyes of holy heaven holy hell'.

Bitchily, I thought this was just the kind of poetry *she* would inspire in Jack; I, on the other hand, would have brought his true voice out.

Because, of course, as soon as I recognised how bad he was, I started making excuses for him. It was as if my self-esteem was deputising for his. I had started to feel humiliated on his behalf – although no public humiliation seemed likely. No one, as far as I could tell, was sniggering or whispering. No one had left or vomited. And when Jack sat down, there was even a round of applause, quite equal to the one Neal – or Otto – got. (There was no real way of judging – dead people always get lots of applause.)

I was interested to see that Jack was letting Neal – who now stood up again – close the show. It was probably because Neal couldn't really read Otto's poems and then go directly on to his own. So, it was either Neal last or Otto – and Jack probably fancied his chances better against Neal. I'm not sure if he made the right decision. (Not till later did I wonder why Jack didn't read Otto's poems. I think it had something to do with Otto's mum.)

Neal was holding a thick-papered writing book with a leather cover and marbled endpapers. He started reading from about halfway through it. This, I found out later, was his life's work: diary, journal, sketchbook, doodle pad. More confidently than before, he began to read: 'This is from my latest collection, *Everybody in the world has an interesting face (so be nice to them, please).*'

                    The wasp,
        yawing
                from side to
        side,
        bumping
                crisply into
        the window-
        pane,

        rattling
                in a jamjar,
        /caught/
        bristling
                against my hand,
        escaped!

Wow!

I was amazed and – despite myself – proud to be Neal's
girl, if only falsely. He got the first laugh of the reading, the
second, third and fourth. He smiled when something he'd
privately thought might work publicly came off. He glowed
until he was almost handsome. For the first time, I wondered
why his mother and father hadn't come along to offer their
support.

The next thing I knew, Neal was saying my name – saying
it again – then reading out what he said was 'something he
had only just that morning written'. It was a love poem and
it was dedicated to me and it was good.

Neal sat down.

Jack now took over – or tried to. He stood up before
Neal had half-sat down. He made sure Neal's applause was
cut short, though he couldn't do much about its volume.
Maggie was first to stop clapping. I felt that I had to be last.

Neal looked over at me for the first time. He was expecting a reaction.

Unfortunately, I think I gave him the wrong kind of smile – the wrong kind of thanks: it was a sisterly-thank-you smile, not a you've-changed-my-life beam. Neal, I could see, was crushed by this – but was trying not to show it.

Jack started to speak as Neal looked down at the cover of his manuscript book.

Neal was aware that he was in front of an audience, but he was even more aware that the audience contained me.

'And now for our announcement. In order to follow through on the success of this evening, to spread the word even further, Neal and I have decided to start a magazine. I'm not one hundred per cent sure what the name will be yet. The obvious answer would be something like one of the great Beat journals: *Neurotica*, *Big Table*. So we might call it *Screwed-up* or *Little Chair* or something.' I had been watching Neal's hands go pink and his knuckles whiten round the edges of his wonderful book. We hadn't made eye contact again. I thought something was coming: I was preparing myself for an outburst, anger – or for him to start crying. (I thought the last likeliest.) 'But we'll decide on a name in the next couple of days. We hope to have the first number – ' Neal stood up, head down. '– out by the end of August. The magazine will be dedicated – ' Neal stepped off the platform and hurried out the door. Maggie's eyes followed him, then turned to me. *Your fault*, they were saying. Jack looked at Maggie, then at me. He'd missed it all. 'Yes, we'll dedicate it to the memory of Otto Lang. Any contributions from you would be extremely cool. I think Neal's right, it's time to go, not stay – it's time to do, not say. If you'd like to put your name down as a subscriber, please speak to Maggie here. Thanks again for your kind attendance. Later.'

Jack then hurried out the door.

Everyone started applauding. I think they thought that, even if it hadn't been planned, this was all very poet-like behaviour. We continued to applaud the empty resounding stage for a full minute or so. Eyes occasionally turned to the door, as if expecting the poets to reappear and take a bow.

Jane stood up, from the other end of the front row.

'I think the best way we can express our thanks, now Neal and Jack have fled, is by subscribing to what I'm sure will be a fantastic magazine. Thank you.'

She stepped up to Maggie, as people were getting their stuff together.

'Can I give you my address?' she said to Maggie.

'Um, Neal's taken all the writing stuff.'

'I'll get something from my office,' said Jane – looking as if she hated Maggie enough to take an age.

I thought for a moment about not doing it, then got out my pen and notebook.

'Another poet?' asked Jane.

Maggie looked at me with reluctant thanks. People were already queuing up to give their details.

'Not really,' I replied. 'It's mostly shopping lists and lists of books I should read.'

'I'm sure they're very poetic.'

I decided I liked Jane.

'Do you write?' I asked.

'Yes,' she said. 'I'm writing a novel. It's set in Stewartby. That's where I live. It's about women.'

Stewartby was a left-turn off the bus route to Bedford.

A whole village built out of one huge batch of bright red bricks – to be lived in by brickworkers.

I couldn't see much of a novel coming out of there, even one about men as well as women.

'I'm writing about what I know about, like they say you should.'

I smiled. I was finding it hard to continue liking Jane.

'I'd love to read some of it.'

'Are you coming to the pub?'

'I think we'll have to find the escapees, first.'

Maggie's queue was down to two people. I hoped she hadn't been peeking at the other pages of my notebook.

I'd written a few bitchy things about her, but I'd called her by the nickname I had for her: 'BB'. (Jack, I called 'Mr Right'. Neal's nickname was 'Muttley'.)

'They're very talented, aren't they?'

'Yes,' I replied.

'Didn't you love Neal's poem to you?'

'I'd like to read it again before I say anything.'

'I'd love someone to write something like that about me.'

'It was probably my fault he ran off like that.'

'Well, I don't suppose you could really have stood up and kissed him and told him how much you loved him in front of everyone. I'm sure he understands that, really. Or he will. Later on.'

'You sound like you know him well.'

'We went to school together. He's a sweetie.'

As Maggie was now free, Jane stepped over to her and dictated, very clearly, her full name, address, number.

'See you in the pub, maybe,' she said.

'Which one?' I asked.

'The Bear,' said Maggie.

'The Bear,' said Jane. 'I'm glad it was a success, after all.'

Maggie handed my pen back to me.

'Can I rip the pages out?' she said.

'I can copy the addresses out.'

'I don't think you'll be able to read my handwriting.'

'Let's have a look.'

Maggie handed over *my* notebook. The cover was sweaty and creased from her holding it too tightly.

'I'm afraid I'm going to have to kick you out,' said Jane. 'I have to turn the lights out, set the fire alarm, etcetera.'

'It's fine,' I said to Maggie, without looking at the writing. 'If I can't read them, I'll photocopy them. I really don't want my notebook ripped to pieces unnecessarily.'

'Thanks for the room,' Maggie said to Jane, then walked out.

'Maybe see you in The Bear,' I added.

Maggie was already halfway down the stairs by the time I got out the door.

7

I didn't catch up with her until she was crossing Silver Street.

'You haven't got your sunglasses on,' I said. 'Look, Marks & Spencer! Look, Dolcis!'

She stopped walking and stood in my way.

'Are you trying to be a bitch? You're not very good at it.'

'*Bitch*? That isn't a very hip thing to say, is it?'

'Oh, fuck off.'

'I started this evening by trying to be your friend.'

'By trying to get in Jack's pants.'

'Look,' I said, 'here they come.'

Jack was hurrying back towards us.

Maggie put her dark glasses on and looked down at the pavement.

'I'm pretty sure Neal's gone home. I think he ran all the way back. There's no way I could catch him.'

He said this as if we'd expected him to.

'Is it over?'

'Yes,' said Maggie, still in a sulk.

'Did you get some names and addresses?'

'*She* has.'

'Can I have them?' asked Jack.

'They're in my notebook.'

'So?'

'It's private.'

'I won't peek.'

'You won't get a chance. I told Maggie I'd photocopy the pages.'

'Photocopying you can't do – it's unhip.'

'Something's puzzling me about this unhip business. I mean, do you read newspapers?'

'Not unhip ones.'

'What about books.'

'Nothing unhip.'

'But you read paperbacks! I mean, you read books that were printed after 1966!'

'There are always going to be compromises. Shall we go to Neal's? I want to see him.'

We started up the road.

'We do our best. It's not easy, stuck out here in the middle of nowhere. We don't have access to all the things we want.'

'Oh, you have my sympathies,' I said.

'I really thought we did.'

Jack suddenly went sadder than I'd seen him. I didn't back off much, though:

'But you spend unhip money! You buy unhip shoes! You brush your teeth and wash your hair with unhip stuff!'

'Look, we'd be one hundred per cent pure if we could. We try to be pure. We try to use pure products. But it isn't a game for us. This is the whole thing. It's our only chance. It's not that we've arrived somewhere, it's just we're trying to move in a particular direction. We're following our own path. If it isn't your path, then go home. Go on! You don't have to come back to Neal's with us.'

Jack shrugged to indicate the road down to the bus station. We were passing it on our left.

'No,' I said. 'I have to go back to Neal's.'

'Why?' said Maggie. 'He won't want to see you and we certainly don't.'

I saw Jack look at Maggie as if he seriously disagreed. It would be worth sticking around just to piss her off.

'My car is parked there.'

They both stopped dead. If they had been cartoons, jaws would be liquefying on the pavement, eyes would be out on springs. Together, with the same amazed intonation, they said: 'You have a *car?*'

'It's my father's car, really,' I had turned back to face them. They looked very confused.

'But you can drive it?' said Jack. 'You have a driving licence?'

'Of course I do,' I said. 'You mean *you* don't?'

I started walking again, thinking that was as good an exit line as I was likely to manage.

The two of them started after me, though, hurrying to catch up.

'No,' I heard Jack say. 'We don't.'

'What? None of you?' I had turned and faced them again. This was getting silly. I decided not to stop again until I'd reached the car. I looked at Maggie, who was blushing. By the time Jack answered, I had already turned away.

'No. None of us. Not me, not Maggie, not Neal.'

I looked at the brick walls of the prison and the high school.

We walked fast – very fast – not talking – until the Union Street crossing. Jack was beside me, Maggie behind.

'It's a very unhip car, Jack. You wouldn't be interested. You wouldn't even want to look at it. It was built in the mid-'70s. It's not American. It's not fast. It's not pure. But I can borrow it, sometimes. If I'm lucky. I'm sorry if Neal got upset by this evening. It wasn't anything I meant to do. I'm sorry if it was my fault, though. Tell him to phone me, if he likes.'

We were now over the road and approaching Warwick Avenue.

'Does he have your number?'

'Do you have anything to write on?' I asked, not stopping.

Jack pulled a fountain pen out of his jacket pocket and cracked open his lever-arch file. I gave him the number, code and all.

We walked round the corner and up to Neal's house. They crossed the road. We didn't say goodbye.

I saw Neal's mother opening the front door for them, not looking distressed or anything. A bit red-eyed, maybe – probably from the dope. Luckily, she didn't look across the road, see me, ask why I wasn't coming in.

I unlocked the car door.

They went inside.

I looked for Neal's face at an upstairs window. I thought about following them in – apologising and making up, asking to use the toilet – but it wasn't worth it. It wouldn't work, I knew.

I got in the car.

I drove up Warwick Avenue and left onto Linden Road, deliberately not using my rear-view mirror. (I didn't want to see Neal running out into the street after me.) I turned off Linden Road and down Lansdowne Road, the leafy road that runs parallel to Warwick Avenue; right, Union Street, roundabout, Greyfriars, straight on, roundabout, right, River Street, lights, fairly calm by now, left, Midland Road, roundabout, left, Prebend Street, bridge, still Prebend Street, roundabout, right, Kempston Road, roundabout, left, Britannia Road, roundabout, right, yes, quite calm, Ampthill Road, straight on, roundabout, straight on, roundabout, right, still Ampthill Road, under the railway bridge, roundabout, straight on, Hardwick Hill, straight on, straight on, straight on, calm, Ampthill Hill, Bedford Street, mini-roundabout, right, Dunstable Street, right, Alameda Walk. And I didn't start crying until I'd turned the engine off.

8

By the following afternoon, I had calmed down enough to start wondering why Neal hadn't called – and when he was going to.

As was becoming usual, though, I thought more about Jack: I lay on my bed in my bedroom, staring at the walls, counting the Blu-Tack stains, wondering.

Had Jack copied my phone number out of his lever-arch file and into his little black book? Was *he* going to phone me secretly? Had he already told Maggie that he had a new love and that it was all over between them? Was he sitting with her, even as I thought about it, upstairs at Alfonse, Saturday afternoon, explaining how she would just have to make do with Neal?

I realised that I wasn't being a very nice person, but I didn't care: I just wanted the phone to ring and to put me back in touch – directly or indirectly – with the object of my desire.

But for that I had to wait until Sunday afternoon; and so I had a lot of time to think about things – lots more time than I really wanted.

When Neal and not Jack phoned, I tried very hard not to let him hear my disappointment. I also avoided mentioning the reading, the love poem, the stomp-out. Neal, though, in a speech that sounded like it had been in rehearsal for most of the previous twenty-four hours, apologised.

'I'm sorry I ran off at the end of the reading and I'm sorry I didn't let you know about the poem before. I didn't intend to embarrass you, or anything like that: I just thought it was one of my best poems, and I wanted to read out my best. I hope you can understand and forgive me.'

I of-coursed immediately – then held myself back from saying, 'How's Jack?' No, I *wouldn't* be the first to mention him. If Neal didn't mention him, that was fine – absolutely fine.

'I hope we'll see you again some time soon.' More rehearsal.

'I should think you will.'

There was a relieved pause, at both ends.

'Jack mentioned you've got a car.'

Bingo-jingo.

'I told Jack it was my dad's car: I can only borrow it.'

'But you've got a driving licence?'

'Yes.'

'Wow. Cool.' There was another pause. 'Would you give me lessons?'

This was unexpected.

'What?'

'Would you teach me to drive?'

'Why me? Why not a driving school?'

'They wouldn't understand.'

'Wouldn't understand *what*?'

'That there are certain roads I can't go down. That I would have to wear dark glasses. Plus, my mother doesn't approve of cars. She wouldn't pay.'

'You need insurance to drive someone else's car.'

'We've thought about that. We're going to use the Buddha fund.'

'The what?'

'It's the money we were collecting to buy a proper Buddha for the altar in the Temple.'

'You want to spend the Buddha fund on getting insured to drive my dad's Vauxhall?'

'We want to travel. We'd like to go to Brighton.'

'You want to go *on the road*?'

'We don't want to travel by train or aeroplane, no.'

'But what's in Brighton?'

There was a dulling of static as Neal's hand cupped the receiver. It lasted about fifteen seconds. 'Otto used to go up there a lot, to stay with his uncle. His uncle is also called Lang. He used to live in Paris. He has some more of Otto's manuscripts. I'm going to edit them.'

'Is someone there with you?'

'Only Koko. Do you want to say hello?'

'Okay.'

I heard the phone being put down on something hard. Footsteps went away, then came back.

'She can hear you now.'

'Hello, Koko. Hope you're having a nice day. Get Neal to give you some lovely cream. See you soon. Can I speak to Jack now, please, Koko?'

Again there was the pause, the dulling.

'No, he's really not here,' said Neal.

In the background, what sounded like feet were walking away. More than one pair. Where was the phone in Neal's house? I tried to picture it. The kitchen? I couldn't remember seeing one.

'Alright, then.'

'Will you teach me to drive?'

'I can't say yet. I need to think about it and I need to ask my father if it's okay.'

'Okay.'

'Is Maggie there?'

'No.'

'Has she said anything about me to you?'

'She's really not here.'

'I think she feels threatened by me.'

'She's just a quiet person. She'll open up to you soon.'

'Give me your phone number.'

He did.

'I'll ask my dad about the car and phone you back in a couple of days.'

'Cool. Thanks. Later.'

As I put the phone down, I realised that my mum had been listening.

The question of the car came up over dinner that evening. I knew it was on its way when my dad stood up and turned the TV off.

'What about *Coronation Street*?' I said.

'We're videoing it,' he replied.

This was serious stuff.

He sat down.

It was steak-and-kidney pie with boiled new potatoes and carrots. The potatoes had been neatly peeled. Parsley had been sprinkled over the nob of butter atop the carrots.

Rufus sat, alert, beside Dad's chair, waiting for the inevitable treats.

I looked down the living room, over the carpet, out into the garden, over the lawn.

Get me out of here!

'Your mother said you might be wanting the car a bit more than usual.'

Mum was still helping herself to new potatoes. When she had a small amount of everything, she would make two little piles – one of salt, one of pepper – on the edge of her plate. But when the time came for her to clear the plates away, the two little piles would still be there. Today, the salt and pepper ritual was a good excuse for avoiding my eye.

'Well, we've talked about it together – and it's fine by us. Since I've retired, we only really need the car to go to Tesco's, or if we're going on a day out. So, we may as well let you have the car – to own – as long as we can borrow it, now and again. If you get a job in London, you'll probably want it there anyway.'

Arriving so unexpectedly, my parents' simple and generous offer was absolutely infuriating. What would have suited me better than anything was a straight refusal. Then I could have flounced out, gone for a long walk, come back, broken down, been accepted, won the argument.

Finally, I was able to catch my mum's eye.

'I wasn't prying,' she said. 'I was just in the kitchen.'

'You could have shut the door.'

'Your mother just wants to help.'

We sat there as our plates went cool.

'Thanks, Dad, Mum,' I said, finally.

With no real excuse for delaying, I phoned Neal later that same evening. I made sure no one was listening in. The TV was on in the living room. Neal's mother answered.

'Mary,' she said. 'How wonderful!' and went to call him.

He was breathless when he reached the phone.

'We can start as soon as you like,' I said.

Neal turned out not to be working at Alfonse for the next couple of days. He didn't work there at all, really, except on Mondays and Saturdays.

There were no obstacles.

My dad had even rummaged my old magnetic L-plates out of the garage.

Neal, now almost incapable of speech, grunted affirmatively.

I wondered, was *his* mother listening to *him*?

'See you tomorrow,' he said.

I listened to him putting the phone down, then went upstairs.

My power over him made me melancholy for the rest of the evening – it was so *useless*.

9

Monday was a lovely bright sunny day.

When I got in the Vauxhall, I closed the driver's door three times and touched the rear-view mirror once with crossed fingers – just in case.

Speeding into Bedford, I had the radio blasting and the driver's window all the way down.

I was wearing a semi-hip summer dress, sandals and no undies.

Again, Neal's mother answered the front door and told me to go on up. I'd have liked more of a conversation, this time, but she seemed rather distracted.

Neal was in the Temple, meditating to calm himself down.

I went into his room to wait for him, but he came through almost immediately. I'd just sat myself down on the sofa, beside a long musical-instrument case of some sort. In front of me, on the coffee table, was a piece of sheet music: a minuet. Koko was nowhere to be seen.

'Hi,' I said.

'Hello.'

'What's this?' I touched the edge of the music.

'I heard you coming up the stairs, if you wondered,' said Neal.

'You play a musical instrument?'

He stepped over to the case.

'Um, the trombone.'

'Can I have a look? You don't have to play me anything.'

After a slight hesitation, he sat down next to me on the sofa. He pulled the case onto his lap, unclicked the clasps.

'I've already done my practice for today.'

'You play jazz, do you?'

He lifted the trombone out of the purplish-metallic plush of the case. It was a dull well-handled gold. It was hip.

'Jazz and classical. I used to play in the school orchestra.'

I took the instrument. It seemed far less balanced in my hands than in his. The slide fell away towards the carpet.

'Is it easy to play?'

'Well,' he said, sitting back, 'the thing is, with the trombone, you have to *know* the note to make it. If a piano plays flat, it's the piano-tuner's fault. But with the trombone, it's always the trombonist. I suppose the violin's a bit the same – I'm not explaining it very well, am I? The trombone – You have to *know* the notes, or they'll sound wrong. You have to be *inside* the note for it to come out right. The trouble is, people think it's nothing but a brass instrument – meaning you have to play it so it sounds *brassy*. But I think it sounds horrible like that. You have to sidle up to the notes – or sidle down to them. *Sidle*, not slide. You have to trick it into sounding gentle – how you want it to sound. It's difficult.'

'Is that how you like it to sound?'

'Yes,' he said. 'I prefer gentle things.'

'Jack isn't gentle.'

Damn, I'd done it already.

'He is really – inside. You just don't know him yet. Shall we go?'

'How does Koko like your playing?' I said, standing up.

'She really hates it. She goes and hides in the garden – unless it's raining, then she'll go in the basement.'

Neal put the trombone gently back in the case.

'Is she in hiding now?'

'No,' said Neal. He went and picked a large wicker travel basket out from under his desk. 'She's in here. She's coming with us. She wants to learn to drive, as well.'

When we got to the car I made Neal get in the passenger seat. He sat there, dark glasses on, the travel basket on his lap.

'I'll just take you somewhere with not too many cars.'

With a learner on board, I exaggerated everything: mirrors, indicators, handbrake, gear changes. I drove to the car park behind Robinson Pool. It was almost empty.

'Right,' I said. 'Ready?'

I undid my safety belt.

'No,' said Neal.

'Do you want to learn to drive?'

'I think so. I'm not sure. Can't we just talk for a bit?'

Oh, no.

'What about?'

'Um –'

He looked over towards the park. Then, almost without looking, he undid the buckles on the basket and took Koko out.

After putting the basket on the floor, he sat her on his lap and began stroking her.

'I liked the poem very much. I was very flattered that you'd dedicated it to me.'

'I didn't just dedicate it. It was about you.'

'Well, thank you.'

Koko started to purr.

'And I meant it as well.'

'I'm very flattered.'

'Do you think we could walk for a bit?'

We got out of the car, all three of us.

'She'll come as well,' said Neal, putting Koko on the tarmac. 'I walk with her here quite often.'

'What about dogs?'

Neal shrugged and kicked the Vauxhall's front-left tyre, softly. 'Well, she hasn't killed any yet.'

Bedford Park was wide and grassy-green, edged with a dark line of evergreen. Further up the hill were the cemetery and the crematorium. A group of boys were playing football, over towards the bandstand.

The path we were following went round the side of the pool.

A girl wearing a Walkman rollerbladed past; Neal inspected the pansies in the opposite flowerbed.

It really *was* summer.

Koko walked five steps ahead of us, tail held high.

I decided I'd better help Neal.

'Is there something you want to talk about, particularly?'

'Um,' he said. 'Not yet. Wait till we get to the benches. That's the best place.'

The benches were about a hundred yards away, flanking the path from the bandstand to the teashop.

'What a strange and beautiful cat you are,' I said, but Koko took no notice.

In fact, Koko ignored everything – grass, flowers, litter, stains. She walked as if we were a procession she had been charged with leading. It was almost as if Neal had scripted her.

'Koko is the best cat in the world. She's much better than

people. I tell her everything. She knows everything about me.'

'More than your mother?'

'If I didn't lie to my mother, I wouldn't be here today.'

'Where would you be?'

'In prison, I expect.'

On the path ahead of us, a squabble of seagulls were making a large piece of bread jump about. As Koko approached they flew up into the air, carrying the bread with them. When the seagulls passed over our heads, crumbs dropped onto our shoulders.

I was so sadly familiar with the scene we were about to play out that I felt like turning round, running back to the car and driving off. But that, again, was another sort of scene. And I didn't want to make Neal run after me. Something told me that making Neal run would be the worst thing I could do to him – to make him run would humiliate him. It would be rejecting him wrongly. What I really wanted was to find something adequate to say. The walk to the benches was too long – if it had been shorter, I'm sure I would have been able to come up with the right words.

What frightened me most was the thought that Neal knew *exactly* what words *he* was going to use; the words were probably, as he sped up slightly, all that he had in his mind – all that he had had ever since our phone conversation the night before. No doubt Koko knew what he was going to say. If she could have spoken, she could have told me – with his intonation, his awkward pauses – the whole conversation. She most likely knew which bench he had chosen for us to sit on, as well.

'Why don't we sit on the grass, instead?' I suggested, stepping off the path.

'I've never liked sitting on grass, really,' said Neal.

'Oh,' I said.

'I don't like spiders and wasps or any insects except lady-birds and moths.'

'What about butterflies?'

'Not as much as moths. I don't mind caterpillars.'

We had reached the first bench. We sat down.

'Yes,' I said. 'I like caterpillars. I don't mind spiders.'

'Oh, no,' said Neal. 'They're horrible.'

I looked over at the bandstand. It was encircled by a low black-painted fence and a small band of lawn.

Now that we were close up, I was no longer sure it *was* a bandstand. The lines of the verdigris roof were scooped out in a pagoda-like fashion. On top of the roof was a bobbled spike.

I could hear people arguing on the tennis courts.

The boys with the football were turning their goal posts back into sweatshirts.

'I'm in love with you,' said Neal. 'I suppose you guessed.'

Koko had come to sit on his lap again. As this would make kissing me rather tricky, I felt safe for the moment.

'I don't expect you're in love with me. I don't think anybody is ever likely to be. I don't know why.'

'Neal —'

This wasn't exactly what I'd expected, but I didn't feel any happier. I still felt pretty sure I would be using the word *friend* quite a lot in the next half-hour — and I hated myself for not being able to find a less girlie way out.

'I expect you're in love with Jack, like everyone.'

'No, I'm not.'

'Oh,' said Neal.

Yes, this was wrong — this was the first really wrong thing I did. I suppose I thought the truth wouldn't help either of us. I think I was trying to avoid following the script. Perhaps

I was even trying out what lying – totally, directly – felt like. I had told the truth most of the time before then, and it didn't seem to have helped. I was in a mood to experiment with things, with my life.

'You don't?' asked Neal. 'What about me?'

I leant over and kissed him lightly on the lips.

'I can drive!' said Neal, suddenly.

'What?!'

He was fumbling in his back pockets, pulling out a driver's licence, babbling:

'I learnt to drive when I was seventeen. I got some money for my birthday. I used it to buy driving lessons. My mother didn't approve. But she didn't want to stop me, either. I used to have lessons after school, when it got dark. I passed first time. I had about £5 left. I bought my mum some flowers for having let me. I'm quite a good driver, I think – or I was. I haven't driven for a while. We don't have a car. This is my driving licence.'

The plastic folder had yellowed slightly.

'Why did you pretend you couldn't drive?' I knew the answer, but didn't really want to admit it to myself.

'I needed to see you again. I needed to see you. But I wouldn't have dared phone unless Jack had told me to. I'm sorry. I wouldn't have used driving lessons as an excuse if it had just been me. But Jack and Maggie don't know I can drive. I didn't have an excuse for them. They told me to phone you. I meant just to tell you that, today, but I thought I might as well tell you everything. The reason.'

'That's everything, is it?'

'More or less, I suppose.'

'Why didn't you tell Jack about your driving?'

'I hate being a disappointment to him.'

'You know you're a better writer than he is, don't you?'

Koko jumped off Neal's lap and went over to the bench opposite. Like all the benches, it had smoothed-off lions' heads decorating the hand-rest part of the arms. I stroked the mane of the lion that lay under my hand. Koko began rubbing herself against the legs of the bench.

'I can't really tell. He's much stronger than me.'

'That's part of his problem,' I said. 'He's too strong.'

For the first time, Neal looked at me directly. I couldn't help pitying him.

Someone on one of the tennis courts swore, extravagantly.

'You really think he's got things wrong with him?'

'Everyone has.'

'I think you're pretty perfect.'

'Neal, *don't* –'

'Well, I think you're pretty.'

'Perfect.'

After a short pause, he leant over and kissed me.

This time, I closed my eyes.

Neal's lips were very soft and his skin felt very soft. He smelt very nice, of rice paper and almonds.

The kiss didn't last as long as I'd expected – but, throughout, I was aware of Neal's happiness. It was as if I had put my face very close up to a four-bar fire. Perhaps this was one of the reasons I didn't want him to stop: I needed some warmth, some tricked warmth.

It's not often I feel like an ice maiden.

When he did stop, I said:

'Why don't we go for a drive? You can drive. I won't tell Jack or Maggie.'

'Cool,' said Neal.

And I couldn't help laughing.

10

We didn't go anywhere exciting. We went to Ampthill.

Almost as soon as we got in the car, Neal had said, 'I'd like to see where you grew up.'

Neal drove perfectly well, though he did hesitate too long at roundabouts. He looked splendid with joy. Behind the dark glasses, his eyes were glowing.

I sat with Koko in her travel basket on my lap. This caused me a little anxiety, but I thought it would be wrong to exile her to the back seat.

As I didn't want to distract Neal while he was driving, I had plenty of time to think. I spent a while wondering whether Neal now thought I was his chick and wondering, also, whether there was any way I could let him know I wasn't.

Already I had begun to feel guilty about what had happened in Bedford Park. The only ways out that I could see at that moment were abrupt and cruel. I would, whatever else I did, have to drive Neal back into Bedford.

But I had no excuses: I had kissed him first and without him really asking me to. What he had been declaring was, he thought, unrequited love. If he felt *so* ecstatic now, then he had every reason to.

I was a deceitful cow.

I half-hoped we would die in a car crash before we got home.

We were just driving past the Houghton Conquest turn-off when Neal asked, 'What's there that's interesting in Ampthill? I've never been before.'

'If there is anything interesting, I wish someone would tell *me* about it.'

Neal laughed. But then he could, *he* lived in Bedford.

'No, it's not that bad. It's just quiet, that's all. We could go to Houghton House. Turn left when we reach the top of the hill.'

It would be nice to motor down the long drive up to the house, I thought: green grass, blue skies, white clouds, silver car.

'What is it?'

'It's an old ruined mansion. It got burnt down by a jealous husband.'

'I'm not sure if I want to see one of those, today. I only like that sort of thing sometimes. Maybe another time. Could we just go to yours?'

'Okay. But I can't guarantee that it'll be *interesting*.'

'I can,' came the reply. Neal paused, then clarified. 'I haven't been out of Bedford for three years – anything's going to be interesting to me.'

Immediately, I remembered that my mum and dad were both going to be at home.

'Three years?' I said, without really knowing what I was saying.

I was pretty sure I could introduce Neal as a friend without him making any objections; but I knew that, whatever I said, my parents would immediately *assume*.

Perhaps it *was* going to be interesting, after all.

'Oh,' I said, remembering another thing. 'We have a dog.'

'Don't worry,' said Neal. 'It'll be perfectly safe. I won't let Koko out of her basket.'

I opened the garden gate with my left hand and spun round, once, when we reached the doorstep – just in case. Neal, I guess, thought I was looking back at the car.

'Do me a favour,' I said.

'Yes?'

'Can you take your glasses off while we're inside?'

He thought about it.

'I suppose so.'

'Mum, Dad – this is Neal. I'm teaching him to drive. And this is Koko, Neal's cat.'

I hadn't consulted Neal about lying, but I assumed he'd go along. It meant we could always have an excuse to meet up, in future. Or perhaps he wasn't as devious as that. Or perhaps he was so nervous, he wasn't really hearing anything.

'Hello, Neal,' said my dad.

'Pleased to meet you,' said my mum, then looked down at the basket. 'Both.'

They had been sitting in the living room, in their easy chairs, one on either side of the turned-off gas fire, slowly vanquishing the *Sunday Telegraph* crossword.

Now, though, they were in the kitchen, standing in front of us, their coupledom emphasising ours.

There was a short pause, during which they looked at me and *assumed*.

I felt the whole weight of this assumption descending upon me, like a goosefeather pillow being pushed firmly down onto my face – I couldn't breathe, I couldn't shout.

What made the suffocation completely horrible was that their assumption was *right*.

I heard Rufus coming out from my parents' bedroom, where he'd been napping under the bed.

'Would you like some tea?' my mum asked.

Neal looked at me for an answer.

Rufus entered the room and went straight for the basket. Trying to avoid an animal scene, I said, 'I think we're going to listen to some music.'

'Right,' said my dad, assumption confirmed. (First rule of boyfriends, keep them classified for as long as you can. Second rule, once introduced, get them away from the parents a.s.a.p.)

A sound started inside the basket. It was as if Neal was holding an actual scream in his hands.

Rufus was visibly cowed, but went on yakking.

'I'll bring it up to you, then,' my mum said.

'Lovely, Mum,' I shouted.

'Thank you,' said Neal. I don't think my mum could hear.

I turned to back out the door and up the stairs.

My dad winked at me and, at the same moment, my mum shouted, 'Biscuits?'

'Yes,' I replied, halfway into the hall.

When we got upstairs, I shut Rufus out on the landing.

'I like your room,' said Neal, who was looking out of the window. 'It's full of light, isn't it?'

'Only when it's sunny.'

With Neal there, I became conscious of how totally unhip my room was. There were postcards on the wardrobe of movie stars who hadn't even been *born* in 1966. My stereo dated from the mid-'80s. (I had christened it with a Culture

Club tape.) The bed (1987) was from Habitat, back when I thought Habitat the height. The carpets (circa 1979), wallpaper (1980), curtains (1994), curtain-matching lampshade (1994) – none of them were old enough to be acceptable. On the bedside table (1984ish) was a half-empty can of Diet Coke (yesterday).

'You can put your glasses on again, if you like.'

'I'm fine.'

'Would you like to listen to some music? It's what we're supposed to be up here for.'

'Yes.'

'I'm afraid it's mostly on tape.'

I kept my tapes all jumbly-jumbled up in a cardboard box. One day, during a bored, hippyish mood, I'd decorated the outside with silver paper and gold stars. Deeply cringesome. (Mitigating circumstance: I must have been about thirteen.) But whenever I decided to get rid of it, nostalgia would win out over embarrassment. Most of the cassettes were tape-to-taped and were unlabelled. I recognised some of them by their colour and some by their smell.

'Let me have a look,' said Neal.

I was surprised, but stepped aside to let him get at the box.

'You don't have to, you know.'

'But we – we *know* each other now.' Neal closed his eyes, his head fell. 'I'm not perfect. I'm not hip all the time. I like – I like disco music. Do you have any?'

I had to not-gasp.

'Disco?'

'Abba!' said Neal. 'I love Abba.' He pulled out a cassette with a green label – ABBA scrawled on it, in fat purple felt-tip. One of my earliest surviving tapes.

'It's their *Greatest Hits*,' I said.

'I've always loved Abba,' said Neal.

'But you're not meant to.'

'I used to listen to them when I was five. I was in love with Agneta. I thought she was so nice. I wanted her to be my mother. A little later I wanted her to be my sister. Then I wanted to *be* her. Then –'

This was, of course, the moment my mum chose to make her entrance.

'Tea and biscuits,' she said, putting the tray down on my desk, as always. 'I'll leave you to it.'

Out she went.

To what?

'Can you put it on? I'm not sure I can work it.'

He handed me the cassette. I pressed the eject and took out the tape that was already in there: The Smiths, *Hatful of Hollow.* I dropped the Abba tape in, switched on the stereo, pressed play, turned up the volume.

Neal was sitting on the edge of the bed with his eyes closed.

The tape was in the middle of one side and started as one song faded out. Next up was 'One of Us'.

'I love disco music,' he confessed. 'It's such happy music – so slinky and kinky, like satin. Disco makes you want to be in its world, to touch it. Jack doesn't know but, secretly, I have a Sony Walkman and about ten tapes. I've got the soundtrack to *Saturday Night Fever*, the soundtrack to *Grease*. I've got three Abba albums, *Arrival*, *Voulez-vous* and *Super Trouper*. I have a couple of *Hits of Disco* compilations. I have *The Greatest Disco Album Ever.*'

'It's alright, Neal,' I said, trying to calm him down. 'I won't tell anyone. I'm good at keeping secrets.'

He lay back on the bed, his eyes still closed. I went over

to my desk and poured out the tea. Neal's feet were tapping against the duvet cover.

'Milk?'

'Yes, please. Lots.'

'Sugar, as well?'

'Two, please. Heaped, please.'

After giving the cup (the second-best set) a stir, I placed it on the bedside table. I sat down on the chair and took a sip of tea. Milk, no sugar. I wasn't sure whether Neal wanted me to join him on the bed, now that the threat of my mum had receded. That, though, seemed very un-Neal – unless I'd misjudged him completely.

When the song ended, Neal opened his eyes and looked up at me. He was close to tears.

'I feel very happy. It's a big relief, being able to tell someone things. I can't even tell my mother about Abba.'

'Why not?'

'She'd tell Jack. She's a big fan of Jack – he gets dope for her. I listen to my Sony Walkman under the covers. Last week, she almost caught me. I feel really guilty about letting Jack down.'

'Oh, I'm sure he's got secrets of his own. He probably reads the newspaper every day, listens to Radio 1, drives a sports car.'

'Do you think so?'

'How can you be sure what he gets up to in private? What's *his* bedroom like – is it completely hip?'

'I wouldn't know. I've never seen it.'

'You've never been to his house?'

'No, never.'

'Do you know where it is?'

'No.'

Bugger.

I wondered if we were going to kiss again. It looked as if I would have to initiate everything.

I was finding Neal's honesty attractive. Okay, a turn-on. I wanted to be nice to him. I wanted to make him feel less anxious about Jack and restore him to himself. I felt that I knew so much more than he did. All this wanting to be kind went to my head, and I started feeling drunk.

After putting down my tea, I went to lie down beside him.

'I'm very happy,' he said.

'Good,' I said, and closed my eyes – expecting a kiss immediately. None came. Instead, Neal said:

'I'm a virgin.'

When I looked at him, he was staring straight at the ceiling.

'Well, we're not going to have sex now, are we?' I said.

'Really?' he replied, as if he had no choice in the matter.

'My parents would hear,' I whispered.

'Is that why?'

'I couldn't have sex if I knew my parents were listening.'

'It's not that I haven't done some things.' Neal sat up. 'I've done lots of things. Some that you probably haven't. I just haven't –'

'Hey,' I said. 'Don't worry about it.'

He turned to look at me.

'So, are we still going out?' he asked.

Sometimes we do things we *know* we shouldn't do – not just afterwards, but while we're doing them.

The problem is that knowing they're wrong often makes us more, not less, likely to do them.

'If you want to.'

'I do.'

I closed my eyes, and this time he did kiss me.

For a few minutes, I was quite glad that my mum had left us to it. Then I began feeling guilty.

About two hours later, I drove Neal back into Bedford. We kissed goodbye in the car. I didn't go in to speak to his mother or meet his father.

We arranged for me to go round the following evening: Maggie and Jack were going to be there for what he called a 'dig' – a relaxed evening of talk, music, snacks and drugs.

I drove home by what was fast becoming my usual route.

I I

When I got to Neal's the following evening, Jack had yet to arrive. So, I went with Maggie and Neal to wait for him at Young Life Corner.

As we stood around, Neal explained:

'You can approach here from five or six different directions. We never know which way he'll come from. Sometimes I think he must even walk past my house to get here.'

'Sounds a bit silly to me.'

'He doesn't want to be bothered when he's writing. Sometimes he just disappears for days at a time. Mostly, though, when there's something to discuss, like the reading, we'll arrange to meet at a certain time at a certain place. He needs his secret life, you see. It's part of his power.'

I'll bet it is, I thought.

There wasn't much to look at while we waited: a roundabout with some bushes in the middle.

Neal had obviously said something to Maggie about me and him going out. She had given me a big maybe-evil smile when I arrived and hadn't spoken to me since. At the time, I thought she was just waiting to see what Jack's reaction was — so she could repeat and amplify it, so she could be sure hers was the correct one: his.

Neal didn't seem to have spoken to Jack since yesterday. I

was interested to see how Neal would tell him. (Verbally? By a quiet word. Physically? By putting his arm round me.) I was more interested, though, in how Jack would react, *if* he would react.

We waited for about fifteen minutes. When Jack did turn up, it was from the direction of Robinson Pool.

I wondered whether I could take this as a clue to where he lived. If he had plenty of time, he might take an indirect route; if he was late, he couldn't afford detours.

'Hi,' said Jack, to everyone.

'Hi,' we said back.

'How's it going?' he said to Maggie, leaning over to kiss her.

'Mmm,' she said, without taking her lips off his.

'We'll let you catch up,' said Neal.

We walked back to Neal's. I wanted him to put his arm round me, just to help get me there.

'Do they always do that?' I asked.

'Mostly,' said Neal.

We waited for them in Neal's room. They turned up ten minutes later. Maggie was beaming; she knew what to say. Jack came up to where I sat on the sofa.

'Glad to have you along,' he said.

'Yeah,' said Maggie, from over by the door.

They both smiled at me.

If they hadn't taken ten minutes deciding, I'd almost have thought it was genuine.

Neal had put some music on (The Dizzy Gillespie All Stars), which Jack now changed (The Miles Davis Quintet). He then picked up the bongos and began to tap along.

The dig began.

Neal went downstairs to fetch some wine from the kitchen. Jack allowed Maggie to roll a joint.

While Neal was out of the room, nobody spoke: me, because I was scared; Maggie, because Jack hadn't spoken; Jack, for his own reasons.

This was the first time I'd seen Jack since the reading. But I'd been thinking of him so constantly it felt as if we should be far more intimate than we were. I looked across to where he sat, at Maggie's side, on Neal's bed.

There *he* was – the reason I was playing all these bad games. I had guessed, or thought I had guessed, so much about him. The most frustrating thing was that, with Maggie there, I had no way of finding out whether any of my guesses were correct. All I could do was watch him as closely as possible, listen to everything he said, then go home and think about him afterwards – adding this new information to what I already had. (He was looking even more unkempt, today. Did that mean anything? Was he struggling with the dilemma? Would he tell Maggie, now or soon or *ever*, that it was over between them? Would he betray Neal, his best friend in the world? Would he try anything on with me if Maggie and Neal left us alone?) I could also, I thought, flirt a little more obviously; although this risked pushing Maggie too far.

When Neal came back, he handed one of the wine bottles and a bottle opener to Jack. It was a light-looking red wine: Chianti. Not hip, but acceptable.

Everyone watched as Jack opened it. Maggie gazed into his face, hoping for eye contact. Neal looked down at his bare feet, waiting for the sound of the cork. I kept my eyes on Jack's long fingers.

The cork popped and Jack poured. My glass came first, then Maggie's, then his own, then Neal's.

Victory.

We clinked glasses. I didn't say cheers – and none of the others did, either.

'So,' said Jack, turning immediately to me. 'We have to figure out what we're going to do with you.'

'To do with me?'

'Yes. Are we gonna make it easy or difficult?'

'What *are* we going to do?' said Maggie.

'I think we should talk about this later,' said Neal. 'Another time. Now should be a celebration. It's a dig.'

'You see, I don't think you can really jump right in. I think there's gotta be some kind of initiation. Decontamination period. Quarantine. Before you become a Beat, you should be a pre-Beat. That way, we can make sure you get hip to things in the right kind of a way. We don't want you going wrong over anything. So, let's say it's not 1966 – because, of course, you haven't gotten anywhere near as advanced as 1966 yet. You're not on that level of consciousness. Let's say it's 1958. Your favourite book, because you like that sort of thing – you're a seeker – is by D. H. Lawrence. It's *Women in Love*. You haven't even heard of *Lady Chatterley's Lover*. You also read introductions to philosophy by Bertrand Russell. Your bestest ever favourite singer is Cliff Richard. You dig his first single, 'Move It'. But you also dig trad jazz. Bix Biederbecke. Louis Armstrong. Sidney Bechet is about as cool as you get. You have lots of hobbies – you collect wine labels and stamps. You ride a bicycle everywhere. You wear a big thick blue dufflecoat and go on CND rallies in Trafalgar Square. You sing folk protest songs against the bomb.'

'Cliff Richard *and* jazz *and* folk music!' It was all I could think of to say.

'Hey, you're a crazy mixed-up kid. We're gonna find you

and convert you to Beat. It's what you were waiting for all along.'

I was ready to leave, but I played it cool.

'Did you make Maggie do that?'

No one answered.

'I don't need any of that. I'm hip to Beat already.'

'You are?' said Jack.

'Sure,' said Maggie.

'Neal has hipped me to the scene.'

Jack's eyebrows went up. I could see he was trying not to be impressed.

'I was getting hip to Beat while he was getting hip to driving,' I said. 'In *my* car.'

'Cool,' said Jack. 'Cool.'

He lay back on the bed, elbow propping him up. An intolerable smile dimpled his face.

'So,' he said. 'You're one hip *chick*, now.'

I took a big gulp of the red wine, praying it wouldn't go down the wrong way and make me cough uncoolly.

'Yeah. I'm one hip *chick*, brother.'

'What day is it?'

'It's July 29th, 1966. Bob Dylan is dead.'

Jack's hand reached into his pocket and brought out his Golden Virginia stash tin.

'Why don't we toke a little celebratory tea?' he asked, his head turning from Maggie to Neal. 'This is a dig, after all.'

His smile was still there. In fact, it was getting bigger by the second.

I couldn't believe myself. I was turning into Maggie.

No, it was even worse than that: I was turning *myself* into Maggie.

My only real thought – to stop myself getting hysterical – was: *Whatever it takes. Whatever the fuck it takes.*

○

I didn't talk much for the rest of the evening. There wasn't much to say. I was beginning to live with the consequences of my actions.

Jack and Neal discussed how they were going to set up the new magazine. They were trying to come up with a title.

Café Bohemia was Neal's suggestion. *Birdland* and *The 5-Spot* were then mentioned, and dismissed. *Café Bohemia* came back a couple of times.

'*Café Bohemia*,' said Neal. 'The talk is deepest where the coffee's cheapest.'

'Yeah,' said Jack, softly.

Something had almost been decided.

I finally handed over the addresses that had been collected at the reading. By now it was obvious that Jack wasn't going to phone me to ask for them, so I might as well give up that hope. I had typed out the list on my dad's old mechanical typewriter, brought down especially from the attic.

Only Neal showed any real interest.

'This is great,' he said.

Maggie pretended to be busy rolling another joint while Jack pretended to be busy smoking the one she'd just finished.

Neal had put on a long-player by J. J. Johnson, who he called 'the greatest bebop trombonist'. Jack nodded his head to the music and, now and again, held the smoke back until the end of a solo.

When he passed the joint on, it first went back to Maggie, then to Neal, then to me.

I'd never smoked so much dope. It felt like someone was making a cappuccino in my head.

Jack stopped the jazz and played some Dylan on the guitar.

At one point, about halfway through the evening, it was decided (I didn't play much part in this) that when I got home, I would have to start clearing out my bedroom. The reason, though this was never made explicit, was that if Jack were ever going to go there, he didn't want to be confronted with anything too impure. I thought what a hopeless task this refurbishment was going to be. However much I wanted Jack there (the point of the whole charade), I wasn't going to redecorate my whole bedroom *just* for him. We would just have to close the curtains and light a candle. Get under the covers. Hide from the world. Forget appearances.

Slightly later on, all three of the others disappeared into the Temple. They'd each drunk at least a bottle and a half, as well as smoking several joints apiece, but some sort of meditation was thought necessary. I considered listening at the door to see if they really *were* meditating or just using that as an excuse to talk about me. I decided, instead, to play it cool and dig the jazz vibes. When I got bored with this, I picked up a book, then the bongos, then another book. I wondered if I'd gain any kudos by leaving. It wasn't worth the risk to try and find out – and finding out was something I might never do.

When they came back in, they didn't seem any closer to enlightenment. (If anything, it was the next three joints that suggested the possibility of imminent nirvana.) And I was feeling far from blissful myself: Maggie had Jack and I had Neal and I was jealous as fuck.

I couldn't stand hearing her talk about him. Whenever she did, I watched her tongue. I was convinced that, in between words, on certain syllables – th, la, lo – she was sticking her tongue out at me. I also noticed that, during conversations of which *he* was the hero, she spent a huge amount of time speaking with her eyes closed – as if she were keeping his mental image always in front of her as she spoke – so as not to betray it. (All this even though she could open her eyes, turn and see him sitting beside her, listening to her.) But I went further than this and became jealous of her even *thinking* of him. I wanted to distract her – to keep her mind from approaching the subject of him. I imagined doing wild, desperate things to stop her – for just a moment, even – being able to think about anything *at all* other than what I wanted her to: I imagined French-kissing her, suddenly and passionately – or flashing my tits at her – or saying nothing but *fuck* for five minutes. But the trouble with people who've been intimate as long as Jack and Maggie had is that the most off-track thing you could possibly think of – blancmange, JFK airport, Hinduism, alarm clocks – is likely, somehow, to remind them fondly of each other. For lovers, no subject is not *the* subject – and that subject is always *them*. And so, as a final fantasy, I saw myself bashing her head in with a brick – stopping the thoughts and memories dead.

At about ten o'clock, Neal's mother came in to say good-night. The room was a box of smoke. It seemed her natural element. She shared a joint with us, to help her sleep. She promised to consult the I-Ching on my behalf. I could see she was very fond of Jack – almost as fond as she was of his stash. I was starting to worry about my lungs.

As the last bus left Bedford Bus Station at 10.35, I had to leave before the others. Neal had warned me in advance that there'd be a lot of drinking, so I hadn't bothered with the car. Also, I'd suspected – if I brought it with me – that Jack would suggest a joyride. And he did, at one point, ask if I'd come in the car.

I said goodbye to Neal – in front of a very giggly Jack and Maggie, still lying on the bed.

We didn't kiss, though they were obviously *expecting* us to.

Neal squeezed my hand behind my back, where they couldn't see.

I was checking myself in the hall mirror when I heard someone banging down the stairs.

I turned, expecting to see a kiss-wanting Neal – but it was Maggie.

My first thought was that I had forgotten something, and that she'd been sent to return it.

'Go on,' she said. 'Outside.'

I opened the front door and she followed me onto the street.

'Leave him alone,' she said. 'If you don't, I'll tell Neal.'

'Tell Neal what?'

'I saw you. You think you're so subtle. All evening you've been looking at him. Leave us all alone. You have no idea what's going on.'

'Well, why don't you tell me?'

'If you stuck around a bit, you'd see what I mean.'

'I have to catch the bus.'

She held back for a moment.

'You can have Neal, if you want, but Jack's mine. You can see Neal during the day. Teach him to drive.'

'If Neal invites me round, I'm going to come. If Jack's here, then I'll see him. What are you going to tell Neal, anyway?'

'There's lots I can tell him. Enough to make him hate you. All he'll have to do is watch, he'll see for himself. So, you won't even know if I've told him anything or not. You'll just have to *behave*!'

'Maggie,' I said. 'I'd like to be friends.'

But she turned and went back into the house.

O

Walking quickly down Union Street, away from Neal's, felt like an escape.

With every step I was making wilder promises to myself. I wouldn't ever go back. I wouldn't speak to them on the phone. I wouldn't see Neal if he came round. I wouldn't even see Jack if he came round, alone, to beg me to come back. (Really?) I would find a job in London. I would move to London. I would get in touch with some university friends. I would escape *properly*.

I tried to convince myself this reaction had nothing to do with Maggie.

Ever since the reading, I'd been desperate to see Jack. But now I *had* seen him, I didn't feel any better. I just wanted to see him again, sooner this time.

It was *killing* me that I could never get to be with him alone. (I had lots of things I wanted to say to him. There were whole speeches I had worked out, whole scenes I'd gone through.) With Maggie on the alert, it seemed unlikely I'd ever get a chance. She was very observant and very jealous, and I hated her for it.

I reached the bus station, got on a bus and, slowly, it took me almost all the way home.

12

Over the next few days, I became more and more obsessed with Maggie.

I thought about her body, her clothes, her smell. I thought about her till it hurt, physically. I remembered details about her that I couldn't even remember noticing.

What I found most intensely frustrating about her was that she knew Jack better than I did. The thought of this was almost unbearable – particularly as I *knew* that, given half her opportunity, I would have known him at least twice as intimately.

I pulled dead leaves off my giant spider plant, then live ones. I lay on the bed, throwing pop-socks up so they almost-but-not-quite-touched the ceiling. I began to compile a list of things I hated about them together: I hated it when one of them used a phrase or gesture that belonged to the other; I hated it when they both began saying the same thing at the same time – then laughed, looked in each other's eyes, and *knew*; I hated the way they could touch each other without having to make that initial movement that announces *I'm about to touch you*; I hated it when she reached into one of his pockets, knowing exactly what she was going to find there; I hated that gesture he made with his hand, the one that turned her into the whole possible world; I hated to think of them ever discussing me, even nicely; I hated the idea that he knew when she was having her period – and didn't know when I was having mine.

Sometimes, I would go downstairs and walk up to the phone, backwards, turn around three times and walk away – just in case.

But when the phone did ring, around six every evening, my mum would answer.

'It's Neal,' she would call out.

I was so bored by the idea, I almost couldn't make it down the stairs.

My parents took the opportunity to increase their worry-factor to 9.5: I wasn't eating or sleeping properly. I wasn't getting enough exercise. I was watching too much TV.

But I really didn't see what was in front of me. All I saw was Jack and Maggie, on Neal's bed, side by side, laughing, together, intimate, exclusive.

Boy, was I confused.

I was in the gang, which was good. I couldn't help feeling happy about having been accepted. (That Maggie didn't want me to join made me, if anything, a little more happy.) I was happy that Neal was attracted to me. I was happy that Jack didn't disapprove of me and Neal. I was happy that I would be able to get closer to Jack.

But there were so many other things that made me unhappy: Ampthill, my parents, my bank account, my body.

Nearly worst of all was lying to Neal, basing my whole life on a lie. But actual-worst was that I didn't feel as bad about lying as I knew I should.

I was feeling guilty about not feeling guilty enough.

But at least I had something practical, if absurd, to do – once I'd finally decided to do it.

First of all, I went up for a rootle around in the attic –

seeing what I had available to help me make my tastefully contemporary bedroom over into the pad of a hip '60s chick.

Then, after a morning of this, I made my mum a cup of tea, sat her down and gently broke the news.

'Mum, I'd like to make a few small alterations to my room – like I'd like to put these up.'

I pulled the pair of curtains out of the black bin-bag on the kitchen floor.

'Oh, Mary,' she covered her hand with her mouth. 'But I've been meaning to throw those out for years. I don't know why I even kept them.' *Because you keep everything, Mum.* 'We had those up in the flat when we were first married.'

I could believe it. The pattern was made up of those 1950s squiggles and rough-edged dots.

'I'd just like to be surrounded by old things, for a while,' I said.

'Aren't your father and I enough?' she said. 'You're always on at us for being behind-the-times.'

One of the things bringing Neal into my house had made me realise was how up-to-date my parents actually were.

My dad had a PC with a modem; my mum had a kitchen full of gadgets (but *no* microwave). They both knew how to use the TV and set the video. There had even been talk of cabling the phone.

'I can't really explain, Mum.'

'If it's what you want.'

'I'll probably put the others back up in a few weeks.'

'Want *me* to put them back up, more like.'

Now the biggie.

'I'd also like to have a look through your wardrobe.'

'What for?'

'Old clothes. I *know* I've been on at you about getting new things, but –'

108

'You don't have to explain. It's your new friend, isn't it?'

'What?'

'It's his style.'

This wasn't *exactly* true, but it gave her enough of a reason.

'Yes. Sort of.'

By the evening, my room was transformed.

Mum remembered there used to be a lampshade to match the curtains. Once I'd persuaded her up the ladder into the attic, she found the right black bin-bag almost immediately. The same bin-bag yielded a quilted duvet cover that would also do.

'I don't understand you, Mary. It'll be all dirty.'

'Would you wash it for me?'

There was an old rug propped against the far wall of the attic, white with grey stripes. I took it out to the washing line and beat it as clean as I could.

I swapped my Habitat chair for an older wooden one, from the spare room.

The desk, I could do nothing about in itself – so I covered it with a tablecloth and then covered this with old-looking objects: vases, ashtrays, knick-knacks.

I took down all my posters and postcards, patting the small spreads of Blu-Tack off the walls. The lack of decoration was a problem, till I noticed a stack of very tacky paintings, again in the attic. These I'd washed and, after buying some picture hooks, hung. One of them, a raging impasto seascape, had its title chalked on the back: *Midnight in Madagascar*. I quite liked it, and put it up over my bed.

There was nothing I could do about the paint *on* the walls, but no one could object to buttermilk. It wasn't really hip, but it could probably pass as time-darkened whitewash.

I covered the stereo with a spare piece of green velvet. I brought down my dad's old record player and the hippest of his EPs and long-players from the attic. I hid the box of tapes.

By the time I went to sleep the room was as hip as I could make it.

That night I dreamt of Jack.

I woke up feeling guilty.

The dream had reminded me that everything I'd done the previous day had been for Jack, who would probably never even see it – Jack, who was arrogant, sexist, uninterested and attached.

As my dad would have put it, *just what do you think you're playing at?*

Neal was considerate, funny, besotted and available.

And Neal was *mine*, if I could only be bothered to want him. In fact, he was mine already, without me really having done anything. (That's how I saw it at the time, minx that I was.)

Over breakfast, I made a conscious decision to think as little about Jack and as much about Neal as possible. If it was going to be possible to reverse my affections, this seemed the best way to start.

Unfortunately, as everybody knows, this kind of thing never works. If you fall in love with someone there's nothing you can do about it except suffer or enjoy; if you don't, you're even more helpless.

But I did what little I could: I phoned Neal and arranged to pick him up that morning for our second driving lesson.

13

It was a light clear creamy day.

Over my hip-enough T-shirt and chinos, I was wearing one of the few decent things I'd found in my mum's wardrobe: a brown suede jacket. The moment I saw it, I remembered I had borrowed it once already, years ago, to fancy-dress myself as a pirate.

During the drive in, I played my Abba tape.

I was just coming off the roundabout onto Midland Road when I spotted Jack. He was wearing his shades, walking fast and staring at his shoes.

The traffic stopped me about twenty yards ahead of him. I felt fairly safe: his eyes were nowhere near the road and I was pretty sure he wouldn't recognise the car, even if he did see it.

I expected him to keep going past me, out towards whatever his destination was: the railway station or Bromham Hospital, Young Life Corner or Neal's house, even. But he stopped, looked guiltily up and down the pavement, then ducked inside a doorway. It took me about five seconds to realise where he must have gone: the amusement arcade.

The traffic moved off.

Driving past, I couldn't see anything through the tinted glass of the shopfront.

I took the first left and parked as soon as I could, down past the church.

I knew that to go back and spy on Jack was to risk getting caught – but because, by entering that den of ultimate unhipness, he was already so much in the wrong himself, I thought that even if he *did* see me he might pretend not to recognise me.

Whatever happened, *he* was the really guilty one, not me.

I walked up to the arcade door, looking anxiously out for Jack.

The room seemed to be both gloomy and, at the same time, full of lights. I remembered that the building had once been a roller-disco. The carpets were a dirty orange-and-black. The walls were mirrored.

A few steps in, I became very aware that I was the only woman in the arcade.

A group of Asian kids in sports gear were gathered round a game near the door. I sneaked a look between their shoulders: on the screen a computerised young girl ninja was kicking wildly at a computerised old man ninja, throwing fireballs at him, doing somersaults to escape his blows. In the background was a redbrick pagoda with dragons sitting on either side of its entrance. I wondered if they ever came to life.

The boys watching the game gave quiet words of advice to the player and shook their heads when they weren't taken. One of them looked back towards me.

He didn't really look *at* me – I was just an object he could refocus his eyes on. I moved away.

Why had Jack come in here? I had no idea. I felt like I'd seen him going into a shop selling dirty books. I knew that now I had knowledge about him he wouldn't want me to have. I knew I was gaining power over him.

When I caught sight of him, he was standing behind another man at the glass-fronted change booth.

I went and stood so I was mostly hidden by a line of fruit machines.

When he'd got his change – a tenner, I thought I saw – he turned and walked right past me, back towards the door. It happened too fast for me to be scared of him spotting me.

For a moment, I was almost disappointed – if he had just come in here to get change, the whole thing would mean less than nothing. I couldn't confront him with it. It certainly wasn't guilt and impurity.

I wanted guilt and impurity.

I wanted power.

I got it.

Right by the door, a couple of machines along from the Asians, was the game he had come in to play.

He walked straight up to it, not looking at any of the others.

He sat down.

And, now I *saw*, I felt stupid for not having guessed.

I moved along into the next aisle of fruit machines. I was now standing almost directly behind Jack.

Still, I stayed back, in case he caught sight of my reflection in the screen of the Sega Virtua Formula 1995 driving game.

My first feeling was joy at my new power over Jack.

I knew him better than Neal or Maggie did; I had discovered Jack's own disco music, his own Abba, his own shameful unhip secret.

I could see that he was very good at the game. He drove

fast, never crashing or leaving the track, anticipating the corners and taking them easily. Other cars came back towards him and he overtook them with a shimmy of the steering wheel. He changed gear instinctively, rhythmically. He looked a better driver than I would ever be.

Already I was thinking about *when* I might let him know that I knew. I wanted to take a photo of him, to have proof if he denied it. Another part of me wanted to go and tell Neal, to make him a sort of present of the secret. Because if he knew about Jack's unhip secret, he'd surely feel less guilty about his own – and Jack's hold over him would be weakened. But I knew that to tell Neal immediately would be to dispose of the information too quickly and cheaply.

This was something to sit on for a while.

All I had to do now was get out of the arcade without Jack seeing me.

I watched him for a couple more minutes, feeding the fruit machine to stay inconspicuous. What would I say if suddenly he leapt up and grabbed me? The thought, and the tickle of fear, weren't completely unpleasurable. I could always try kissing my way out of the situation.

Escape turned out to be easy. Jack was concentrating so hard on driving that I could probably have called out his name or poked him in the back without making him turn round.

Looking the other way, I walked quickly past and out into the sunshine.

Easy, but I still didn't dare to look back till I'd reached the car.

I needed to sit still in the front seat, breathing, to calm myself down, breathing steadily. With crossed fingers I tapped out my lucky rhythm on the steering wheel – just in case.

'Thank you,' I said. 'Thank you.'

Already I regretted not confronting Jack, there and then – in the middle of all that unhip technology, on the scene of his guilt.

It would have been the first time we had been alone together, away from the others. I could have told him – things.

But confrontation – any kind of melodrama – had never really been my style.

No, this needed thinking about.

I drove straight to Neal's, already a little late for the 'driving lesson'.

He was waiting for me upstairs, and so was Koko.

We talked for a bit as he stashed his trombone away.

I thought it funny I hadn't heard him playing as I came up the stairs. I wondered if he could really play after all.

Neal picked up Koko's travel basket.

'Let's go!' he said, putting on his dark glasses. It was a pure Jackism.

We headed out to Cardington.

Neal wanted to have a look at the huge grey airship hangars.

'They're my favourite buildings of all time,' he said.

'I saw your postcard,' I said. 'In *On the Road*.'

Neal's driving seemed to have deteriorated. He waited far too long at junctions, forgot to check his mirrors and stalled twice. It was only later I realised it must have been nerves.

We got out of the car and stood by the road. The hangars were about half a mile away – square-doored sarcophagi for inflatable Titans were about half a mile away.

'Is it the airships you like?'

'Blimps,' Neal said. 'We call them blimps.'

'Not a very airship-sounding word, is it? Zeppelin's better. More futuristic.'

'They say that the ceilings in the hangars are so high that clouds form inside them. Indoor clouds.'

The idea seemed to make him very sad.

'Would you like to go up in a blimp?' I asked

'Sometimes I think I'm already up and the real problem is going to be getting down.'

'Neal,' I said, 'write a poem instead.'

He looked at me very simply.

'Is it me you like or Jack?'

I would like to remember hesitating, but I didn't.

'It's you.'

Immediately, Neal said, 'We'd like you to come with us to Brighton. I mean, we'd like you to take us to Brighton, in your car.'

'When?'

'As soon as possible. We didn't want to wait until I've learnt to drive. Not now you can take us.'

'So you still haven't told them?'

Neal shook his head as he said, 'We want to go while it's still summer. Soon.'

'What will we do when we get there?'

'Lang invited us, a long time ago, at Otto's funeral. We're going to stay with him, in his house. He has a printing press in his basement. The first issue of *Café Bohemia* has to be out by September. I'll give up my job. Maggie's on holiday from her course. We'll work together, get inspired. I'll edit Otto's journals. Maggie's doing the design.'

I didn't ask what I would be doing.

'You decided on *Café Bohemia*?'

'Jack liked it best. He said 5-*Spot* sounded like pimples.'

'And what did you think it sounded like?'

'Ladybirds.'

Neal was having a fey-day.

Brighton was better than Ampthill. If we had somewhere to stay, it would be cheap. Jack would be around enough for me to grow sick of him. *Yes*, I thought.

'I could probably take you next week. I'd have to ask about the car.'

'I thought it was yours.'

'How long would we stay for?'

'Till *Café Bohemia* is done.'

'I'll phone when I know for definite,' I said.

'Do you really want to come?'

Instead of answering, I gave him a big kiss. A passing car honked at us. Neal didn't seem to notice.

Now I had accepted the invitation, Neal lost interest in continuing the driving lesson.

'Let's go home,' he said.

Though he hadn't made it clear, I was somehow certain – straight off – that he meant *his* home, not mine.

I could hear Neal's mother, in the kitchen, singing, when we walked through the door. It sounded something like opera, though it might also have been jazz. I wondered if her presence made it any less likely that Neal would try and get me into bed.

She was sitting at the kitchen table, smoking a roll-up.

'Is she going?' she asked, immediately we walked in.

Neal went to one of the cupboards.

'But she's only just got here.'

'To Brighton.'

Neal's mother turned to me.

'I hope you said *yes*. He was very worried you wouldn't.'

I was about to answer when Neal said, 'She's going to have to ask her parents.'

Neal's mother looked at me as if I had suddenly become both more and less interesting. There was a pause.

'Why on earth would you want to do that?'

'It's *their* car,' I said.

'Well, they won't stop you stealing it, will they? They wouldn't call the police?'

'Probably not.'

'So you may as well steal it.'

I began to wonder what per cent proof Neal's mother's lunch had been. I felt about twelve.

'Neal's probably told you I don't like cars. In a way, I hope you crash it and all have to walk back.'

'Please don't,' said Neal.

'Not seriously. And you don't have to walk, you could take the train. It goes directly, anyway. I don't see why you don't take the train down there. It's a lovely fast train.'

'You know we can't,' said Neal.

Neal was patting ground coffee down into an old-fashioned aluminium percolator. There was, I noticed, a cafetière upside down on the washing-up board.

'Of course you can. If you stopped playing Jack's silly game for a couple of hours.'

Neal's mother gave me the opportunity, while Neal wasn't looking, to return her conspiratorial look.

'I think we'll go and play some music,' I said.

'I love music,' said Neal's mother. 'Don't you?'

'Yes,' I said.

'It's always such a good excuse for leaving the room when someone else's mother is being terribly embarrassing.'

'I'll come up in a minute,' said Neal.

Neal's mother shouted after me: 'I did your I-Ching!'

I could hear the argument beginning as I went up the stairs.

By the time I got my coffee it was tepid. Neal was too ashamed to explain.

'She's like that, sometimes,' was all he said.

I said, *I understand*, though I wasn't sure I did.

I finished the coffee – very strong, very creamy – and said I had to go.

'I'll call and let you know about if I'm coming to Brighton.'

'But it should still be alright?'

'Well, we're not going to take the train, are we?'

'What train?' asked Neal.

We kissed goodbye, but only lips.

As we walked through the hall, Neal's mother called out from the kitchen.

I sat in the car for a minute, calming down.

I thought about going back to the arcade to see if Jack was still there. But, judging from how little money he had, I doubted that he would still be playing.

The idea of following him and finding out where he lived was very appealing – and I regretted having blown what was probably my only chance to do so.

Driving back through Bedford, I kept hoping to see him.

My parents agreed to the trip without hesitation.

'The car's yours now, you can go where you want in it,' said my dad.

But I couldn't stop thinking of it as theirs.

They asked a few questions about Lang, but seemed more interested in local colour than his morality. *What does he do? Is it a bed and breakfast he runs, then? Does he have any children himself?*

I didn't have any real answers for them.

Dad suggested they get the car serviced and Mum made me promise to send them a postcard with my address on it.

This time, I was genuinely glad for their lack of opposition: I wanted to go to Brighton, whatever was going to happen there. At least *something* would happen. It was bound to.

I phoned Neal with the news. Jack was with him, making plans for the magazine. We decided to leave on Saturday morning.

14

I didn't see Neal, or either of the others, in the week leading up to the road trip. I had decided to be quiet and by myself for a while. We would see enough of each other, I was sure, once we got to Brighton. I thought about taking the bus down to London and doing some clothes shopping, but I felt that even this would somehow be a betrayal; though I wasn't sure any longer of what or of whom. Jack, Neal, Maggie – not one of them was pure. And I could always have kept my dark glasses on.

Neal phoned, every evening; Jack didn't phone.

Each conversation with Neal was full of tips on what I should and shouldn't bring.

My mum's beautiful beige honeymoon suitcase came down from the attic, eliciting some well-meaning jokes from my dad and some tender glances from my mum. I wondered if they still thought I was a virgin.

It seemed as if I had transformed my room for no reason – Jack wouldn't be visiting it before Brighton. Irrationally, I continued to hope that, one unexpected day, he would just turn up.

By the end of the week I wasn't sure if I could really be bothered to put myself through whatever would happen. But then I thought of how disappointed Neal would be, and how disappointed Jack might be, and, of course, how pleased Maggie would be.

I was going.

Neal phoned up on Friday night to tell me I should turn up at about four o'clock on Saturday afternoon. The idea of an early start had been vetoed by Jack: he had never been sighted before noon. We were to arrive at Lang's in time for a welcome dinner.

I thought that was the last I would hear, but the phone went again around eleven o'clock.

I was upstairs packing. My mum answered.

'Mary!' she called, up the stairs.

From her uncertain expression as she stood holding the phone, I could tell it wasn't Neal. Could it at last be Jack?

'It's a girl,' said my mum, cupping her hand over the receiver.

She handed it over.

'Maggie?' I said.

I could hear lots of people in the background. It could only be a pub.

Mum went back into the living room. I closed the door behind her.

'You think you're so clever, don't you?'

'Not really.'

'You think you're so *fucking* clever.'

I waited for whatever was coming.

'But you can't see what's going on. You're *blind*.'

'Why don't you tell me then, Maggie?'

'Because I can't.'

'Why not?'

'Because of Jack.'

'So, what's the point of phoning me up?'

'Tomorrow night, I want you to drive us down to Brighton and then I want you to just turn around and drive yourself back.'

'But I've been invited.'

'Oh,' said Maggie, 'everyone's invited. That's not what's the problem — the problem isn't that.'

'What's the problem?'

'The problem is invited to *what*?'

I don't like being sober and talking to people who are pissed, especially down the phone, even more especially when my mum might be listening. The only advantages, I suppose, are that you can't smell the pissed person and the pissed person can't hit you.

'Who gave you my number?'

'I got it off Jack.'

'Did you see him today?'

'Yes. When we had sex.'

I thought about putting the phone down, but there were still things I might learn.

'I'll see you tomorrow,' I said.

'Jack wants to fuck you.'

'Maggie —'

'But Jack fucks everyone — everyone, all the time. Jack's a fucking fucker.'

My father walked past, carrying the local paper.

'I'll see you tomorrow, Maggie. I hope you get home safely. Oh, and I *will* be staying in Brighton. Good night.'

I heard Maggie say one word before I put the phone down, but it didn't make any sense. It sounded like *yum-yum*.

○

I said goodnight to my parents and went up to bed.

In the bathroom, I stood looking at myself in the mirror.

My face, I thought, used to reach the horizon; now I can see its edges, coming towards me.

There was a toothbrush sticking out of my mouth and foam round my lips.

I was starting – or so I thought – to get some idea of what Maggie was talking about. Her jealousy suggested that Jack really *had* told her that he wanted to sleep with me. The fact she had asked me not to stay over in Brighton was further evidence for this interpretation.

I spat out the toothpaste.

The dental floss was in the medicine cabinet. I decided I had better not floss – not if there was a chance that I might kiss Jack tomorrow. I didn't want to risk bleeding gums.

So, anyway, it seemed as if Jack wanted to be able to have me and had asked Maggie's permission. Or maybe he hadn't – maybe he'd just told her that was what he wanted to do. After all, she was just a chick. Why should he bother what she thought?

But if he intended to spend our nights in Brighton hopping from her bed to mine, where was Neal going to end up? With Maggie? On Lang's sofa? With Lang?

And if that was the set-up Jack envisaged, did I *seriously* intend to play along with it? Could I stand to share him with Maggie? Would I be able to let him go back to her once he'd been with me? Wouldn't I even try to make him choose between us?

I decided to floss. My gums bled a little.

I needed some time to think about this.

Plus, I thought, *I need to see what happens tomorrow.*

O

I drove up Warwick Avenue about ten minutes late.

I had intended to be five minutes early, but discovered that both my parents had speeches they wanted to make.

What surprised me was that they seemed to take this departure more seriously than when I'd gone off to university. I don't know how they knew, but, looking back, they were right – it was.

Jack and Maggie were standing outside Neal's. They were arguing. The only words I heard were Maggie's, who ended a sentence by shouting, '. . . but not together!'

Neal came out of the house with a beautiful brown leather suitcase and a scuffed-up old satchel. He added them to the other luggage: three more suitcases, the trombone case, the naked guitar, the bongos, a box of records, a hatbox and, of course, Koko's travel basket.

The combination of Neal coming out and me driving up quietened if not calmed Maggie and Jack down.

I parked in front of Neal's house and got out of the car.

Without saying hello to me, Maggie stepped off the kerb and crossed the road. Although I hated to admit it, she was looking deeply glamorous today – if not particularly Beat.

She was wearing a fake leopard-skin coat, and getting away with it. But what I noticed most of all were her feet: open-toed high-heel slingbacks displaying ten neatly painted toes. The varnish was an outrageously slaggish blood-red. There were plasters on both her heels. Her hair was up. She had on a darker pair of dark glasses than usual – to hide her pink and hideously puffy eyes, I hoped. She was wearing foundation and lots of powder. It made her appear disconcertingly like an old woman trying to look younger.

'Hi,' said Jack.

'Hello,' said Neal.

'Problems?' I asked.

'Neal will help you load up,' Jack replied, then crossed the road to talk to Maggie.

I unlocked the boot. My mum's honeymoon suitcase, as yet unexposed to Jack's approval, was pushed as far back as it could go into one corner. Everything would fit in, just.

Jack's voice was louder than Maggie's, and he seemed to be doing most of the talking, but their discussion was still disappointingly inaudible.

Neal reached for the biggest suitcase. With some effort he lifted it up, and slid it on top of mine. Then he decided to take mine out and put the biggest suitcase on the bottom.

I picked up the hatbox, intending to slot it in down the side.

'No!' shouted Maggie, trotting back across the road. 'Take it out!' she shouted at Neal.

Jack followed her back over the road.

Maggie turned to me. 'Give me that!' I handed the hatbox over. Neal, however, stood looking at Jack, his hand resting on Maggie's suitcase.

'I'm not going,' Maggie said to Jack. 'I'm not going if she is going to be fucking –'

'Don't!' shouted Jack.

Maggie looked at him through comically narrowed eyes.

'Why not? She's going to have to know soon enough.'

'I think I know already,' I said, and smiled.

Neal seemed surprised.

'Maggie, you can come or you can stay,' said Jack. 'Because, whatever *you* do, *we* are going.'

He reached into the boot of the Chevette and pulled out Maggie's suitcase. Neal stepped back. Jack threw the suitcase onto the pavement. One of its locks clicked open. It span round slowly a couple of times, making a scraping sound.

Jack picked up two suitcases at once and threw them into the boot. I had never seen him so angry.

'We are going right *now*!'

He seized the other small suitcase and violently dropped it on top of the other two. Then he opened the back door and launched the satchel, guitar, bongos and typewriter onto the back seat.

By this time Maggie had started to cry. She was standing, looking down at her painted toes. Her shoulders were slumped.

Neal gave me a look that confirmed we could be nothing but onlookers.

'Get in,' ordered Jack, pointing into the back of the Chevette.

'You bitch!' shouted Maggie. It was a second before I realised she meant me.

Jack opened the front passenger door and got in. He rolled down the window and shouted out, 'Neal, get in!'

Neal stepped over to Maggie.

'Come on,' he said, in his quietest voice. 'We'll sort something out when we get there. Don't make him angry.'

'I don't care. He's so selfish. But I'm not playing his game any more. He can't have everyone. I'm saying no.'

She moved towards the back of the car. I thought for a moment she was going to kick out the back lights, but instead she slammed the boot shut.

After giving her one imploring look, Neal picked up Koko's basket and got in the back of the Chevette. He left the door open and started to arrange things so there would be room for her.

Maggie looked at me directly. I knew that I had to stare her down.

'You can have them,' she said. 'You can have them *both*. I hope you enjoy them. He just wants to have everyone.'

Then she picked up her suitcase and started to drag it along. One side was badly scraped. The hatbox was in her other hand.

'Please come with us, Maggie,' I said. 'I'd like you to.'

She walked towards the car.

Neal turned back to look at me. I don't think he'd ever liked me more.

'Maggie!' he called, as she went past.

But she just kept walking.

Part Two

I

No one said anything until we were out of Bedford.

'Dumb chick,' was Jack's response.

'I think we should write to her and invite her down,' said Neal. 'And maybe apologise.'

'Could someone map-read?' I asked.

'Neal,' said Jack, 'map-read.' He was lighting a cigarette.

Having both Jack and Neal in the car embarrassed me. It felt, for some reason, daring – even though my parents had given their permission for it. At the first roundabout we went round, I made a little *niaow* sound – and they both started laughing. Then, when we got onto the open road, I began – like I always do – to sing. Again, they laughed. If they carried on, I was going to get nervous and, as I do when I feel nervous in a car, I was going to drive too fast and miss my turn-off and get lost – and that would make me drive even faster.

Slow down, I told myself. *Take a chill pill.*

I wouldn't get lost just yet, though: I was driving back the way I had already come, back towards Ampthill.

'The road map is in the door,' I said.

'What?' said Jack.

'Down there,' I pointed.

'It's okay,' said Neal. 'I've got mine here.'

In the rear-view mirror I saw Neal taking a red hardcover book out of his satchel.

'What's that?'

'It's a hip road atlas,' said Neal.

'Should have guessed.'

Jack, even though he was wearing his dark glasses, seemed to be taking some notice of the landscape. There were the chimneys. There was Hunting Engineering.

How long was it since *he'd* been out of Bedford?

It was such a hot day that we had both the front windows wound down.

As we drove up Ampthill Hill, Jack said, 'So, this is where you live, is it?'

'It's further on,' said Neal.

'I'll show you when we drive past. We could go in, if you want. It's a very hip pad, these days.'

'Another time,' said Jack.

We drove through the Market Square, past the Moot Hall.

'Who lives in that funny-looking clock?' asked Jack.

'It's an estate agent's,' I said.

'Upstairs as well?'

'I think so.'

Jack looked out the window, seeing or not seeing The White Hart, Weatherheads, Ampthill Fish Shop, Today's Pine, Central Hairdressing Salon.

'It's on the right here,' I said. 'Down the alley, past the pub.'

Jack looked through me as the glimpse flashed past.

'Will you come and check it out when we get back?' I asked.

'I don't see why not,' said Jack, smiling for the first time.

He glanced at the empty seat beside Neal.

'There's no reason why I shouldn't.'

He flicked his butt out the window.

As we drove past the Mid-Beds District Council offices, Jack put his hand on my shoulder. I know I should have shrugged it off – at least once, at least the first time.

Jack turned to look at Neal.

'We're on the road,' he said. 'We're on the road.'

I glanced up at the rear-view mirror. The Magic Tree was swinging from side to side. Neal was looking, or pretending to look, at the hip road atlas.

'Cool,' he said.

Jack pinched my earlobe gently before dropping his hand back onto his lap.

'We've escaped,' said Jack. 'When we go back – *if* we go back – we'll be different – Things will have changed with us – We will have learnt things and seen things – Life will be different – It may not be better, but it will have changed.'

Exactly, yes.

We had passed through Flitwick and Westoning, and were on our way to Toddington – dull, duller, dullest – when Jack said: 'Which way are we going?'

Neal was silent.

'Well,' I said, 'I looked at the map before we set out. The easiest way is to join the M1 at Toddington, change onto the M25 for the drive round London, then join up with the road – whatever it's called – which takes us all the way to Brighton. It's an A-something.'

'The M1 I've heard of,' said Jack, 'but it doesn't start in Toddington. This M25, though – what is it?'

'Jack –'

'We're best off sticking to the A- and B-roads.'

'Jack,' I said, 'it'll take twice as long.'

'Twice as long as what? We can only ride the roads that exist.'

As the turn-off to the M1 was coming up, I pulled into a lay-by.

Neal was looking back and forth in his hip road atlas between the index and the maps.

'We can either go round London or through it,' he said.

'Round,' I said. 'Definitely.'

'Through,' said Jack.

Neal looked from Jack to me and back, several times.

'Through,' he said, finally.

I was determined not to get angry.

'Okay, if that's what you want. It'll probably be dark by the time we get there and –'

'Perfect,' said Jack.

'And London will be far unhipper than the M1. When was the M1 built anyway?'

Neither of them answered, though I was sure they both knew. We pulled out of the lay-by.

'Go straight on,' said Neal, map-reading.

We passed through Toddington, leaving the chance of the motorway behind.

Our new route would take us through Dunstable and onto the A5. We would follow that down to South London, where we would join the A23, which would take us all the way to Brighton.

Lunacy.

The landscape was nothing special: houses, hedges, pedestrians, trees. It looked like Ampthill, only slightly more spaced out – in both senses.

The cool of evening was welcome after the swelter of day.

I enjoyed the hot smell still coming off the vinyl seats.

This was how my childhood summer holidays had always begun – only *then* I'd been in the back, on the side where Neal was sitting, with my favourite doll on the seat beside me.

Neal asked, 'Can I let Koko out? I'm sure she'll behave.'

'Of course,' said Jack.

I thought it might be dangerous, but didn't say anything.

I needn't have worried: Koko immediately made her way onto the rear window shelf.

Once the basket was off his lap, Neal announced: 'I'm going to write Maggie a letter, to explain.'

'What's there to explain, man?' said Jack. 'The chick just flipped – She wigged out and split because she couldn't stand the heat – She just lost it – Went loco – She cut out on us, brother – Right from in front, she's always been crazy – Maggie couldn't make the scene, you dig?'

This burst of jive shut everyone up.

I thought about putting on the radio, but then – of course – Jack wouldn't allow that. There was no way I could guarantee the records we'd hear would all be pure – not even on Radio 2.

After a while, I heard clattering noises behind me. I assumed it was just Neal arranging things to make himself comfortable. But, a couple of moments later, I was astonished to hear the regular clacking of a typewriter.

Jack turned round slowly. His look, pretty obviously, was intended to stop Neal right where he was.

'I'm writing to her,' said Neal. 'I'm writing whether you like it or not. We shouldn't have left her like that.'

'Let her come on after us, then,' said Jack. 'Let the dumb chick do what she wants. Don't go wasting paper on her.'

But Neal didn't stop typing.

O

We were just coming out of St Albans when Jack started up:

'It's such a drag we aren't in America and this isn't the beginning of a three-thousand-mile drive — off into the heart of the wild neon American night — coast to coast — along all the long heavenly roads — having wild adventures and high times and sad times — meeting up with old buddies and making new ones — making crazy detours for guys thumbing rides.'

Neal chimed in immediately:

'England is such a small island. You drive to the edge, then all you can do is stop. There's nowhere else to go. Unless you keep driving. Unless you go over the edge — off the road — into the sea. I want to keep going. I never want to stop. North, south, east, west — I don't care. Just get me off this island! Take me away! Take me to America!'

I'd never heard him speak so wildly.

He kept going:

'We're stuck here, hemmed in. That's why there's no rhapsody of our roads. England has no Whitman; could never have. There's no fucking acceleration here. As soon as you start going fast and mad enough, you have to slow down and stop, turn slowly round and start speeding up again. We're stuck here. But I want to get out! Brighton isn't far enough for me. I want to go all the way: New York to San Francisco, via Denver — and then down to New Mexico. Maybe stop off in Lowell, see Kerouac's birthplace, or Woodstock, where Dylan died. Or find Desolation Peak. Or Hibbing. Or Big Sur. But just cruising through, you know, windows down. Stopping only to pick up hitchhikers. Picking up speed, picking up more speed. Being there only as long as you're passing through. I want to stop being a point, I want to be a line. I want to be an arrow, a meteor, a highway.'

Jack had wound down the window all the way. He stuck his head out and started screaming: 'I'm getting out of here! You're still here, I'm already gone!' He whooped. 'I'm gone!'

Eyes were following us: a woman with her kids outside McDonald's, a man in a cardigan waiting at some traffic lights, a policewoman ticking off a couple of skateboarders.

Jack stuck his head back in.

'Drive faster!' he said. 'And honk the horn!'

'No,' I said.

'What?'

'I'm going at thirty. If I go any faster, I'll get caught on a speed camera.'

'A what?'

'I don't care if you don't know *what*, I do – and I'm not paying.'

Jack quieted down a bit.

'Don't you wish this was America, Neal?'

'There's *nowhere* I want to go more than America.'

'We'll get there, brother,' said Jack. 'This is just the sad and early first stage of the trip. We're accelerating towards it. When we get going fast enough, we'll broom away across that holy ocean and really *be* there.'

'All of us,' said Neal. 'Mary and Maggie as well.'

Whether it was intended to or not, this finally brought Jack back to reality.

'But Brighton first,' he said. 'First and fast.'

I tried to stick to thirty. But it was difficult.

I wish something interesting had happened on our road trip, but nothing did. We didn't even stop for petrol.

Going into London was okay, but coming out we found ourselves in the middle of a mini Saturday rush hour.

Looking out the window as we rode over the downs, Neal, in a very quiet voice, said: 'It's very Englandy, isn't it?'

I knew what he meant – green and pleasant and lumpy and overpopulated.

Most of the time, though, we all sat in silence. Neal had packed up the typewriter after finishing the letter. Jack stared out of the window and chain-smoked Woodbines. I tried to think if there was anything I'd forgotten – or anything I shouldn't have brought: I was particularly worried what Jack would say when he saw my brand of shampoo.

We arrived in Brighton at about eight o'clock.

Lang lived in a boxy white house in the middle of a long row of boxy white houses: Kensington Place.

'Honk the horn,' said Jack, as I was drawing up outside the number he had given me. I did.

I watched for the front door to open. Neal got out of the car and went round to the boot.

'Toot it again,' said Jack.

'Can't you just knock?' I asked. In truth, I was embarrassed by the Chevette's wet fart of a horn.

But Lang appeared before anything further was necessary, walking up the stairs from the basement. His fingers flicked along the black-painted railings.

I got out of the car. Lang was shaking hands with Jack. Neal was standing to one side.

From what I could see, Lang was perfectly hip. He wore a charcoal-grey suit, white shirt and green tie. All conventional enough, if rather '50s looking – but on his head he had a French beret. When he later removed it, I saw that he was completely bald.

As I walked around the car, he reached into the breast pocket of the suit and brought out a pair of dark glasses.

Jack laughed and patted him on the back.

'Cool,' he said.

'But where is Maggie?' Lang asked.

'She couldn't come,' said Neal.

'She *didn't* come,' said Jack.

'She *wouldn't* come,' I said.

'And you must be Mary.' Lang stepped over.

For a moment I thought he was going to kiss my hand. Instead, he contended himself with: '*Enchanté, mademoiselle.*'

He smelt of ashtrays and unflossed teeth.

'Let us go indoors,' Lang said. 'Tonight we are going to have lightly boiled asparagus, chicken's livers in a sauce of white wine and wild mushrooms, *crème brûlée*, Roquefort and truffles.'

He stepped towards the front door, patted his pockets, then turned back to us.

'I'll just go round and let you in.'

After he'd disappeared down the basement steps, Jack turned and spoke to both of us: 'Don't mention Maggie again.'

We unloaded the suitcases and other stuff onto the pavement. Lang opened the front door from the inside.

'Welcome!' he said. 'Jack, you are in the guest room.'

Jack took the biggest two suitcases. Neal followed him with the next two biggest. I took the typewriter and Koko's basket.

Inside, the house was very dark. It smelt even worse than Lang himself. We walked through a dusty, book-filled hall. I didn't have time to notice any titles.

We passed a closed door.

'You can leave Koko here,' Neal said.

I placed her basket on the lowest stair.

The upwards staircase was to our right. It wound round, very tightly. The suitcases Neal was carrying bashed into my knees.

On the first floor, there was a small bathroom, a small study and two bedrooms: one small, one medium-sized. Jack led us into the medium-sized bedroom.

In the centre of the room was a big brass bed. There was a proper dressing table, a couple of wardrobes, a chest of drawers. Bare black boards made up the floor and the walls were unadorned whitewash. The window looking out onto the back garden was net-curtained.

'Where am I?' I asked.

'You're in here,' said Jack.

'And where are you?'

'I'm in here, as well.'

'Jack, there's only one bed.'

'I think that'll be enough,' said Jack.

He brushed past me and went back downstairs. I didn't move. I didn't say anything.

Neal was standing with me.

Between us, we managed to distil a pretty heady silence. Someone had to say something, preferably before Jack got back.

'Do you mind?' I asked.

'Mind what?'

'If I sleep with Jack.'

'Only if . . .'

'What?'

'I better go and let Koko out.'

'Neal!' I said, but he didn't come back.

I sat down on the edge of the bed, the typewriter lying heavy on my lap.

The counterpane was a beautiful eggshell blue. The sheets seemed to have been recently laundered.

Downstairs, Jack was laughing at something.

I put the typewriter on the bed. Nothing had prepared me for this, even though I still wasn't sure what *this* was.

Before I'd given myself a chance to think what I was going to do, I took myself downstairs.

Jack and Neal had brought the rest of the stuff in from the car. I realised that I still had the car keys in my pocket.

Jack's laughter came again from the back of the house.

I went through. I could smell cooking. It was the kitchen. Though it was still light outside, the room was candlelit.

'I'd like to go for a walk on the beach,' I said.

'After we eat, surely,' said Lang. 'It's almost ready.'

'I'd like to take a look at the sea.'

'Would you like some wine?' asked Jack.

'It's a very good wine,' said Lang. 'To celebrate.'

'I need to lock the car,' I said.

'I've done it already,' said Neal.

In the centre of the table were a couple of candles in raffia-covered bottles. There were four big white plates, four places laid. There was a clunky glass cruet. Lang had a tea towel folded round the wine bottle.

Koko was on the floor with a bowl of milk.

'The asparagus is almost ready,' said Lang.

'Come on,' said Neal.

I joined them at the table. Lang filled my glass.

Neal and Jack were to my left and right; Lang was opposite me, to be nearer the cooker.

'Let's eat,' he said.

The food was excellent. When he could be bothered, Lang was an exceptional cook – a chef, almost.

During the meal he talked, mostly to Jack, about how

141

they were going to produce *Café Bohemia*. The printing press was in the basement. He'd just been pulling the covers off it when we turned up.

After the cheese tray had been cleared away and espressos had been served, Lang begged our silence.

'I have seen you arrive, my friends. You are not in high spirits. You are suffering – and suffering badly – from the ennui of the provinces. You are the Provincials – sons and daughters of the respectable *petite bourgeoisie*. But do not despair! All great men, and women, emerge from the provinces – or, at the very least, the suburbs. The great become great by fighting their way out of obscurity; not only their *personal* obscurity, but also the obscurity of their province. Great destinations require humble origins, pass through bizarre suburbs, traverse lost roads – but, in the end, arrive! Definitely, my Provincials, you will arrive! You feel stuck, embedded, wasted. But Brighton for you will be but a resting point, an intermediary between you and your futures – your glorious futures. More wine. A toast. Welcome to the Provincials!'

We all stood up and clinked glasses. We all sat down again.

As no one seemed inclined to add anything, I said: 'I would like to go down to the beach, when we're finished.'

'You Provincials are so impatient,' said Lang.

'Wait a bit,' said Neal.

'No!' said Lang. 'Go! *Be* impatient! I'll do the washing-up.'

'I'm happy to go on my own.'

'We'll come with you,' said Jack.

2

As we walked down to the beach, I deliberately fell behind Jack and Neal. They realised what I was doing, and didn't make it difficult.

Even though I was preoccupied with trying to think, I couldn't ignore the Pavilion. It was floodlit, and looked as if it was heavily flavoured with vanilla. While I gazed at it, I felt like I was somewhere far more interesting than England.

The only thing I knew about it was that the outside was all Indian in style and the inside was Japanese – or Chinese – or something.

A crazy mixed-up building. I could relate to that. *Inside*, I was crawling to the beach on my hands and knees; *outside*, I seemed to be capable of walking – though not necessarily in a straight line.

To my left was an area of green and trees, a sort of huge traffic island. This, I was sure, was the road we'd come into town on. Up ahead were pale hotel-looking buildings and, in between them, the gaudy lit-upness of a pier.

Neal and Jack seemed to be talking. It was probably only paranoia that convinced me that I was their subject.

We crossed over a couple of roads and went down onto the beach.

The lights on the low dome in the middle of the pier

crawled along in long lines, like ants entering and leaving their nest.

The stones of the beach weren't the best surface for walking on – sometimes they gave a lot and sometimes they didn't give at all. You never knew what to expect.

We turned right.

Ahead of us, stuck a little out to sea, was another pier – grey, derelict, not illuminated, more ghostly than the other. I knew immediately which I preferred.

Jack and Neal were still up ahead.

I wondered if they were deciding what to say, or who would say it, or who would say what.

In a funny way, I missed Maggie. At least she was another female. Now it was just me, alone among the men.

Then, all of a sudden, I felt very glad she *wasn't* there. It was very glamorous, being the centre of attention – though glamorous probably wasn't the right word. The whole thing was up to me. I had important decisions to make.

I crunched to the very edge of the sea, bent down and dipped my fingers into the water.

Jack and Neal had stopped walking. They were standing, looking back at me. No doubt about it – I was being doubly chaperoned.

I picked a couple of stones up and threw them as far as I could, without really trying. Then I started walking again, on towards the derelict pier.

Jack and Neal kept ahead of me.

We went past a few groups of two or three, sitting on blankets on the beach. Some were smoking and passing bottles, some kissing.

When we reached the pier, I looked at it as closely as possible. There was a sign visible, which made a little poem:

West Pier
Dangerous Structure
Keep Off
& Keep Clear

I walked back and sat on the concrete wave-break.

'Hey!' I shouted. 'Come here!'

Jack and Neal ambled over and sat down on either side of me.

'Tell me what you're suggesting.'

'It's called *yabyum*,' said Jack.

I remembered Maggie's parting shot on the phone: *yum-yum*.

'What's that, the Buddhist word for *threesome*?'

'You could say that,' said Jack. 'It's to do with a sharing of mind and body. But there's no real limit to numbers.'

'Really?'

I thought of Lang.

'Theoretically.'

'And Maggie did this?'

'Of course,' said Jack.

'That's what upset her, isn't it? She was okay about me coming down here, but she didn't want you two to go to bed with me.'

'Or maybe she didn't want to go to bed with you herself.'

Right.

'Neal?' I asked.

'Maggie always had problems with *yabyum*.'

I told them about the night before, about Maggie's phone call.

'She was a very uptight chick.'

I turned to Neal.

'You told me you were a virgin.'

'I am.'

'A *very* uptight chick,' said Jack, then laughed.

'So, what did you do?' I asked Neal.

'Other things.'

'Neal, do you *want* this?'

Jack was bashing two pebbles together, annoyingly.

'I don't know.'

'Neal's really into it. You know how he digs you. It'll be a ball.'

I looked back towards the lit-up pier. There was a mini fun fair on the end of it: a Big Dipper.

'What about you two, then?' I asked. 'Are you into *yabyum* together – with each other?'

'Sure we are,' said Jack.

'Are you?'

Neal nodded and continued to look at his shoes. I stood up and took a couple of steps away from them.

'Kiss each other,' I said. 'I want to see.'

For a moment I thought I *had* Jack.

Neal as I'd expected was stamping his feet and crumpling his body up into a ball.

Jack bashed the stones together a couple of more times, then dropped them. He moved over to Neal, put his arm round his shoulder and kissed him on the cheek.

'No,' I said. '*Properly.*'

Neal looked up at me, his eyes were almost crying.

Jack put his hand on Neal's cheek and forced him to make eye contact. Then he kissed him.

Properly.

I felt winded, thrilled.

It was as if I had just jumped off something, something very tall.

I had dared them to kiss but now their kiss had become a dare to me; it was up to me to do something to match it.

There was only one thing I could think of.

I went up to Neal. He didn't want to look at me. I lifted his head up and kissed him. His cheeks were clammy wet.

Then I turned to Jack and kissed him as well. As I did so, I heard Neal walk away.

The kiss with Jack went on for much longer than the kiss with Neal.

When we parted Jack said: 'Shall we go back to Lang's?'

'Okay,' I said.

Neal was already halfway along the beach.

We ran to catch him up.

We walked along the street, holding hands, all three of us, me in the middle.

When we got back, Lang was still in the kitchen. We went straight upstairs.

The overhead light was a bit too much, so Neal went and brought some candles up from downstairs. He also made a second trip to fetch our glasses and another bottle of wine. For a moment I worried, ridiculously, about which of the glasses had been mine before.

We took our shoes off and lay on the bed. Neal was to my right and Jack to my left.

Part of me wanted to ask them if this had been the arrangement with Maggie and, if it had, get them to swap round.

The room felt very warm and close all of a sudden. Jack spilled a little wine onto one of the pillowcases.

After the freedom of the beach, everything here seemed to have retreated back into constraints. For once, Jack seemed to be leaving the breaking of them to me. I was grateful for that.

'We're not going to sleep in our clothes, are we?' I asked.

Jack stood up and, in a very few seconds, was naked. His clothes fell in a ring at his feet. He got back in, under the covers.

'If we're going to have sex,' I said, matter-of-factly, 'it's got to be safe – and please don't pretend you've never heard of *safe* sex.'

'You mean we use rubbers?' said Jack.

'Call them what you want, but you're putting one on.'

'That's fine,' said Jack, quietly.

'I'm just going to the bathroom,' I said.

I opened my suitcase and took out my washbag.

The bathroom was at the top of the stairs. It was small, and everything in it was porcelain or stainless steel. The bath was quite clean, but the toilet was disgusting.

I badly needed a pee.

As I sat down on the loo, I felt one of those huge shivers go through me – as if someone had frozen me, then poured hot water down my spine.

I wasn't going to think about what I was going to do, I was just going to do it. Whatever happened afterwards happened: I would take an equal third of the responsibility. For the moment, I would call the whole thing having fun, an experiment, *yabyum*.

By the time I got back, teeth brushed and nerves steadied, Neal had undressed and got under the covers.

The two boys didn't seem to have been doing anything – not even touching each other.

Undressing wasn't so bad, in the flattery of the candlelight.

Neither of them stared or even looked at me. Their clothes were on the floor; they'd left the chair for mine.

I crawled across the counterpane and got in between them. Jack drew his feet up, so I didn't crush them.

The sheets were old and soft and many-times washed. Compared to the grime of the rest of the house, their cleanliness was a surprise and a turn-on.

The only other time I'd been in bed with two other bodies, I realised, was when my parents had made an exception during thunderstorms. Of course, my dad wore pyjamas and my mum wore a nightdress – and so did I.

The bed was already very warm, so I pushed the counterpane down.

Jack turned slightly towards me, then reached across and stroked my breast.

'You're very beautiful,' he said.

'Shh,' I said. 'No talking.'

I was a little worried that Lang might hear.

Neal copied Jack, and stroked my other breast.

I put my hand behind Neal's head and brought his face down close to mine.

'Are you okay?' I asked.

'You said no talking,' said Jack.

'I meant *you*,' I said. 'Shh.'

'I'm okay,' said Neal.

I kissed Neal.

Jack had my nipple between his fingertips. Neal began to kiss my neck. One of my hands was playing with his hair, the other was slightly crushed under Jack.

Jack kissed me.

To kiss two people, one after the other, is to end up comparing them: Jack's mouth was large and cigarettey; Neal's small and sweet. There were other comparisons to be made: Neal smelt of marzipan and apricots; Jack smelt of coffee and coal.

I pulled my arm out from under Jack and began to play with his nipples.

Slowly, we relaxed – I relaxed – and we began to kiss and touch more randomly. I still hadn't seen Jack kiss Neal, but I felt them touching each other – over me.

Being in bed with two other naked bodies, rather than the single one I'd always been used to, was very strange. It felt as if there was too much and too many – too much weight, too much flesh; too many mouths, too many choices. That was the worst thing: the constant having-to-choose-between. There was always someone being rejected or dis-placed – there was always someone you were turning away from – and that person, more often than not, seemed to be Neal.

I was now holding them both. Neal's penis was the larger and more erect of the two.

Jack was sucking and biting my nipple. Neal was sucking and biting my ear.

I realised that it now *meant* something, how much pleasure I showed. But competition was a stupid way of looking at it. I didn't want to be constantly judging between them. That wasn't fair. I was still thinking that I was a girl in bed with two boys, not that we were three bodies all in bed together: I was still thinking that it was *their* job to do things to me, to give me pleasure.

I realised that I hadn't closed my eyes once. I was keeping tabs, itemising, judging.

Didn't I trust them?

The fact Neal was a virgin worried me.

I kissed him and closed my eyes and, immediately, I started to become confused. I kissed mouths at random, not knowing whose they were until the kiss had begun. I got onto my knees and they moved together, beneath me. Our movements became wilder. Sometimes, I was shocked to find that an area of flesh I had been caressing was, in fact, my own. After a certain stage of abandonment, though, this didn't seem to matter. Pleasure, although unfixed and moving, was always there as something I could aim towards. They were kissing and touching each other, now – I was sure. Suddenly, I got that seasick feeling – of it all being too unanchored, too stormy – but I relaxed and let it pass. I could take pleasure now without feeling guilty. I wanted it.

I lay back down, eyes still closed.

My nipples were being sucked, tongues ran round and round them – flicking, stroking.

Hands met in the space between my legs. I was wet already. One of them would finger me while the other circled my clitoris. (They had done this before, I thought, and almost laughed. There was teamwork in it.) One of them hadn't cut his nails, and I felt small cuts being made in the walls of my vagina. Jack, I thought. It wasn't unpleasant. I would tell him about it, privately, tomorrow. It didn't hurt that much.

Their identities became clearer again. Now Neal was nibbling my ear, now Jack was kissing my neck; now Jack flicked butterfly kisses over my lips, now Neal brushed his fingers along my eyelashes.

Then Neal moved aside for a moment.

There was a gentle ripping sound, foil being torn.

Jack was fingering me.

Neal got between my legs and eased himself inside me.

I put my hands on his buttocks.

This was his first time, ever.

I had never had sex with a virgin before.

Neal started to fuck me. He was very intense. At the edges

of everything, there was pain. He seemed to be attacking me, as much as anything. I could hear him grunting.

Jack tried to kiss me, but I pushed him off.

Neal fucked me faster and faster.

'Go on,' I said, moving my nails over his sides. 'Oh, yes.'

Suddenly, he came.

I could have, too; I was almost there. If he'd kept going a little longer.

When I opened my eyes to look up at him I saw, under his arm, Lang, standing in the doorway, watching.

Neal bent down to kiss my forehead. He was still inside me, though I could feel him getting smaller.

I felt as if I was going to shit myself.

How long had Lang been there? What the fuck was going on? Why hadn't Jack told him to fuck off? Had this been prearranged or had he just heard our noise? Was this our way of paying the rent? In the midst of this live bed show, was he most interested in me or Jack or Neal? Was he about to join us?

Neal pulled back a little and smiled at me.

'Thank you,' he said.

He slipped out of me and fell to one side.

Lang saw me looking at him, I'm sure, but he didn't smile or anything. He didn't go away. He didn't change his stance. I couldn't see whether he had an erection. He was wearing a dressing gown.

Jack was now unrolling a condom onto his penis.

Neal was stroking my arm.

I closed my eyes.

Jack started to fuck me.

I smelt cigarette smoke. Lang had lit a cigarette!

Jack was slower than Neal, and more controlled. He knew what he was doing – which, in a way, made it less exciting.

He reached down and stroked my clitoris. He kept kissing me.

Somehow, I forgot Lang and started to think about Jack. This was him, here, now – fucking me. This was what I'd wanted from the moment I saw him. I'd seen off Maggie – I'd accepted Neal – now, I *had* Jack.

After this, I came very quickly.

Halfway through a particularly loud cry, I remembered Lang, but let it go anyway.

It wasn't the best orgasm ever, but it was a huge relief as it felt like the foreplay had been going on for weeks.

Jack, who seemed to have been holding back, hurried to finish off. I would have been more comfortable if he'd stopped, but I let him bring himself off inside me. I could smell the cigarette smoke again.

Jack pulled out of me faster than Neal had. He sat on the edge of the bed furthest from Lang, tying a knot in the condom. Neal had just let his slip off, wetting the sheet.

Neal started to kiss me.

Jack was gently touching my breasts.

Gradually, our movements became slighter and slower. The gaps between kisses grew.

I pulled their hands away from my vagina and onto my breasts – patting them down, telling them to lie still. They obeyed.

Lang shut the door behind him.

I dozed off, then woke to feel Neal pulling a single sheet over us.

Again I woke up, feeling tipped to one side as Jack got back in. The candles had been blown out.

I sleep on my left side, so I was lying turned towards Jack. But I could feel Neal spooned up close around me and hear his slow breathing.

Jack whispered, 'Good night.'
After that, I slept till morning.

3

I woke up alone, surprised.

There were smells rising from downstairs – the heavy salty smell of bacon and eggs, the edgier smell of blackened toast, the softer smell of tea.

The net curtains were a field of white-grey light. I looked about for an alarm clock, but there wasn't one. The skin on my face was sore with shag-rash.

If I waited long enough, breakfast would surely appear on a tray – surely Neal would bring me up something.

But that would be taking advantage of him and not taking advantage of Jack. I had to be careful.

The floor felt cold against my bare feet.

I looked out the window. The garden was a square of concrete surrounded by weedy flowerbeds. Koko was there, burying something. It was going to be another cloudless day.

This was exactly the right sort of room, I decided, for what had happened: neutral, hotel-like. If there had been a conspiracy to seduce me, then the room had been the fourth conspirator. I didn't mind that much.

I couldn't be bothered to unpack properly, so I put on yesterday's clothes.

The dressing table had three equal-sized oval mirrors. (Two more, at least, than I needed.) I looked a complete whippy-head. It took me ten minutes to comb the fuck-knots out.

The question wasn't, *Did I feel guilty?* but, *Had I done anything wrong?*

Lang was standing at the cooker, his back to the door.

'Hi,' said Jack, as I walked in.

'Good morning,' said Neal.

'I hope you slept well,' said Lang, without turning round. Was he embarrassed?

'It's a very comfortable bed.'

'Bacon and eggs do you?'

'Lovely.'

Jack and Neal were at the dining table, emptied plates in front of them. I joined them.

'You can type, can't you?' said Jack.

'One finger. Why?'

'We were just talking about it. Maggie was going to be typist on *Café Bohemia.*'

Lang draped two strips of bacon into the crackly pan.

'I can type,' said Lang.

'Really?' said Neal.

'Many talents.'

'What's going to be in it?' I asked.

'It's going to be new,' said Jack. 'Completely new. All except for Otto's stuff. We're going to write it right here.' He banged his palms on the table. He was never more attractive than when he was pretending to be literary. 'It's got to be spontaneous. We'll write it first, then print it.'

'What about the addresses you took?'

'None of those cats were hip to the scene. Except Jane. She may post something down. She knows where we're at.'

'And if I write something?'

'Cool,' said Neal.

'We'd just have to see about that,' said Jack.

I poured myself some stewed tea.

Neal offered to make some fresh.

'Yes, thanks, Neal,' I said.

Lang cracked a couple of eggs into the pan.

I was watching him, to see if he would look at me directly.

'And what are the Provincials doing today?' asked Lang.

'I think we'll just get with it,' said Jack.

'Very good,' said Lang.

Get with it –

That turned out to mean sitting round the kitchen, smoking or not smoking, drinking cups of tea, talking about what we'd do *if* we were to do something.

Lang had gone out, after finishing the washing-up.

'What does *he* do?' I asked.

'Shopping,' said Jack.

'But for a living.'

'He doesn't work – he's got enough money not to.'

I phoned my parents to let them know I'd arrived safely.

'Is everything alright?' asked Mum. 'Did you pack the towel with the blue stripes?'

While Jack and Neal were talking, I was able to have an explore. Lang's front room was full of clichéd junk-shop discoveries. But somehow he'd made it okay by having two of everything, side by side: two phrenologist's heads, two box Brownies, two wind-up phonographs, two sets of Russian Matryoshka dolls, two Victorian samplers. There were also two of every book. Mostly, these were existentialist classics: Kierkegaard, Nietzsche, Sartre, Beckett, de Beauvoir, Genet, Ionesco, Camus. From what I could see, Lang operated some fairly strict rules of hipness himself. But as he'd been doing it for longer, he could be even more exacting: all the books were hardback first editions – in English and French.

When nothing seemed to be happening, I started reading *Nausea* – but Sartre soon bored me.

I put him aside and looked at Ionesco, but he lost me, too.

At about one, we had a quiet lunch.

Lang returned in the afternoon. He came straight into the front room and put a couple of packages on the desk. He said *Bonjour*, but didn't look at me.

I went back to Sartre. (I think I preferred Kerouac.)

After an hour or so, Neal came in and sat down.

'I said I was going to teach you to meditate. Would you like to learn now?'

'Okay,' I said.

'Shall we go upstairs?'

'Is Jack coming?'

'He thinks I should teach you.'

We went up to the bedroom.

'Take your shoes off,' Neal said. 'You don't want to be wearing anything constraining.'

He got onto the bed. I joined him.

'Can you do the lotus position?'

After an interesting moment, I realised he meant sitting. 'No.'

'Well, you can just sit cross-legged. None of us can do the lotus, either. Maggie can do a half-lotus. She used to do gymnastics.'

'Did you finish your letter?'

'I got Lang to post it for me.'

'Does Jack know?'

'Can we start?'

'Are you okay, Neal?'

'Have you ever meditated before?'

I told him no, and he began to teach me. Mostly, he said, I should concentrate on my breathing. I should count ten breaths, thinking about the in breath; ten breaths, about the out breath; ten breaths, about where the air first hit my nostrils. Then I should go back to the beginning of the cycle – though I could start on any one. He said not to breathe any slower or faster than normal, but deeper and more regularly. Trying too hard to empty my mind of all thoughts wasn't a good idea. It was better just to let the breathing happen.

'I understand,' I said, looking as serious as I could.

When his explanation finished, we tried for about fifteen minutes. As soon as we stopped talking, I started to hear things in the room and outside. The loudest sound was Neal's breathing – immediately regular and self-soothed. Neal's wristwatch, an old-fashioned wind-up one, was the next microsound to come through. Then there was the hushing-straining of water running in old pipes: Jack must be filling a kettle. Next was a car going by in the street outside. After that were the cries of a seagull, the gurgling of my stomach, the creak of the bed springs, a TV or a radio next door.

My ankles started to feel crampy under my weight. There was an itch developing behind one of my ears. I was worried that it was an insect, trapped in my hair.

My hands never seemed to be comfortable. I zipped the fingers up, laid one palm on top of the other, made a prayer tent, let them flop at my sides. I wondered if I had arthritis or Parkinson's.

Throughout all this, I kept losing count, kept forgetting

which part of the breath I was meant to be concentrating on.

I was getting stressed out at how badly I was doing.

Although Neal had told me not to worry about clearing my mind, I couldn't help thinking of things: sex with Jack, sex with Neal, Lang watching, being in Brighton, being in Lang's house, Maggie being left behind, Neal's secret, Jack's secret, my car, how hungry I still was, breakfast, whether that bulge under my hand really *was* my belly, a diet, the contents of the fridge downstairs . . .

'Okay,' I heard Neal say. 'Start coming out.'

But I haven't even been in!

'That's enough for now.'

I was taking a last few breaths when I felt the bed springs dipping. Neal kissed me on the mouth.

'You did very well,' he said.

I opened my eyes.

'I didn't do anything.'

'Exactly,' he said. 'Most people can't even sit still. Not-doing-anything is everything.'

'Don't go all Buddhist on me, Neal.'

'But that's what we're trying to do.'

I gave him an affectionate kiss.

Jack was still sitting at the kitchen table when we came down.

'Where's Lang?' I asked.

'He's gone to see the man. I asked if he could get us some real gone grass. He said he knows some spade cat can lay it on him. I'd like us all to get turned on, tonight, before we make out.'

'Are *we* going out today?' I asked.

'Not till the evening. Not till it's dark.'

'What?' said Neal, disappointed.

'There's too much bad stuff around. We're here because Lang's is a hip pad, not because Brighton is a hip place. It's hipper than Bedford, but it's not all that hip.'

I tried for a moment to accept this, but:

'I'm going out,' I said. 'I'm not suffocating in here. Neal, do you want to come?'

'It's a bad idea,' said Jack, to both of us.

'I don't know,' Neal said.

'Have some tea,' said Jack.

'Okay,' said Neal. 'Let's go.'

'Don't!'

But we were out the door.

'Are you okay?' I asked Neal, as soon as we got onto the street.

'I'm okayer than I've been for a long time.'

'Are you sure?'

'Not really,' he said.

'Where shall we go?'

'Let's go to the Palace Pier. I like the Palace Pier.'

We walked towards the seafront.

'Is it last night that's bothering you?'

'No,' he said hurriedly, 'I don't mind that. Not in itself. It is difficult, though, isn't it?'

'It's not something I've done before.'

'I find it quite hard to share people.'

'Was it okay? I mean, to lose your virginity like that – with other people there.'

'It was with you. That's good enough for me.'

'We're going to be okay,' I said, and put my arm round

him. 'We can do things without Jack — like the meditating or like this.'

'Of course,' said Neal.

We walked down to the front and out along the pier without saying anything else.

I wasn't sure if Neal would want to go near the amusement arcades, but he showed no reluctance.

We walked into a wall of sound: fuzzy buzzes, deep beeps, singing ringings. Digitised voices cried out — threats, advice, come-ons. There was music, if you could call it that: irregular arpeggios (high, ascending; low, descending), victory jingles. Bass drums kicked out a race-rhythm for the driving games. There were the different sounds of coins: the edgy sound of coins going into slots, the dashing sound of coins being won, the scrunching sound of coins being scooped up. But most of all there were just *sounds*: explosions, gunfire, ker-pow punches, car skids. A woman was hoovering, and you couldn't hear the Hoover for the sounds.

The driving games couldn't help but remind me of Jack.

I thought for a moment about telling Jack's unhip secret to Neal. It might make him feel better.

We reached the Dodgems. We could go no further.

'We'll have to look after Jack,' said Neal. 'He isn't as strong as he likes to think.'

'Really?' I said.

'He feels vulnerable. It's best to let him have his way. I think we should do what he says — we should stay in the house till he suggests we go out.'

'Then why did you agree to go out now?'

'I wanted to work out what I thought.'

'I don't think I can manage,' I said.

'Try,' said Neal. 'For me.'

We turned back.

O

I *tried*.

Over the next few days, the whole house settled into a routine. In the late mornings, when we eventually got up, Lang would cook us breakfast. He would then go shopping. We would sit round, talking. Neal would work in the bedroom. (He was reading through all Otto's poems and journals, right up to Otto's suicide.) Jack would sit typing at the kitchen table. (He was writing a long poem, I think.) Sometimes they would have private discussions, upstairs. I was allowed the front room. (I had started reading *The Second Sex*.) I couldn't disturb *them*, but *they* could interrupt *me* at any time. As the only chick, I was expected to brew up for them, wash up after them, talk when they wanted. When lunch (prepared by me) was cleared away, Neal and I would have a meditation lesson. Lang would come back for tea, usually having bought a couple of things in a junk shop. We would sit round, talking. Lang would start to cook us dinner. Maybe Jack would play the guitar or Neal the trombone. Koko was around. Dinner would be served, eaten, cleared away. Spliffs would be rolled. (I got quite good.) We would sit round, talking. Lang would expound on the links between the Existentialists and the Beats. Koko would be put out. Jack, Neal and I would go to bed and have sex. Lang would watch. Each night, standing a little closer.

I *tried*, but I failed.

But it wasn't my fault.

4

One afternoon, while I was reading and lounging about in the front room, Lang came in.

When he sat down opposite me, I looked up.

'Do you like de Beauvoir?' he asked, noticing my book.

'I find her easier to read than the others – and more relevant.'

'Ah, *relevance* – the great cry of the Provincial. Make it *mean* something relevant to *me*.'

'It's not such a bad cry,' I said.

I could hear Jack in the kitchen, typing.

'She is a very good writer, but she is not Sartre.'

'Thank God. There's more than enough of him already.'

Lang shifted on his chair. He was, as usual (during daylight hours), wearing his grey suit. His smell hadn't improved.

'You are very intelligent – and you have a very attractive body.'

I thought about saying *Thank you*. Instead: 'Well, I have *seen* you watching us. I hope you enjoy it.'

'But of course. It is a very beautiful thing to see. But do you enjoy it?'

'Enjoy *someone* watching or enjoy *you* watching?'

'If you want to really flatter me –'

'I think I'd prefer it if you weren't there.'

'That is a shame. It gets very frustrating – all that looking, and *no* touching.'

'You seem to touch yourself quite a lot.'

'It's no substitute.'

He gave me a disgustingly coy look.

'Perhaps you ought to find one, then.'

I walked out of the room, carrying de Beauvoir with me.

'Mary,' said Lang, quickly. 'Could you leave the book behind? I don't want to disrupt the *symmetry.*'

I handed it over, making sure our fingers didn't touch.

Jack didn't seem to have heard anything that had passed. He carried on typing when I entered the kitchen.

I was thinking of how to tell him, when Lang came in behind me.

'I intended to do beefsteak for dinner,' he said. '*Sanglante*, with *petits pois* and new potatoes.'

'Fine,' said Jack.

'I'm going out,' I said.

Jack looked up.

'I have to get out.'

Lang, standing with his back to Jack, smiled at me.

I ran upstairs to get my purse.

Neal was on the bed, meditating, and didn't move.

Jack, I thought, might try and stop me. But I left the house to the quiet sound of typing.

Outside.

Outside seemed so wonderful. The weather didn't need to be as fantastic as it was: I'd have felt better even if it had been raining. Just stepping out into smokeless, dustless, odourless air was a complete joy. And the light, actual light, light that came to me directly, not through grubby net curtains – God, that felt good.

With no real plan, I first walked our usual route down to the Palace Pier. This would have made me easier to find, if anyone had bothered following me. There was a chance, I thought, that Neal would try and find me – once he heard I was gone. But I didn't bother to hurry or look over my shoulder or do anything unpredictable.

Instead, I strolled along the promenade and noticed stuff – all the people and things that Jack would have me ignore: huge groups of identical fluorescent-backpack-wearing kids, heading from McDonald's to their language school (or back); healthy-looking pensioners in grey, oatmeal, brown and – daringly – *faun*; a pair of wide American women with khaki shorts and white socks, dipping into their fannypacks for change; some fatigue-wearing Crusties, sitting with a dog on a carpet, doing hair braids; an emaciated man walking the spacey baby giraffe walk of latter-stage AIDS; a crew of kids in long-sleeved deathmetal T-shirts carrying skateboards and spitting; a rollerblader with a ratty little pigtail and Celtic tattoos on each of his calves; two fat-armed girls with pink flower-shaped hairgrips in their mousy mops; a mountain-biker with a Day-Glo helmet and bug-eyed mirrorshades.

Out to sea, brightly sailed windsurfers and catamarans were moving through a slight haze. A Li-Lo was in danger of being blown under the West Pier.

The beach was crowded with sunbathers, some topless.

Parallel to the promenade, flash cars cruised up and down the front: fake off-road vehicles, low-slung saloons, creamy cabriolets with bull-bars. Motorbikes revved unnecessarily.

Above it all, the seagulls made their rusty swing noise, their doggy yelp, their drowning child squeal.

My simple summer dress and sandals made me feel antique. Everyone around me seemed to be so contemporary. They were all wearing sports gear: trainers, baseball caps, cycle shorts, T-shirts. Hardly any of them were going to actually *play* any sport, but that didn't matter: they were *now*, they were *relevant*. My dress put me in another era. Like it or not, I was closer to Jack than to them.

When I'd walked along to the West Pier, I decided to find somewhere I would fit in a bit more.

I was very aware that I hadn't really approached the *real* Brighton – not unless Lang's house counted as that (which, looking back, I suppose it did). But the front and the beach were there for the tourists – or the tourists were there for them. And, like a real tourist, I wanted to get away from all the tourists.

I crossed the road and walked away from the sea.

Almost immediately, I came to a busy shopping street. No difference here, I thought.

I carried on inland – and things were immediately quieter and more residential. Lots of the tall white houses had FOR SALE or TO LET signs up. There were no shops.

My feet were starting to get a bit sore.

When I came to the end of the road, I turned right. This would take me back, eventually, to somewhere near Lang's.

I hadn't yet decided what I was going to do. Either I told Jack about Lang or I didn't. The question really was whether Lang would back off or not. *That* I couldn't predict. Perhaps, I thought, I should wait until I knew for certain. I didn't want to ruin Jack's chances of doing the magazine. I was a bit scared of Lang.

Somehow I ended up back on the busy street again – or on one very like it.

I saw a Waterstone's, which gave me an idea. I didn't go in, but I started looking out for second-hand bookshops.

I crossed the road, and found myself on a long interesting-looking street: North Laine. I went into each second-hand bookshop I saw and asked if they had *The Second Sex*. In only the third, they did.

It was quite a recent printing – a big fat paperback. Someone – a woman, I hoped – had read it about halfway through, then given up. The spine was soft and didn't feel like it would crack. (These things are important.)

The second-hand price was only a little less than the cover price, but I bought it anyway.

Now I wouldn't have to go into the front room if I didn't want to. I could stay up in the bedroom with Neal – and, if he didn't want me there, I could go down into the kitchen and be with Jack. I could even colonise the garden, which no one but Koko ever used.

But more importantly, the book was my ammunition, my self-defence, my own hip Bible.

A little further along the same street, I found a café with flowery tablecloths, ordered an apple juice and for a couple of hours sat, blissfully, by myself, reading and people-watching.

As I turned the corner into Lang's road, I saw Neal entering the house. It looked like the search parties had been out after all.

I hugged de Beauvoir to my chest and got ready to confront Jack. This time, I wasn't going to say sorry or give in. I wouldn't accept being called a chick any more. I wouldn't slave after them.

They could hide themselves from the really happening world, but I was going to go out and enjoy it. The up-to-date was much more fun, more colourful, more free than their world.

Coming through the front door, I heard Neal speaking to someone at the rear of the house.

'Jack?' he called, hearing my footsteps.

'It's me.'

I walked into the kitchen.

'Where have you been?'

'I went for a walk, then I bought a book, then I sat in a café for a while. It was great.'

'Jack's still looking for you.'

'Why did you bother?'

'That's what I said,' put in Lang, bitchily.

'Jack seemed to think it was very important.'

'He got very agitated,' said Lang.

'There wasn't any need.'

'He said we mustn't allow you to come into contact with too much unhipness. He said it would pollute the whole house and damage our work. He said we had to find you, bring you back.'

'Well, he didn't come after me when he saw me going out. What time did you start looking?'

'We said we'd meet back here at six,' said Neal.

'It is now —' Lang checked his watch '— half past six. I would like to know how many there will be for dinner.'

We exchanged a glance. *All your fault*, it said.

I became very aware of the book in my hands and the car keys in my pocket.

I would have to tell Jack about Lang.

'I got lost,' said Neal.

'So did I,' I said. 'A bit.'

Then I realised.

'I know where Jack is,' I said. 'Let's go and get him.'

I put the book down on the kitchen table, cover up.

Lang saw.

'There will be four for dinner,' I said.

Neal followed me the whole way, not saying anything. I don't know what he thought I was up to.

The Palace Pier was itching with lights and smothered in smells.

We hurried through the Palace of Fun.

Jack, just as I'd guessed, was in the Pleasuredome – playing on the huge Sega Virtua Formula Grand Prix 1995 driving game.

He'd taken his dark glasses off and was concentrating totally on the race.

Four brightly coloured plastic Formula One cars were lined up in front of four large screens – Red, Green, Blue, Yellow.

Jack was Yellow.

A small crowd of men and women were watching the action.

As the drivers jerked the steering wheels round, the cars jerked in hydraulic response.

The big screen graphics showed the whizzing pixellated landscape from the driver's point of view – plus, a map of the whole circuit, a speedometer and a race position.

Jack was 1st.

In smaller TV screens, up above the big screens, you could see black and white shots of a couple of the drivers.

I was smiling, pleased with myself.

Jack's black and white face was utterly deadpan.

I glanced across at Neal.

He looked as though he were standing at the roadside,

watching some terrible pile-up, some long screaming uncontrolled skid, everything moving as if in slow motion – skidding, skidding, skidding, screaming – and there was nothing he could do to stop it. His mouth was open and his eyes were bright.

The intensity of his reaction horrified me. I wondered what I'd done.

When he managed to look at me, eventually, he saw my horror – but he thought it was because of Jack.

'I don't understand,' he said. 'How did you know?'

I put my hand on his arm. Should I lead him away? I was sure he'd come with me.

All I'd wanted to do was prove my hunch. All I'd wanted to do was pull Jack down a little in Neal's eyes. Show him that Jack had secrets, too.

'It is Jack, isn't it?' said Neal.

We'd been watching for a couple of minutes. The race would soon finish. We'd been lucky – or unlucky – to catch Jack actually at the wheel. For Neal, it would have been enough just to *see* Jack in this place.

I didn't want Jack to catch us watching him.

I felt Neal turn away. I saw him start running.

He ran along the pier – past people lounging in deckchairs, trying to win cuddly toys, buying Belgian waffles, doughnuts, chips.

I ran after him, but he was always getting away.

He turned right as he came off the pier, that was as far as I was able to keep him in sight.

When I reached where he'd turned, I looked after him. The beach was a narrow muddy-coloured wedge. He could have gone down the steps. There were two roads he could have followed. In the middle-distance were huge golden cliffs.

I stooped down, hands on knees, catching my breath. My heartbeat was booming behind my ears. I couldn't decide if I was going to puke or not.

A young man came up and handed me a flyer. A gang of muscley-legged girls came by, all leaning onto each other for support. They surrounded the young man with the flyers and started laughing at him.

No, I *wasn't* going to puke.

I looked in the other direction: along the front, along the lit-up façades of the expensive hotels.

Where was Neal going?

What was he going to do?

Whatever it was, I couldn't stop him.

I walked back to the Pleasuredome.

Jack was hurrying towards me, back down the pier. He must have realised the time.

I stepped into his path, still puffed.

'Did you win?' I asked.

'Mary,' he said, stopping.

'Is this the real reason we came to Brighton – so you could play computer games?'

'What are you talking about?'

'I saw you. Neal saw you.'

Jack started walking again.

'Saw me what?'

'Saw you in there. Then he ran off.'

'Where is he?'

'I don't think he went back to Lang's. He was very upset. He went that way.'

I pointed.

'I was out looking for you,' Jack said.

'So, you've never played that game before? It was just beginner's luck you were so good?'

He didn't reply.

'I've seen you, Jack. I've seen you in that arcade in Bedford.'

'I don't want to talk about it.'

He started walking towards the road.

'Neal knows. You're going to have to talk about it.'

'Let's go back to Lang's.'

'Aren't you going to go after him.'

'We'd never find him. It's better to wait.'

'Oh, fine.'

'Shit,' said Jack.

5

Lang was surprised to find there were only three for dinner, but we gave him no explanation.

'His steak will be ruined, absolutely,' he said.

As soon as the meal was over, we went upstairs to wait for Neal.

Jack rolled a joint, which we shared. Then I went and sat at the dressing table. Jack lay on the bed and groaned.

'Where did he go? Maybe we should look for him, after all.'

'Jack, I'm not *that* angry with you. I just wish you'd stop pretending.'

'Look, I'm worried about him. You don't know Neal like I do.'

'I know that you've badly disappointed him.'

'I know I have.'

His head was in his hands, long fingers through thick hair.

'But you haven't disappointed *me*. I already knew. I knew even before I had any real proof. All your act of being so pure and not seeing anything you didn't like – there was bound to be *something* that attracted you, something you couldn't admit.'

'Neal's not like that, though.'

'Neal's exactly like that.'

I told Jack about Neal's obsession with disco music.

'You're joking,' he said.

The image of Neal listening to *Saturday Night Fever* under the bedcovers made Jack laugh almost as much as it depressed him. He sat up.

'Is that supposed to make me feel better? You don't understand. I'm trying to *do* something. I'm trying to make something happen. We have to have principles.'

'Not ones you can't keep. Not ones that are impossible to keep. The world is against you, Jack. Admit it.'

'Where do you think Neal went?' he asked.

'I think he went for a long walk. He probably got lost. He'll be okay as long as he can find his way back to the sea again. Maybe he's just walking along the beach until he gets tired.'

'I hope so.'

Jack looked so depressed, sitting on the edge of the bed, that I went to sit down beside him and give him a hug.

'It's not easy,' he said, 'being the leader.'

'I know,' I said.

I ran my fingers into his hair. This, I realised, was the moment I had been waiting for, the situation I had desired.

We were together, with no one else, in a room, on a bed. It was a shame it was so crap, but ultimately that didn't matter.

With both my hands, I raised Jack's head. We looked each other very closely in the eyes, then kissed.

It was different this time.

I found it much easier to relax – no Neal, no Lang. Maybe it was because Jack was in such a low mood, but the way he touched me felt gentler and subtler. Foreplay was more of a conversation, not a shouting match – as it had been before.

Now he was listening to me as I had always listened to him. No one here was trying to impress anyone, just to give them pleasure. I discovered that his nipples were very sensitive, becoming erect when I stroked them. (A big turn-on.) This was private – something he wouldn't have wanted Lang to see. I was in control; Jack was letting me do what I wanted.

Neal came in without us hearing him.

Jack was underneath me. He held my breasts in his hands and my hands were pushing against the wall. The counter-pane had slipped onto the floor.

When I looked up to the shape in the doorway, I thought it was just Lang.

'Fuck off,' I said.

Then I saw it was Neal, turning away, very slowly.

His eyes didn't meet mine – he was looking at Jack.

We hurried to dress.

Jack's erection looked ridiculous in his underpants. I wanted to laugh, but didn't want to admit how cut off from Neal's emotions I was feeling.

We kissed before going downstairs.

Neal hadn't run out into the street. He was sitting quietly at the kitchen table. Koko was on his lap.

Lang wasn't in evidence.

It was about ten o'clock.

'Can I have the keys to the car?' he asked, a few moments after we walked in.

'Do you want us to go for a drive?' Jack asked.

'I'd just like the keys.'

'What for?' I asked. 'Are you going to go somewhere?'

'But he's just learning to drive,' said Jack. 'He can't go anywhere.'

'I *can* drive,' said Neal, standing up. 'I know how to drive.'

'You never told me,' said Jack.

'I just want to sleep in the car. I don't want to sleep in the same bed as you two.'

'When did you learn to drive?' said Jack.

'You can sleep downstairs,' I said. 'On the sofa.'

'Maybe not in the same house.'

'Neal,' I said. 'We need to sort this out.'

'Can I have the keys or not?'

'Yes, you can have the keys. But I think you and Jack should talk first.'

Neal hesitated.

'When did you *learn* to *drive*?' Jack said.

'You betrayed me,' said Neal. 'I can't trust you any more.'

'Then you betrayed me, as well – or at least lied to us.'

'I'm going to wait by the car. Will you bring the keys out?'

'Here they are,' I said, taking them out of my jeans pocket and handing them over.

'Neal,' said Jack. 'I'm sorry.'

Neal picked Koko up from where she had been circling his feet. He didn't say anything in reply.

As there seemed to be little more I could do, I took a blanket, a cup of coffee and a plate of bread and jam out to Neal.

Lang, it turned out, had taken a downer of some sort and crashed out on the study sofa.

Neal was sitting in the back seat with Koko on his lap. She was purring like a sewing machine as he stroked her.

'We'll leave the front door unlocked,' I said. 'You can come in any time you feel like it.'

He asked me to bring out his satchel. I did.

'Good night,' he said.

Jack was lying in bed. I looked at him as blankly as I could.

'I said sorry,' he said.

'You'll have to do more than that. We both will.'

Outside a police siren went by.

Jack wanted to have sex, but I said no.

6

The car was still there the following morning, to my great relief; and, to my even greater relief, Neal and Koko were still inside it.

Only Koko seemed to have got any sleep.

'How are you?' I asked.

'Jack slept upstairs, didn't he?'

'Yes, we slept in the same bed. But that was it.'

Neal had his journal on his lap.

'Will you come in for breakfast?' I asked.

'No, I won't,' he said. 'Can you bring me the typewriter and some paper?'

Jack and I didn't speak much over breakfast. The kitchen seemed empty without Koko's soft presence. Lang was already gone on his rounds. We had tea and toast.

As I was washing up, I heard something coming through the letterbox. Jack was upstairs, shaving.

The front door opened as I walked into the hall.

'Neal,' I said.

'It's from Maggie,' he replied, picking up the letter. 'She always uses pink paper.'

'Who's it to?' I asked.

He read the address on the pink envelope.

'It's to Jack.'

'Do you want to bring it in? We can read it after Jack.'

Neal dropped the letter back on the mat and went out, closing the door behind him.

When Jack came down, I gave him the letter.

He kissed me, his skin so soft and smooth.

'Neal saw it arrive. He wanted to read it. Perhaps you could take it out to him afterwards. You need to talk to him.'

'I hope that cat isn't pissing in your car.'

Jack ripped the letter open and read it standing in the hall.

'Neal can't see this,' he said, when he'd finished. 'It's not to him.'

'Well, will you talk to him?'

'What's there to say? I've already said sorry.'

'I'm going to talk to him. Are you coming?'

'No.'

Neal had no objection to me sitting in the car with him. He had moved through into the passenger seat, propping the typewriter up against the dashboard. The car keys were in the ignition.

'I've been getting some funny looks,' he said.

'I bet.'

'A policeman asked me if anything was wrong.'

'What did you say?'

'That I'd had an argument with my wife and had slept in the car.'

I was laughing.

'And he bought that?'

'He said it happens more than you think.'

'Will you come inside?'

'Didn't you bring the letter?'

'Jack said it wasn't to you. I think it was about him and Maggie.'

Neal looked very distressed: red-eyed and unshaven. His stubble was several shades lighter than his hair. I remembered the goatee he'd had at the party.

'I have to think,' said Neal. 'I can't think inside.'

'Is there anything you need?'

'Some milk for Koko.'

I brought him out a full bottle and a saucer.

Jack sat down at the kitchen table and started typing.

I hadn't been allowed to read anything he'd written. (I don't expect it had improved much over the earlier poems.) And even when we were lying in bed together, without Neal, we hadn't actually *talked*. At the time, this didn't worry me: I thought Jack was just trying to be enigmatic.

There wasn't much I could do on my own. I thought about going for another walk, but the first had caused such mayhem that I didn't dare risk a second. Surely it couldn't *all* be my fault? Lang was to blame for forcing me out. I would have tried meditating, but I associated that too closely with Neal. Surely Neal would have caught Jack out sooner or later? With Lang absent, I considered taking over the front room again. But that seemed to be inviting him to return and catch me there and to assume that *that* meant *yes*.

So, I lay on the bed upstairs, reading de Beauvoir and daydreaming. When I got totally bored, I had a bath.

I wanted it to be an Indulgence Bath, but I didn't have enough Indulgence Bath ingredients – no candles, no maga- zines – so I had to make do with a Maintenance Bath.

My legs had already started to get prickly again. I thought about asking Jack if I could go to Boots and get something chemical to defoliate them with. I wasn't sure if we were still pretending that such things didn't exist.

Even a Maintenance Bath gave me too much time to think. It had now been confirmed that I was the biggest bitch in the whole history of the world, ever. I wasn't surprised that Neal didn't want to be in the same house as me.

I washed my face with Lang's horrible oily soap.

Lunch was the first opportunity to talk. I made Brie and tomato baguettes.

'How was this morning?' I asked.

'Great,' said Jack. 'It's going great.'

'It sounded like you were typing a lot.'

'Spontaneous compositions, written fast and furious.' (Bollocks, in other words.)

'Have you thought about speaking to Neal?'

'I've been trying to think about other things.'

'He shouldn't be that upset, you know. He has his own little secrets, too.'

'Such as?'

'Disco music – remember?'

Jack didn't speak for several seconds.

I mimed listening to something funky on a Walkman.

'Really?' said Jack. 'I always thought those looked a lot of fun.'

This was unprecedented.

'Neal learnt to drive when he was seventeen. He never told you that, did he? So, he hasn't got much reason to be upset. He's been just as hypocritical as you have.'

'I haven't been hypocritical. I've just been weak. I was

trying to give it up. When I went to look for you, I didn't mean to go down there. I knew the arcades were there, of course. Then, when I saw the game, I thought, *I just better check*. And because there was no one around to see, I started playing. I'm very good, you know. I beat the others. Everyone.'

'I guessed that.'

We sat not talking for a while.

'Shall I ask him in again?' I said.

'Go on and try.'

When I got outside, I saw that Neal had moved over into the driver's seat.

I bent down and spoke to him through the rolled-down window.

'I think it's time you came inside, don't you?'

He didn't immediately say, *No*.

'Jack is in the kitchen,' I said. 'You can talk to him. Then, if you want to, you can come outside again. I'll even drive you back to Bedford, if you want.'

Neal had his hands on the steering wheel. Koko was on his lap.

'I'll sit here in the car while you go in.'

I opened the driver's door.

After another moment's hesitation, Neal stood up out of the car and carried Koko through the open front door.

The car smelt strongly of cat, but not of cat pee – which was more of a relief than I wanted to admit.

I tried the ignition. It went first time. Neal didn't seem to have been draining the battery in any way.

Anticipating a long wait, I switched the radio on.

God, I hadn't heard any decent music in *days*.

The idea of a drive along the coast was very appealing, but I knew I couldn't go anywhere. If Neal rushed out and found me gone, I would have betrayed him again. I couldn't afford to do that.

I thought about all that had happened: about the party and the reading, about the dig and the magazine, about Maggie and Lang, about Jack and Neal.

In the end, I was left waiting for a couple of hours. Then Jack came through the front door.

'He's back,' he said, and smiled.

7

I walked into the kitchen. It was empty.

'Where is he?' I asked.

'He's upstairs in bed,' said Jack. 'He didn't pay his usual visit to Sleepsville last night. Man, was he knocked out.'

I noticed that Jack had taken his shoes off. Perhaps he and Neal had been meditating together.

'Jack, you aren't going to start speaking like that again, are you? It won't do any good. It's gone.'

'Watch what you're saying, chick.'

'But it's so . . .' I'd been trying to think of the right word even since I met him. Finally, it came to me: 'It's so *ersatz*.'

'Ersatz!'

I couldn't tell if Jack knew what it meant.

'Yes. It's all far too late. You can't change things by pretending they don't exist. If you're really *against* something you're going to have to face it, to protest against it. What you're doing is just hiding yourself from things. But they are continuing. They are out there getting worse, happening faster.'

'Ow,' said Jack. 'You're pretty zappy for a chick, you know that?'

'I'm not a chick. I might have been one, for a while, but I'm not any more. I'm a feminist.'

'Unhip.'

I'd been waiting for an opportunity to make this declaration.

'No, it isn't. *The Second Sex* was published in 1952. Simone de Beauvoir says there is no reason for women to feel inferior to men. We exist independently. We are not your slaves. I am a follower of de Beauvoir. I am perfectly hip.'

This seemed to stop Jack completely. I don't think he'd ever considered the possibility of a hip rebellion.

'We are back to how we always were,' he said, very slowly. 'Neal digs that. I dig that. If you don't dig that, then you might as well cut out.'

'I'm not going anywhere until I'm sure Neal is alright. What did you two talk about while I was outside?'

'That was between men.'

'I think I might sleep in the car tonight, you know.'

'I have no problem with that.'

'And you're not keeping me in this house. I can go where I want and do what I want and look at what I want. I'm a free woman! I'm not a chick! This whole argument is ridiculous!'

I was about to pack up and leave.

Neal walked in, wearing T-shirt and pants.

'Mary,' he said. 'Kiss Jack.'

'What?' I said.

I realised that Jack and I had been shouting.

'Kiss him. On the mouth. For me.'

'Why should I? We're in the middle of an argument.'

'Exactly. But you love him, really. And he loves you. And I love you and I love him and you love me. I hate arguments.'

'So do I,' I said. (Big lie.)

'Me, too,' said Jack.

'But I am standing up for my rights.'

'We respect that,' said Neal. 'And we love you for it.'

Neal walked up to me and kissed me on the mouth. Then he turned to Jack and kissed him. Then he put his arms behind our backs and pushed us together.

'Go on,' he said.

I put my hands against Jack's chest, ready to push him away. His arms were still by his sides.

'I didn't realise you were such a hippy, Neal,' I said.

Jack leaned towards me. I could have jumped back. I could have run out. Jack dropped a miniature kiss on my lips.

'Let's go to bed,' said Neal.

And, for some reason, we did.

8

I wasn't going to let Jack win so easily.

The following day, Saturday, I went out on my own, without asking. I bought a newspaper, the *Independent*, and picked up *Hyper*, a local listings magazine. I sat in my already-favourite café, drinking apple juice and raspberry tea. I relaxed.

While browsing *Hyper*, I spotted something in the Club Guide: *Disco Dollys: seventies disco, eighties pop, Hector's House, 8–11 p.m.* I looked for the day: Monday.

The idea followed almost inevitably – I mean, how many Disco Dollys did I know?

As it turned out, I wasn't alone with Neal until Sunday afternoon: I'd suggested we start meditating again, and Jack hadn't objected.

We were up in the bedroom. The bedsheets were by now pretty disgusting, so we sat on the counterpane.

I'd decided to ask Neal afterwards, when he was calm. The lesson began.

It was all going badly, as usual. I was thinking too much about Monday. Then, about halfway through, I decided to start again. I took a deep beginning-breath and counted, *One*, aloud in my head. Within about five breaths, something had started to happen. It wasn't mind-blowing, more like mind-tickling. First of all, a series of dark curtains seemed to be moving past my eyes. The breath counting became more natural. My head began to feel a little woozy. Was this getting it right or getting it wrong? For a few seconds it seemed as if I was on a sort of internal Big Dipper ride: soaring, plunging, yawing, halting.

Just when it was getting really good, I felt Neal tap me on one knee.

'I think we should stop now. That's three-quarters of an hour.'

'Really?' I said. It was the first time I hadn't been totally bored in five minutes.

'It worked that time.'

'How did it feel?' he asked.

I described what had happened.

'You're making progress,' said Neal, monkishly.

'I'd quite like a coffee,' I said, not wanting to confess all of my feeling-strangeness.

'That can be arranged.'

Neal uncrossed his legs and was about to get off the bed. Only then did I remember.

'Um,' I said. 'Neal, how would you like to . . .' And I told him about my idea.

At first he said *No*. Things were only just getting back to normal with Jack. We should concentrate on keeping him happy. But slowly I began to persuade him. Jack could do what *he* wanted. *We* weren't going to stop *him* going along to the Pleasuredome, were we? Why should *he* be able to stop *us* going to Hector's House? Neal obviously found the idea very seductive. Without really knowing it, he had started to smile. He began to persuade himself, out loud: 'We wouldn't be doing anything secret,' he said. 'We can always ask Jack along, can't we?' I knew he really wanted to go –

but, by the time we went downstairs, he still wasn't one hundred per cent won over.

'Okay?' asked Jack, still at the kitchen table, still typing.

'Yes,' said Neal.

Jack didn't look up.

Neal's smile appeared again.

We were going.

Neal didn't break the news to Jack until we were in bed that evening. I'd left it up to him. Jack was still pissed off with me for not staying in the house.

('You're screwing up my work,' he'd said when I got back. 'You're bringing shit into this house.' He meant the listings mag, which I was still carrying.

As a peace offering, I'd put it in the swingbin — but he hadn't been satisfied until I'd emptied the entire contents of the swingbin into the dustbin outside.)

His reaction to Neal's announcement wasn't as negative as I'd expected. He said *No*, of course — and started to argue against it.

'But I'm on holiday,' said Neal. 'I want to do things I wouldn't normally do.'

Jack didn't want to get back onto the subject of the Pleasuredome. As far as he was concerned, no one was to mention it ever again. So, when I started in — saying how Jack could do what *he* wanted with *his* evenings — he shut up pretty quickly.

'Do you want to come with us?' asked Neal.

'I'll stay in and work,' said Jack.

'You can always change your mind,' I said.

But he wasn't going to do that.

Already, he had started to regain control over Neal. Compared to how it had been, though, his power was very weak. It was better, he obviously believed, for Neal to go off with me than go off for good.

Just before we turned the light out, Jack announced that he'd almost finished what he'd been working on – a long poem about his life. He said it was called 'Bedniks'.

'We'll start designing *Café Bohemia*,' he said. 'Neal, you'll have to hurry up with Otto's stuff. We'll need it soon.'

'Not tomorrow,' I said. 'We have some shopping to do.'

Neal touched me under the sheets, meaning *enough*.

Jack turned the lights out.

Ever since his pass at me, Lang hadn't watched us in bed. He turned in early, zonking himself with downers.

That night I had one of my second favourite kind of dreams: a shopping dream.

I'd found *just* the place.

We spent the morning in the house, keeping Jack happy. Neal worked diligently at Otto's journal and I performed chickish tasks.

To be honest, the house was so disgusting I'd felt primally compelled to clean it from the moment I went inside. I'd resisted this urge so far, but now was a good time to give way.

In the cupboard under the stairs, I discovered an old-fashioned Hoover. Once I'd given it a good dusting and emptied the bag, I took it upstairs and started on the bedroom. I did the hall, the stairs, the front hall, the front room. I didn't do Lang's bedroom.

Koko went and hid in the garden.

From the same cupboard, I produced a broom.

Jack carried on typing and Neal carried on reading as I swept the kitchen floor.

Back upstairs, I changed the smeggy bedsheets and hand-washed a few pairs of knickers.

By the time lunch came round (onion soup and hot rolls), Jack might even have thought we'd forgotten. But as soon as the washing-up was done, Neal and I set out.

The place I'd found was called Snooper's Paradise, a huge bric-à-brac emporium and second-hand clothes market. It was only just round the corner from Lang's. The mannequins in the window probably had the best-dressed bods in Brighton. My only worry was that this was one of the places Lang visited on his rounds.

Neal started beaming as soon as we walked in.

'Wow!'

I led him away from the orange-and-green '50s tea set he had started ogling.

'Some trousers, some shoes and a shirt. What size are you?'

He didn't know, so I borrowed a tape measure from a girl in pink vinyl clogs and an acid-trip of a dress.

Waist: 32″. Neck: 15½″.

As I was handing the tape measure back, the girl asked what we were looking for.

'Flares,' said Neal.

'We're going to Hector's House,' I said. 'Disco Dollys.'

'Well, you'll need one of these then.'

She led us off towards another stand, where I could see a long line of Afro wigs on polystyrene heads.

'Yes!' said Neal, and gave a little skip.

'I'm Mary,' I said, 'and this is Neal.'

'Bella,' the girl replied.

'Thanks for your help,' I said.

'I haven't even begun,' Bella said.

And she was right, she hadn't.

Jack didn't want to see our purchases when we got back, around four.

Apart from the Afro wig, Neal had bought a brown wall-paper-pattern shirt with Boeing 747 collars, some khaki flares in a veloury-textured fabric and a pair of stack-heeled shoes.

When I found out that he really *was* being serious, I'd treated him to a medallion.

For myself, I'd had to choose from: a two-tone boiler suit (lime green with yellow pockets); a sequined boob tube with matching sequined mini; a coffee-coloured flower-print dress with big wavy frills at the neck and sleeves; or a tight yellow silk blouse and tasteful black pencil-leg slacks.

With a little encouragement from Neal, and a lot of reassurance from Bella, I'd finally plumped (which I hoped wasn't the right word) for the sequined boob-tube ensemble. I also came away with some spindly high heels.

Hey, I was on holiday, too.

Neal wanted to try it all on at once the moment we got back, but I could see that would be pushing Jack too far.

'What about Otto's journal?' I said.

'Oh, yes,' said Neal, and settled down to work.

We had tea. Lang returned. Lang made spaghetti Bolognese. (He really was slipping.) We sat and talked.

At about seven-thirty, Neal and I disappeared upstairs to get ready.

He took the bathroom and I got the bedroom. Half an hour later, we were ready to roll.

Neal looked great, and didn't seem at all embarrassed.

I just wished I'd had something a bit more glitzy in my

make-up bag. In the end, I made do by putting on far too much eyeliner and dotting on a beauty spot.

'Back at half-eleven,' I shouted through from the hall.

No reply came.

'Shall we go and show them?' asked Neal, very keen.

'Come on,' I said. 'We don't want to be late.'

To my surprise, Hector's House did actually look like a house – admittedly, a brightly coloured one with very loud music inside – but definitely a house and not some concrete hole-in-the-wall.

Walking in and paying the cover charge was a relief: the boob tube had attracted some close attention on the evening streets. As soon as we passed through the door, though, our oddness became average: here were other Afros and flares, here were more sequins and strapless tops. If there wasn't anyone revealing *quite* as much flesh as I was, then I didn't really mind. Neal was looking round the room beamily. I could see he was proud to be with me, and that made me proud to be with him.

The record that had been playing (which I hadn't recognised) started to fade out.

'Yeah,' said the moustachioed DJ. 'Get down tonite, people, and strut yo' funky stuff. Woah, bay-bee! Will D. Beeste, yo' man here, comin' atcha, puttin' a hex on the decks, keepin' it raw on the disco floor. So, put a dip in yo' hips and a glide in yo' stride. Funk it up, sugar-kitten!'

Candi Staton's 'Young Hearts Run Free' kicked in.

Neal's hips were already dipping alarmingly.

'Do you want to get a drink?' I asked.

'No,' he said. 'I want to dance myself dizzy.'

Neal immediately skipped down the steps onto the dance floor and started to do the Hustle.

I really wished I'd been able to get that drink. A drink might have reassured me that the boob tube wasn't about to ping off towards the ceiling, it might have made me believe that the mini wasn't so short that everyone could see my knickers, it might have deluded me into thinking that I really *could* dance in heels without looking like a six-year-old let loose in Mummy's wardrobe. A *couple* of drinks would have been even better – then I wouldn't have cared that much what any of my clothes did.

Neal leaned towards me.

'This is one of my all-time favourites,' he said, taking my hand and twizzling me round a couple of times.

'We Are Family' by Sister Sledge slunk in.

Neal whooped.

BOOM-tssh BOOM-tssh BOOM-tssh. You couldn't miss it – and if you did, you could always catch it a little later. BOOM-tssh. It was infectious. I was infected.

Surprisingly, Neal was a pretty good dancer – better than me. Perhaps he hadn't *always* had to do his disco-listening under the covers.

The heels weren't feeling too bad, as long as I didn't make any sudden lurches and no one bumped into me from behind.

I started to relax. Neal, I realised, wasn't making a fool of himself. If he whooped, then there were plenty of others to whoop in reply. If he was pulling a few cheesy dance moves (dial-the-phone, hitchhike, swim-the-crawl, hand-jive), then there were people round us who would actually copy him.

Looking round the dance floor, it was as if the mannequins in Snooper's Paradise had come to life. Every variety of bad-taste '70s fashion was present and incorrect: stack heels, flares, shirts open to the navel, medallions, fake moustaches and sideboards, rainbow wigs, purple, gold, blue and green blusher, halter tops, hot pants, go-go boots. Boys were wearing black shirts under white suits; girls wore white ankle socks with black high heels.

No one was here because they wanted to be at the cutting edge of dance music. No one was trying to be in any way 'hip'. They were here to be a little silly, a little nostalgic, a little ironic.

We danced three or four more numbers, then Neal led me to the bar and ordered us some tacky cocktails.

Sweat was cascading down from under his Afro.

A table came free, and we grabbed it.

'This is great,' he said.

'Yeah,' I agreed.

'Cheers.'

Our glasses didn't make much of a clink – they were plastic.

'Thanks for bringing me,' Neal said. He was dancing in his seat.

I doubted we'd be able to finish our drinks without him jumping up, demanding that we get down to another of his all-time faves.

'Isn't it good?' he asked.

'It's wonderful,' I said.

'I feel so *free*,' he said, smiling. 'I find it very difficult, you know, being hip, doing what Jack says all the time. It takes a lot of effort. We have to do lots of research, to find out what existed in July 1966. Like, Jack had to know all about the M1 before we set off down here. That's why he knows Jane so well – she gets library books for him.'

'You mean, she knows where he lives?'

'I think, maybe.'

Fuck.

'And we have to remember all this useless stuff. We live in a world where England have never won the World Cup, where Neil Armstrong hasn't walked on the moon, where the Beatles haven't split up, where the Cold War is still going. Then there are these glossaries of Beatnik slang we have to learn. And I'm always saying something I shouldn't and getting caught out, which is why I don't talk much around Jack.'

'You can do what you want, you know? You can live in whichever world you choose.'

'Look, Mary.' Neal leant closer. 'Jack and me – '

But then 'One of Us' by Abba kicked in.

Neal had been grabbing my hand quite a lot, recently.

We joined the whooping stampede.

Neal didn't stop dancing until the house lights came on.

Jack was already in bed by the time we got back – eleven-thirty, as promised.

Neal wanted him to take a look at how we were dressed.

'We were fabulous!' he said.

Jack just lay there with his eyes closed.

'I'm asleep,' he said.

But Neal was on such a high that he insisted.

'Come *on*,' he said, bouncing the bed springs with his palms.

Jack opened his eyes and looked us over.

'You look stupid,' he said. 'Go and take it off.'

This calmed Neal down a bit.

Jack fell back onto the pillow.

'Did you go out?' I asked.

'No,' he said, 'I stayed in and got stoned with Lang. Are you getting in or not?'

'I'm going to have a bath,' I said.

'After you,' said Neal.

He blew me a kiss and then span round a couple of times to the BOOM-tssh BOOM-tssh that only he could hear.

9

Jack's new tactic for domination, as became clear over the next couple of days, was sex. Mostly, I think this was because he didn't want Neal and me to be alone together. Meditation was out. Instead, straight after lunch, we all went upstairs to bed.

Jack had been trying to get me to suck him off ever since that first night, but I'd always refused. I hated the taste of sperm and, even more, I hated its texture. *Slimy white tadpole soup*, I called it – though not out loud. Neal had never seemed that bothered. He certainly never tried to persuade me into it. But Jack became more and more insistent.

By Wednesday, he was getting angry.

'Come on,' he said. 'What's so bad about it?'

'I just don't want to. Isn't that enough? Isn't it enough that I just say I don't want to?'

'You didn't want to go to bed with Neal and me at the same time, did you? But you did. And you don't regret it, do you?'

'No,' I said – though I was far from sure.

'I kissed Neal and then you were happy to come along.'

'Jack,' said Neal, 'she just doesn't want to. Leave her alone.'

'Maybe you'll copy us this time, as well.'

We were still lying in the same arrangement as always. Jack climbed over me and got on top of Neal.

'You don't have to do this, Jack,' I said. 'It won't make any difference.'

'But I want to,' he said. 'And so does Neal.'

He started to kiss Neal's chest.

Even though I'd wanted them to kiss and to touch, I hadn't expected it to go any further.

'Don't you, Neal?' said Jack.

Jack's hands caressed Neal's thighs. Neal's penis was already erect.

'Don't you?' whispered Jack.

I watched, unable to believe this was really happening – that it wasn't just some weird wank-fantasy going on in my head.

Neal snuck a guilty look at me.

'No, I don't,' he said.

'Yes, you do,' said Jack. 'You really want it.'

His tongue flicked out over the top of Neal's glans.

Neal shuddered and tried to turn on one side, but Jack jumped up and caught his arms.

'Oh no you don't,' he said.

'Please, Jack,' said Neal.

'Please what?'

'Please stop.'

'Only one person can stop me,' said Jack, and looked at me through narrowed eyes. 'Because I *know* you're not going to.'

Even the idea of it was making me moist.

'I'm not going to stop you,' I said.

I wanted to watch.

Jack took Neal's penis in his hand and started to wank him off.

'It's the ultimate turn-on,' he said, looking at me. 'Fucking one person and fucking with another person's head.'

He moved down Neal's body, kissing as he went.

I started to masturbate myself.

Neal groaned, and didn't stop groaning for quite a long time.

Afterwards, Jack fucked me while Neal watched. I could taste Neal's come in Jack's mouth as he kissed me.

We fell apart, exhausted, and dozed gently off.

The room was made distant by heat. An empty condom foil lay under my shoulder, but I couldn't be bothered to reach round and move it. Neal's head was resting on my arm, almost cutting off the circulation. Jack's hand lay between my legs. Our slick bodies were covered by a single, crumpled white sheet.

I heard someone knocking on the front door, and again, and again. When my eyes opened, I stared at the ceiling for few seconds. Even without being drunk, I felt like I was having a bad episode of room-spin.

Neal got up to answer the door, and I heard him shouting Maggie's name.

I turned to wake Jack, but he was awake.

'*Maggie*,' I whispered.

'Uh-huh.'

'Is that what her letter said?' I asked. 'That she was coming down?'

'Well, just that she was thinking of it.'

'You should have said.'

'She only said *maybe*.'

'Which usually means definitely.'

'Are we going to get up?'

I wanted to kiss Jack, to mark him as mine.

'Come here,' I said.

Footsteps were coming up the stairs – fast and clacky.

Jack was now in my arms. His face was turned to mine, though he must have known what was on its way.

He wanted us to be kissing when she came in.

This was my moment of triumph. He was deliberately offering it to me, teasing me with it – and because of that (his deliberateness, his teasingness) I felt like not taking it.

I looked towards the door. Jack put his lips to my ear. A shiver flashed through me.

'I'm going to whisper in your ear,' he whispered, as Maggie walked in. 'I'm going to say the name *Maggie*, so *she* thinks I'm talking about *her*. *Maggie*, yes.'

God, this looked even worse than kissing.

Maggie stopped on the threshold.

'*Maggie* hates that,' Jack whispered. '*She* really does. *She* hates being called *she*.'

She took a step into the room.

'I caught the train,' she said, bravely. 'I wanted to see if you were okay.'

'Having a ball,' said Jack, half crowing to Maggie, half whispering into my ear. 'Having a ball.'

'He's a bastard,' Maggie said. 'I tried to tell you.'

A bit too late, I realised that both my boobs were exposed. Rather than cover up, which was my first instinct, I tried to act like an even bigger slut – I just lay back, all *fuck you, okay*.

'I know he's a bastard,' I said. 'That's why I like him.'

Slowly, and very obviously, even though it was under the sheet, I moved my hand onto Jack's cock. It was really stiff – which shouldn't have surprised me, but did.

Catfights must be his thing, I thought.

Maggie was close to tears.

'Why are you encouraging him?' she asked.

I lifted the sheets a little and glanced down at Jack's erection.

'It doesn't look to me like he needs any encouragement.'

I couldn't believe I was capable of being such a bitch.

'You *will* regret this,' said Maggie. 'What you're doing is very dangerous. You don't understand.'

I almost said that, on the contrary, it was always very *safe*.

'I'm glad I came,' Maggie said to Jack. 'But this is the last time you're ever going to see me.'

'Oh dear,' I said. 'I am sad.'

'Won't you stay?' asked Jack. He twitched the sheet off us. There were my fingers, gripping his cock. There were my pubes. 'Go on – get in. Plenty of room, here.'

'Look at yourselves,' said Maggie, then turned and walked out.

I caught sight of Neal, stepping aside to let her pass. That meant he must have been there all along. Which meant he must have heard everything. Which meant –

I heard them talking downstairs. Sometimes, I think I heard Maggie say, *Come with me*, and Neal say *No, I have to stay with them*. Sometimes, I think I heard Maggie shout, *How can you?* and Neal reply *I'm in love with them*. Sometimes, I think I made these words up afterwards.

The front door closed.

Neal's soft footsteps slowly climbed the stairs. When he entered the room, he said, 'I think I'll sleep in the car again, tonight. If that's okay with you.'

I felt so *bad*.

Neal was sitting in the driver's seat when I came out to talk to him. It was five in the evening. One of Otto's journals – the very last, as I soon found out – was in front of him, resting on the top of the steering wheel. With the pages lifted close up to his face, Neal didn't notice me approaching. He jumped when I rattled my fingernails down on the roof. The Vauxhall was now squittered with seagull shit. The back seat was full of Neal's belongings: his trombone case, his satchel, his typewriter, Koko's travel basket. All the windows were rolled up. Neal hesitated for a moment before leaning over and unlocking the passenger door.

As I walked round the front of the car, Neal lifted Koko off the seat beside him and onto his lap.

I sat down on the cat-hairy brown vinyl.

What was I going to say? I still didn't know.

I pulled the door shut, and we were suddenly together in the dead acoustic of the car.

The best thing was probably to wait for him to say something – and so, for five minutes, neither of us spoke. The loudest sound inside the Vauxhall was Koko's warm purr; the loudest outside were the seagulls' slicing cries. I wondered if Koko could hear them, and if she knew they were birds, and if this tormented her.

'It's funny,' said Neal. 'Otto seems to be quite happy, at the moment.' He flicked through the journal pages he still had to read. 'And there isn't that long to go.'

'What is he writing about?'

'He's rereading *The Subterraneans*, trying to decide what's wrong with it. I'm not sure if he really liked Kerouac that much, after all.'

'Oh,' I said.

'And he's thinking a lot about his father. Otto's father died when he was twelve. He thinks he wasn't told the truth about it. He's wondering why it was a closed-casket funeral.'

'How are *you* feeling, Neal?'

He looked at me, very directly. For some reason, he seemed more adult then than he ever had before.

'I don't know – I don't know what I feel. I'm not sure if what I feel matters any more.' I was about to say it did, but he carried on. 'I feel that everything has gone wrong since – But I don't blame you. It started when I asked you to the poetry reading, when you came into Alfonse. Everything until then had just seemed to work. Maggie wasn't one hundred per cent happy, but I was – and I think Jack was – I think he probably was. But I'm not blaming you. Something was always going to happen to us. It didn't have to be you, it just was. We carried on for a whole wonderful year. We should be grateful for that. You were just trying to make friends with us.'

'Maybe you *should* blame me,' I said.

Neal sat, staring forward through the dirty windscreen. He took his hands off Koko and put them on the steering wheel.

'I don't know. Maybe I should.'

Otto's journal slipped off Neal's lap and fell into the gap between the seats.

I reached to pick it up, but Neal got there first.

'I'll drive you to Bedford – tonight – right now – or anywhere.' Then I had a thought. 'Or you can drive me, if you like.'

'We shouldn't have come here,' said Neal. 'It was a bad idea to get stuck in another town, in another house. We should have gone on the road and followed it the whole way. I think we were afraid of doing that. We let ourselves down. In the end, we'll look a bit silly because we wimped out. We should have just gone.'

'Is that what you'd like to do?'

'I'm sorry,' said Neal, still smiling. 'I still don't know.'

It wasn't worth trying to persuade him back into the house.

He let me bring a few things out – something for him to eat, some more milk for Koko.

Lang returned, and we had a quieter than usual meal.

After we'd cleared up, Lang went and sat in the car with Neal for an hour or so.

Jack and I sat in the kitchen.

'What do you think they're talking about?' I asked.

'No idea,' said Jack, as if he wasn't even interested.

'Will you let me see "Bedniks"?'

'When it's finished.'

'Am I in it?'

'Maybe.'

When Lang came back in he looked very serious, but didn't tell us anything.

'Good night,' he said, taking a bottle of wine upstairs with him.

All this time I'd wanted to tell Jack about Lang coming on to me, and I still couldn't.

We turned in.

'He'll be okay tomorrow,' said Jack, after we got in bed and turned the lights out.

We had sex, I don't know why, and then we went to sleep, I don't know how.

10

In the morning, the Vauxhall was gone.

Lang had looked out at about seven, just to see that Neal was okay.

The car had disappeared from its usual place. After going out onto the street to check it really wasn't there, he came back into the house and woke us up.

'Come downstairs,' he said, without switching the light on. We both immediately knew what he meant.

Sitting at the kitchen table, we waited until he finished making the tea. Jack lit a cigarette and I took a couple of drags. When Lang had poured out, he sat down opposite us.

'Neal's gone,' he said. 'And he's taken the car.'

From the moment I heard for definite, I knew it was serious. Neal wouldn't have taken my car unless he felt it was the only option left. I said we should call the police straight away. But Jack said maybe we should wait a few hours.

'He might come back,' he said. 'Or he might just have decided to drive back to Bedford. We should call his parents and get them to call us if he turns up there. There's no need to get all freaked out over it.'

'No, Jack,' I said, 'We should phone the police. I'm freaked already.'

Lang agreed, which surprised me.

'I was very unhappy about leaving him in the car last night. But he insisted. It was his choice.'

I almost felt sorry for Lang, now. He seemed a lot older this morning. It had been easy to forget that his nephew had committed suicide.

Oh God, I thought, *Otto's journal.*

I didn't say anything.

'Okay,' said Jack.

Lang went and phoned from his bedroom.

Jack and I didn't speak while he was gone.

'The police have already located the car,' Lang said, after he sat down again. 'It was found up at Beachy Head early this morning.'

'Shit,' I said.

Jack grabbed for his cigarettes.

'It's just standing there on the clifftop, about six inches from the edge. No one saw it arrive.'

'And there was no sign of Neal?' I said.

'Not actually in the car, no. They are searching the beach below the cliff at the moment. Some officers are on their way here.'

The phone started ringing.

'Maybe it's Neal,' I said.

Lang went upstairs again.

I offered Jack my hand to hold and he eventually took it.

'Mary, it's your father!' Lang called down, after a long couple of seconds.

'Coming!' I shouted.

This was only the second time I'd been inside Lang's bedroom. (The first was when I phoned my parents to let them know we'd arrived safely.) The phone stood on the bedside table, in between the ashtrays. I jogged the fullest of them as I picked the receiver up. Ashes fell onto my bare feet and onto the floor.

'Dad?' I said.

'Mary?' he said, his voice cracking.

The police had been able to trace the Vauxhall's number plate and had called my parents to find out if it had been stolen.

I realise now that my mum and dad were phoning up to find out if their only daughter was – just possibly – missing or dead. I think, perhaps, under the circumstances, their only daughter could have been a little more sympathetic.

'You're sure you're alright?' asked my dad, again and again.

Eventually, I convinced him that I was. Then I had to convince my mum as well.

'Who was driving the car, then?' she asked.

'Neal,' I said.

'But wasn't he the boy you were teaching to drive?'

'Yes, Mum.'

'So he couldn't even really drive? Oh, that's terrible.'

How could I ever explain?

I heard a loud knock on the front door.

'I'll have to go, Mum. The police are here.'

We all wanted to go and have a look at the car, but the police wouldn't let us. First of all we had to answer their questions.

There were two of them. They interviewed us, one at a time, in the front room: Lang, then Jack, then me. The two they weren't interviewing waited in the kitchen, smoking and not talking.

By the time Jack asked me to go through, they had discovered Neal's real name. Perhaps Lang told them.

They had me sit down on the sofa, but remained standing themselves.

What was my name? Where was my usual place of residence? How long had I resided in Brighton? What was the nature of my relationship with Matthew? How had Matthew seemed to me on the last occasion I saw him? Had he said anything that indicated depression or mental imbalance? Did I know of anywhere he might have left a note? Could I think of any reason he might have had for wanting to commit suicide? What was the nature of my relationship with Jack? Really? Did I think that *that* might have contributed to Matthew's actions? Did I consider that kind of behaviour as *normal*? What did I think my parents would think of that kind of behaviour? What was the nature of Matthew's relationship with Jack? Would I care to *enlarge* on that? Did I think that *that* might have contributed to Matthew's actions? What was the nature of my relationship with Lang?

And so on.

I didn't know what Jack had told them, but I'm sure I told them a lot more.

After they were finished with me, they called Jack and then Lang back in.

At about nine, another couple of policemen turned up. They joined the rest of us in the kitchen for a cup of tea.

'Are either of you the owner of a black cat?' one of them asked.

'Neal has a black cat,' I said. 'She's called Koko.'

'We've taken her back to the station,' said the second policeman.

'She's evidence,' said the first.

'She shat in the car on the way.'

I started laughing.

'Oh, you liked that, didn't you?'

'Fuck, did it stink.'

'We found her in a basket inside the car.'

'The basket also contained some writings that made reference to suicide. These were Matthew's, were they?'

'No,' I said. 'I don't know. Not all of them. Some of them were probably Otto's. Otto Lang.'

'*Otto?*' said one of the original two policemen, then turned to me. 'What was the nature of your relationship with Otto?'

And so the questioning began again.

Eventually, they read my statement back to me and asked if I'd sign it. Everything I'd said had been translated into policespeak.

If I hadn't known what had *really* happened, I'd have been shocked by what I heard.

But there's so much more to it than that, I wanted to say. *You don't understand. Just listen, won't you?*

There was no point in objecting – they had made up their minds that I was a complete pervert and that Matthew and Jack and Lang were, as well – so I signed, silently.

Lang was in the kitchen, washing up the cups and saucers when I came out.

We had to wait another half an hour before they finished with Jack. I smoked a few of Lang's Gauloises and looked at the light coming in through the window.

We didn't speak about what we thought might have happened. Talking to the police had killed all desire to communicate. We both knew how the whole thing would appear to other people, if they heard about it.

Surely the papers wouldn't be interested, I thought.

I'd felt so aggressed during the questioning that I'd almost asked to speak to a woman police officer – but I don't think that it would have helped at all. At least the men made me laugh a couple of times; a woman, I think, would just have made me cry.

Lang went to call a taxi when he'd shown the four policemen out.

Jack sat next to me at the kitchen table, looking really wrecked.

The loudest sound in the room was the electric trundle of the fridge.

I think he was angry with me for not lying to them – for not covering up what had been going on. But, of course, it would have been hypocritical of him to admit there was anything to be ashamed of. We had just been practising *yabyum*, after all. One of his most basic beliefs.

The police hadn't mentioned anything about hipness to me, though they had asked whether Matthew was *like Jack*.

I remembered what a hard time I'd given Jack over what he was trying to do. I thought back to that scene we'd had in the street, after the reading. It wasn't hard to imagine what the police would have had to say about the pure Beatnik existence.

'Here in five minutes,' said Lang.

I went upstairs and put my jacket on.

o

By the time we got to Beachy Head, the police had completed their examination of the abandoned Vauxhall. There it stood, just as Lang had said, right on the very edge of the clifftop. The front wheels were no more than six inches away from a two-hundred-foot vertical drop. When I looked down at the stony beach, I thought I was going to puke. I imagined the car, burnt out by the explosion, lying below on the beach, upside down on its smashed-in roof, what was left of Neal hanging within it. Even if he hadn't come here to kill himself, he had certainly risked his life getting this close to the edge – which didn't suggest he was in a particularly healthy state of mind. I was glad his parents weren't going to see this particular sight.

We were asked to move further off: a police pick-up truck was about to tow the Vauxhall back from the clifftop.

Lang explained who we were.

A policeman came over and spoke to us.

The manager of the pub next to the Beachy Head car park had discovered the car around six a.m.

We watched as another policeman bravely reached through the Vauxhall's open door and took the handbrake off.

The car probably only moved an inch towards the drop, as the rope took up the slack – but it was enough: I gulped back a yell.

Jack and Lang put their arms round me.

'Fuck off!' I said to Lang, who stepped back.

The pick-up pulled the Vauxhall away towards the car park.

The brave policeman ran after it, laughing with relief, and pushed the driver's door shut.

The policeman answering our questions decided the best way to stop me getting hysterical was to carry on talking.

He'd been the first to get there, after the call was put in. When he arrived, he said, the keys were in the Vauxhall's ignition, but all the doors were locked. He could see the travel basket, but wasn't sure if anything was inside it. He radioed for some more officers to come along and help search the beach. He quickly examined the surrounding area.

I was calmer now. I looked out over the sea.

In a way, I would have felt better if the weather had been worse – if the sun hadn't been bright, if the sky had been full of grey clouds, if the sea hadn't looked so healthy. Beachy Head couldn't help but be scary and windswept, but the rest of the world didn't have to seem like it was on holiday. Even the police were in shirt-sleeves. I felt like telling them to put their jackets back on. Couldn't they see they were dealing with death?

The policeman walked off and left us alone.

For the first time that day, I started crying fully.

I was to cry many more times over the coming months, but this time was probably the worst. It felt like I had never cried before – that my body was having to teach me how. It felt as if I was being kicked and punched by something trapped inside me – a hyperactive child. I couldn't see and my nose felt snotty. Lang loaned me a handkerchief. It was grey and dirty. Jack still had his arms around me.

I broke away from him and strode along the clifftop. When I saw they weren't following me, I sat down on the grass.

Further up the coast, back towards Brighton, back into the past, I could see more golden-white cliffs. They looked like what you leave behind when you bite through a choc-ice – only nothing was at all chocolatey. All the colours I could see were at their purest: grass-green, cliff-white, sky-and-sea blue.

The drive to Beachy Head had been along lazily turning, smoothly surfaced roads. The streets were lined with retirement bungalows and nursing homes. This was where people came to die, whether they were young or not.

After I had been sitting alone for a while, I began to think I was being self-indulgent.

I walked back over to Jack and Lang.

'He isn't dead,' said Jack.

'Where is he, then?' I asked.

'I don't know. But I'm sure he's okay.'

'Jack's probably right,' said Lang. 'I'm hopeful.'

'Why did he leave the car behind?' I said.

'It's a good sign,' said Lang.

'I'm sure he's not dead,' said Jack.

'It's all my fault,' I said. 'I'm sorry.'

Part Three

I

We flew in to JFK airport.

It was July 1996.

As we carried our suitcases out of the terminal, I saw my first yellow New York cab.

The Carey Bus would take us all the way to the Port Authority Bus Terminal.

As we drove over an overpass in Queens, I saw my first New York skyscraper.

Jack was concentrating on the book in his lap, just as he had for most of the journey – train, underground, 747. He was reading *On the Road*. Again.

(I'd spent the flight gazing out the window, thinking how from thirty thousand feet the sea looks like pale blue cellulite.)

'At least look at the Empire State Building,' I said. 'It's *there*.'

'Why?' he asked. 'Is King Kong taking a piss?'

This whole trip was already feeling decidedly shaky.

As we came out of the tunnel and onto Manhattan, I saw my first New York mad person – pushing a shopping trolley with a full-length mirror on top of it.

I had phoned ahead from England to book us into the Chelsea Hotel – as hip as they come.

The spine of my *Let's Go* was already covered in splits.

In a couple of days, we had arranged to go to a driveaway agency on West 35th. This would give me time to get over my jet lag. The agency would give us a car for delivery to San Francisco. We then had ten days in which to cross the country.

'New York,' I said, staring out at it, still feeling this wasn't the real thing but the opening sequence of some cop show.

Jack had said he didn't intend to stay in New York any longer than was necessary. We would set off, whether I liked it or not, as soon as we got the car.

The bus pulled up in the terminal.

We got out and waited for our suitcases. We took a yellow cab to the Chelsea Hotel, though we could probably have walked.

The cab driver had his radio playing loudly – some ethnic station. South American.

I gave him a huge tip.

The Chelsea Hotel. 222 West 23rd Street, New York, NY 10011.

Even Jack took some notice of its famous black-balconied exterior.

We'd made it.

2

The police had given Jack and me a lift back from Brighton. Not particularly out of kindness: they were going to Bedford anyway, for the purpose of interviewing Neal's mother and father.

Jack and me sat in the back seat, feeling like we should be wearing handcuffs.

The two policemen up front occasionally shouted a question back to us, but otherwise there was no conversation.

It was the day after Neal had disappeared.

Around lunchtime, the panda car dropped me off on Alameda Walk.

'See you,' I said to Jack, but he didn't reply.

My parents had been looking out for me all morning. I was only halfway up the path when they came through the front door.

Mum hugged me and Dad thanked the policeman who'd been carrying my suitcase.

I wasn't able to say anything. I was so glad that the police car drawing up outside their house had *me* in it. Neal's parents weren't going to be so lucky. All the police car would bring *them* was a typewriter, a trombone and a suitcase full of clothes – some of them very un-Neal.

The policeman said *Goodbye*.

My dad carried my suitcase inside.

Over tea, I told my parents what had happened and what was happening: Neal was officially a missing person – the first one I had ever known.

I went upstairs to my room. Somehow, because Neal had disappeared, I'd expected it to go back to how it was before.

There were some things I hadn't told my parents:

How Koko was staying on in Brighton to live with Lang.

(Neal's mother had said on the phone that she couldn't bear to see Koko without Neal. If Koko stayed with Lang, it was just possible that Neal might turn up one day to collect her.)

How the police believed that 'Bohemian and immoral living' had had a great deal to do with Neal's disappearance.

(But I could see the fascination in their faces.)

How we had made the third page of the *Brighton Argus*, no picture.

During the weeks that followed, my parents let me completely veg out at home. They had seen that I needed some quiet time. (If anything, Quiet and Time were their specialist subjects.) No pressure was put on me to find a job – or even to leave the house. When we got the Vauxhall back, I did the shopping for them at the Flitwick Tesco. That was as far from home as I went. But even this made me feel anxious. And driving the Vauxhall on my own for the first time was a big step. I wasn't really capable of action or thought, however minimal. Instead, I watched a very scary amount of daytime TV and a truly terrifying number of weepie videos. I followed every soap in terrestrial existence. After abandoning *The Second Sex* halfway through, I started to reread my Virginia Andrews collection. I put on weight without even noticing. (Mum was happy about this: I helped her make cakes, and didn't try to skimp on the butter and sugar.) Jack's doctrine of unhipness had left a residue of guilt in me that I made up for by bingeing on the forbidden. Anything really trashy and up-to-date seeming, anything stuffed with e-numbers and preservatives, I was *there*. The worst thing was that I *still* was governed by the laws of unhipness, only in reverse. I didn't want to allow myself anything that pre-dated 1966. The newer, the better – as far as I was concerned. Disco music always made me cry, so I avoided that. But chart songs were great. I lived for Radio 1, *Top of the Pops*, *The Chart Show* and the Top 40. Even more unhip than this was the Internet. I spent hours browsing the weirdest wonderful-lest websites I could find. Dad set me up with my own e-mail address and I made several depthless pan-global friendships.

Eventually, with a little persuasion from my dad, I applied to Mander College – and, with a little persuasion from my dad, Mander College accepted me. By June, if I managed to make it through, I was going to be a qualified secretary – oh joy.

At the time, all these things were just stuff I was doing. Only later was I able to see that they were all attempts to get as far away from Jack's world as I could get. Irrelevance was what I wanted: things that he would have disapproved of, if he'd heard. Everything I did was a form of communi-cation with him.

I still love you, they were saying, *I still love you, you bastard*.

I did have his home number (he'd given me it in the police car), but didn't use it.

The police had continued to make inquiries into Neal's disappearance, but had made very little progress.

A young man had been seen close to Beachy Head, hitchhiking, at about the same time. He was said to have been heading into Eastbourne, away from Brighton.

After that, nothing.

No one had seen him in Eastbourne. No one had seen him getting a lift. He had just vanished.

The likeliest scenario, according to the police, was that he was sleeping rough. He might be in London or another large city. He might even still be in Brighton. If this was the case, they said, he might return home when winter arrived.

But he didn't.

And there was no letter, no card, no phone call.

I met up with Neal's mother a couple of times. We had tea in the Tavistock Café on Tavistock Street.

She said she was totally convinced that Neal – as she kept on calling him – was alive.

'He would never kill himself,' she said. 'He had too much hope. And besides, the I-Ching says so.'

But she chain-smoked and her hair had gone all frizzy.

One time, she suggested we go to the Polish Orthodox Church on St Cuthberts and light a candle for him.

'But Neal wasn't a Catholic,' I said, being no use whatsoever.

This was the first time I'd had a grown-up depending on me for emotional support. It felt wrong.

When I asked how Neal's father was doing, she didn't reply.

Lang didn't contact me for a long time.

He was embarrassed and ashamed, or so I chose to believe.

When he did get in touch, it was by postcard. This was around Christmas.

He wrote to ask whether I minded him writing a proper letter, about something to do with Neal.

The note I sent in reply made it clear that, if it really *was* to do with Neal, I would be happy to hear from him. But that, if it was to do with me or him or an *us* that didn't exist, I wouldn't reply or read anything else he might write.

Lang's letter, when it did arrive, was mostly about Koko. He was very worried about her – she was becoming very thin and had developed a compulsive self-grooming disorder. She had licked most of the hair off the backs of her legs. Lang was writing to suggest that she might be better off with Neal's parents, or with me.

I wrote back, telling Lang about Rufus. No way could Koko live with us and our psycho-dog.

As for Neal's parents, I wrote, I couldn't say – he'd have to write and ask them directly. But, as far as I knew, Neal's mother still thought it would be too distressing to have Koko around.

My secretarial course was okay.

I learnt to type properly. I acquired shorthand. I pretended to understand spreadsheets.

Some of the other girls in my class became sort-of friends. We'd go out to Chaplin's ('Bedford's Premiere Fun Pub') on Friday nights and bitch about men in general while lusting after this or that exceptional individual – usually one of the bar staff.

I even saw Claire again.

She tried to get me to go to another party. I said, *Thank you but no.* She didn't understand why, and I didn't explain.

My exams were to finish in June. It was now February.

I had only seen Jack once in all those months and had been trying hard not to think of him.

The one time I saw him, he was walking along the embankment. I was crossing over the bridge, on my way back from a shorthand class. It was only when I got home that I realised I knew the girl who had been with him – Jane, from the reading. Jane, who had stood so close. Jane, who had been writing the great Stewartby novel.

I hadn't recognised her at first because she had dyed her hair jet-black.

Didn't this make her look a bit like me? I wondered. Could Jack be looking for me in other girls? Had he, perhaps, persuaded her to have it done?

These were the sort of questions that I spent far too long thinking about. I'd hoped I'd been getting over him. But seeing him with Jane brought all my old possessiveness back.

What made it worse was that I'd *had* him, and been happy having him, but then – when Neal disappeared and left us really alone – I had pushed him away. When he phoned up, a week or so after we got back from Brighton, I told him not to call again.

Disentangling my love for Jack from my guilt about Neal seemed impossible: they were the same, and always had been. While pursuing Jack, I'd been lying to Neal, leading him on, betraying him – right from the start. This had affected me so deeply that I was no longer sure if I could trust my own emotions. They seemed to have lost some kind of innocence – an innocence I didn't even know they had, and would have laughed at the idea of, before it was gone.

Being in love was meant to make you into a better, nicer person. At least, that's what I'd always thought. (Perhaps I'd been reading the wrong books.) Love wasn't meant to cause the sort of havoc with other people's lives that mine for Jack had.

In March, Lang sent another card.

Koko, he said, had stopped eating a couple of weeks before – and had died the previous night.

He had already arranged to have her cremated.

Yours sincerely,
Harold Lang.

A pencilled PS added:

Please phone Emily.

It took me several minutes to work out that Emily had to be Neal's mother.

When I phoned, she insisted that we meet up in Bedford – there was something that we had to discuss. Urgently.

We went to Poppins, just round the corner from Alfonse.

I'd never been inside before – put off by the orange plastic façade.

'Why here?' I asked.

Neal's mother gestured round the room.

'Notice anything?'

I didn't.

'There's an ashtray on every table.'

And so, sitting on the spongy red seats, over cooling coffees, in between puffs, she disclosed her revelation.

'The I-Ching told me: you and Jack must take Koko to America.'

'Why?'

'Because of Neal.'

'Why because of Neal?'

'Koko and Neal were so close – don't you understand? In many ways, Koko *was* Neal. If you take Koko to America, you will be laying her spirit to rest – and, if you do that, I'm sure Neal's spirit will be eased, as well. He'll be able to come home. He will cease wandering.'

Neal's mother was wearing a huge peony-covered dress and her wrists were clacking with wooden bangles.

'Lang agrees,' she said, as if this would help persuade me.

'What about Jack?'

I was very curious.

'I'm meeting him this afternoon. I'm sure he'll say yes. He's always wanted to go to America, but could never afford it. This time, though, we're paying for it.'

'*You'll* pay?'

'Lang and I.'

'But it's a complete waste of money.'

'Not if it brings Neal back.'

'Because the I-Ching told you?'

She started to explain, but it was all patchouli-scented nonsense.

When we parted, I was still very anti.

'Let me know what Jack says first.'

'I'd like to be able to tell Jack you've agreed.'

'Well, I haven't.'

'I'm sure you will,' she said.

The phone call came through that evening.

Jack had agreed straight away.

He was ready to set off next week, tomorrow, now.

I'd spent the afternoon thinking about whether I should go or not.

Undeniably, I was still in love with Jack. And, when Neal's

mother made her suggestion, my immediate reaction had been to think about spending all that time with him – away from Bedford – away from Jane.

The supposed reason for the trip – the laying of Koko's spirit to rest, the mystical return of Neal – seemed to me both hippyish and sentimental.

None of Neal's mother's actual arguments convinced me.

In the end, it was the way she had grasped my hand as we said goodbye that made up my mind.

Excessive as her manner was, I could sense that her pain over Neal was the deepest thing she had ever felt. However much I might love Jack, it was nothing to her love for her son. I began to see that this trip might be my only way of doing something for her.

I was worried by the idea of seeing Jack again. But six months of hiding from him hadn't done any good. Perhaps this *was* the only way.

'Okay,' I said. 'I'll go –'

'I knew you would,' said Neal's mother.

' – *after* I finish my exams.'

'But Koko is in torment.'

And you are as well, I thought. *But I'm not dropping out for anyone – man, beast or ghost.*

'I'll go in July,' I said.

3

In June, Jack and I got together to discuss things.

Lang had written to both of us, making suggestions for our trip.

Alfonse seemed the obvious place. We met in the street outside – shaking hands, not kissing.

I had thought Alfonse would be neutral territory, but the girls behind the counter knew Jack's name, his usual order, where he always sat. Having to say I wanted a cappuccino, upstairs, immediately put me at a disadvantage.

We should have met up in Ampthill, I realised. *I should have made him come to me.*

We went upstairs – Jack going first.

Though I hated to admit it, he was looking really good. He'd lost weight from his face. When he took his dark glasses off, his eyes looked greener and brighter. There was something more edgy, more alert about him.

Was this the effect his guilt had had on him? Mine had just slowed me down and made me fatter.

In the weeks before the meeting, I'd been going swimming regularly. I hoped I was getting back to normal.

Jack made the whole physical thing worse by stirring three heaped teaspoonfuls of sugar into his coffee.

'How have you been?' I asked.

'Cool,' he said, and left it at that.

'But you miss Neal?'

Jack gazed out the window, as if Neal might be flying by outside.

'I'm sure Neal is cool, as well,' he said. 'I'm sure Neal is doing his own thing, following his own path.'

'Doesn't it worry you he might be homeless?'

'He may be bumming around, yeah.'

I took a sip of cappuccino and burnt the roof of my mouth. This only made me angrier.

'Are you *sure* you want to go to America with me?' I asked.

'Yes,' Jack said. 'Are you?'

'Lang thinks we should drive across from New York to San Francisco.'

'Hitting the road.'

'But *I'd* be the one doing all the driving.'

'We'll take it easy. Koko's in no hurry. The cat can wait.'

'I think we should consider flying across.'

'The car would be cooler,' said Jack. 'It would be cool to spend all that time with you. I've missed seeing you, you know.'

He reached for my hand, but I pulled it back.

'Have you been seeing anyone else?'

If he lies, I won't go.

He looked at me – and I knew that he could see *exactly* what I was thinking. I felt incredibly see-through, and stupid because of it.

'Yes,' he said. 'I've been hanging out with Jane, the chick from the library.'

'Really?' I said.

'Is that a problem?'

This was the kind of moment that had made me start smoking.

I reached into my bag, pulled out my cigarettes and my lighter.

Jack would have to wait as I went through my routine – the little taps, licks, pinches I'd learnt from watching other smokers, including him.

The first drag filled my lungs – the hit rushing up my spine and shooting into my brain like a thermometer of bliss.

Slowly, I let the smoke seep out through my nostrils.

I stroked my lips with my little finger. Took a second pull.

By now, I was sure, Jack had the most unbearable erection.

'No,' I said. 'I'm cool.'

Driving the usual way home, I thought – as per usual – about Jack.

Even though he hadn't mentioned unhipness, I could tell he was still living by its rules. He didn't even have to speak for me to be sure of that – it was in the way he stood, the way he moved his hands, the way his cigarette smoke curled.

In one way, I was glad: *this was the Jack I knew and knew how to deal with*; but in another way it made me very sad: *hadn't he learnt anything from what happened to Neal?*

By about halfway, I'd almost decided to phone Lang and tell him I wasn't going. But I knew the only way for me to finish this whole thing was to go to America.

There were also realities that Jack needed to face up to – and it looked as if no one else was prepared to make him.

We spoke a couple of times on the phone but didn't see each other before the day of the flight.

4

A week before we were due to leave, I drove down to Brighton to collect Koko's ashes. Lots of the things that I saw on the journey reminded me of Neal. Another summer was on the way. It was all very Englandy again.

'May I ask you to come in for a cup of coffee?' said Lang, as we stood leaning against the railings outside his house.

We had been talking for five minutes. He had been telling me about the police's latest non-result.

No new information had emerged for several months. The police were saying that it was all a matter of patience. They were sorry, but their resources were very limited.

And all the time that he'd been speaking, I'd been assessing him: *What is he like? How safe am I? Will he try anything?*

'Or I could just fetch the urns out to you.'

'No,' I said. 'Coffee would be fine.'

True to form, Lang had managed to find two identical urns. They stood side-by-side on the kitchen table – smooth, very small, heavy, verdigris.

'One for Jack and one for me,' I said, sitting down. 'Do you think we'll still be on speaking terms by the end of it?'

'No, it's not one for each of you. It's one for the East Coast and one for the West. One, if you like, for the Brooklyn Bridge; one for the Golden Gate, perhaps.'

'This is all getting a bit symbolic, isn't it?'

'It's a journey,' said Lang. 'Therefore it's symbolic.'

He fussed around for a while with the percolator. Then with his back to me he said: 'I apologise for – I think you know what I apologise for.'

'Sexually harassing me?'

'Yes, if you want to call it that.'

'I do.'

'There is an explanation –'

'You don't have to give one.'

'It was jealousy. To see you and Jack and Neal – so young, so together. It made me feel very jealous and old and useless. I wanted to be one of you. I wanted to be one *among* you. I am very sorry for what I did.'

'If it won't happen again, we won't mention it again.'

It was strange to be sitting in Lang's kitchen. Over the months since Neal disappeared, I had dreamt repeatedly of several places: Neal's bedroom, the Vauxhall, Bedford Park, the beach, the pier, Lang's guest room. But, I realised, I had never dreamt about this kitchen – which was strange because it was where most of our waking time together had been spent.

'How did you think I was going to react?' I asked. 'With joy?'

Lang looked very surprised. I was in control, and he knew it.

'That wasn't really what I was thinking about.'

'So what *I* wanted didn't have anything to do with it?'

'No, it wasn't that,' he said. 'It was more like trying to join in. I've said I'm sorry. I don't think I've done anything quite so vulgar for a long time.'

'I hope not.'

He put a cup of black coffee on the table in front of me. A jug of milk was there already.

He sat down.

'I still haven't forgiven myself for letting Neal go off like he did.'

'You couldn't stop him,' I said. 'It wasn't your fault.'

'Do you blame yourself, then?'

I had hoped we weren't going to talk about this — guilt was my weakest point. I don't think Lang was consciously trying to take advantage of this; he was just curious.

'It was my fault,' I said. 'It was more my fault than anyone else's.'

'That's the thing,' Lang replied, looking excited. 'I think we all feel that way — Jack, me and you. None of us wants to admit the others had anything to do with it. And, even more, we don't really want to admit that it was Neal himself who ultimately made the choice.'

'No, I forced him into it.'

'Don't you think it's curious that none of us can allow ourselves to think *we* weren't the most important thing to Neal? You have your own reasons. Jack, I think, feels he could have been a better friend to him.'

'He hasn't said anything to me.'

'I'm sure you will talk about it, in America. That's what your journey's for, after all.'

'Our journey is to do with *this*,' I said, putting my finger on top of one of the urns. 'These.'

'You haven't asked me what I think my guilt was.'

'No, I haven't.'

'Aren't you interested?'

I looked round the kitchen, trying to spot any changes Lang had made. I couldn't see any.

'Not particularly. I think, if I wanted to, I could guess. It doesn't seem that difficult.'

'Probably not,' he said. 'So what do you think it was?'

'You were the last to speak to him that night before he went off. You had a conversation out in the car. I expect you think there's something you could have said to stop him.'

'What do you think we talked about in the car?'

'Well, it wasn't suicide.'

'It wasn't.'

'But maybe it was Otto.'

'I mentioned him, a couple of times. Neal had finished reading the journals.'

'Have you read them?'

'Only afterwards. The police returned them. Neal and Otto were similar in a lot of ways. Otto was a lot more like Neal than Jack.'

'I don't think Jack would like to hear you say that.'

'Otto didn't really like Jack all that much. He mentioned him to me in a letter. He said that he was too disciplish, too clingy.'

'Really?' This was interesting. I could use this.

'I didn't tell Jack or Neal about the letters. Otto wrote to me quite often. He liked Neal, when he met him. After that, he doesn't mention him much. I think Neal gave him some of his poetry to read.'

'Didn't Neal start writing *after* he met Otto?'

'Surely not. No.'

'I wonder what Otto would have thought of being turned into such a cult figure.'

'He'd have found it very amusing – and embarrassing. He didn't like too much attention. I think that's why he didn't like Jack.'

'So, what did you talk about, mostly, in the car?'

'We talked about you and we talked about Jack.'

This brought me up. I took a sip of coffee.

'Are you going to tell me what he said?' I asked.

'No,' said Lang. 'I don't think I am. That would be wrong.'

'But it's alright to tell me what you have so far.'

'I'm not sure, but I think it is.'

'Is that meant to make me feel *less* guilty?'

'I said we talked about you *and* Jack.'

'But not *you* – he didn't talk about *you*.'

'I was the one he was talking *to*.'

The light came in from the garden, weakly.

'What are you playing at?'

'Ask Jack, when you get to America. Ask him why he feels guilty about Neal.'

'Grow up,' I said. 'It's bad enough Jack still pretending that the sixties never ended, but you're a grown man. All this play-acting is so adolescent. Why do you have to hide in a time warp? I'm sure Neal wouldn't have had so many problems if he could have just been himself.'

'I *am* just being myself – as is Jack – as are you – as was Neal. We all are. I don't think we are capable of doing anything else. We don't have any excuses. What we are guilty of is not inauthenticity. We, at least, avoided that. If anything, we have been too authentic. You took yourselves too seriously as the Provincials. That was my fault. I shouldn't have encouraged you.'

'Say goodbye to Koko,' I said. 'I'm taking her to her spiritual home.'

'I have already said goodbye, Mary. You forget – I was with her when she died.'

Our room at the Chelsea Hotel had a balcony. I can't recall too much more about it. There were going to be hotel and motel rooms the whole way along – and they were mostly indistinguishable. Now and again, there would be a room with a particularly gross painting above the bed (*Sunset with Buffaloes and Wagon Train*) or something else particularly gross underneath it (yes, a used tampon). From time to time we would get a bargain (free matches and paper slippers!) or be ripped off (doors that wouldn't lock, windows that wouldn't open; dust, fleas, roaches). But as this was our very first room, I might be expected to remember it more exactly than the others. I'm pretty certain that the window looked out towards some dark-bricked façades zigzagged over with fire escapes. That sounds like New York, doesn't it? There was a TV, I'm sure of that – because Jack wouldn't allow me to turn it on. I think it stood on a dark brown chest of drawers opposite the foot of the bed.

The bed was a double. This had caused a bit of an argument on the sidewalk outside the hotel. We were trying to decide whether we were married or not.

On the advice of *Let's Go*, I'd decided to wear a wedding band – it reduced the chances of street hassle, they said.

The double room was reserved in my name, but we could always try getting two singles.

'I don't mind either way,' said Jack.

'It's for the money,' I said.

'We can afford separate rooms the whole way across, if that's what you want.'

'The money is for us to *use*, not to *spend*.'

'They don't care if we're married or not,' Jack said, gesturing at the Chelsea Hotel's plaque-surrounded doorway.

'No, but they will in Iowa, so we may as well decide now.'

Jack dropped his cigarette onto the sidewalk and screwed it out with his heel.

'Mary,' he said. 'Will you marry me?'

'Fine,' I said, pulling off one of my two rings and pushing it into his palm.

'Does that mean *yes*?'

'I'm not having sex with you.'

I picked up my mum's honeymoon suitcase.

'Hey,' he said, 'when did marriage ever have anything to do with sex?'

We checked in as Mr and Mrs, even though my credit card said Ms.

They didn't care.

Once we got into the room, Jack refused to go out.

His reasons were the usual; his arguments hadn't changed.

'But we're in America,' I said.

'*So*,' he replied.

For an awful moment, I thought that he was going to keep me forcefully imprisoned in the room.

(I'm not sure how I'd have reacted to that.)

'You don't expect me just to stay in here?'

'It's your scene,' he said.

As it was, he let me come and go as I pleased – only

hitting me with resentful looks whenever I was anywhere near the door.

I don't know what he did while I was out. I thought maybe he'd been meditating. However, when I asked him, he said he hadn't done anything like that since Neal disappeared. 'The Zen period is over,' he explained. (It was like me with superstitions: I'd given them up completely – they hadn't done any good, had they?) Jack brought a small pile of books with him, but had time to read them at least ten times. (Perhaps, like Neal, he was learning them by heart.) He also had writing materials, though he can't have found much to write about.

What he was playing at, I have no idea. I think now that maybe he was just lying on the bed, petrified by the sheer *volume* of America: jingling, blasting, knocking, scraping; horn beeps, brake squeaks, gear shifts; shouting, swearing; sirens, whistles, alarms, footsteps; the subsonic vibration of the subway (at least I hoped it was the subway).

Even if I *had* stayed in with him, one of us would have had to go out and get food.

But this wasn't going to happen.

Both days we were there, I headed off on my own to be a terrified tourist.

I walked everywhere I went: up 5th Avenue, across 42nd Street, through Central Park, back down Broadway. I got lost in Chinatown. I ate pretzels and drank coffee in Washington Square. I found lots of second-hand bookshops with signed photos of famous authors (some of them Jack's gods) on the walls.

I couldn't believe how small Manhattan was.

At the end of my first day, I went up to the observation deck of the World Trade Center and watched the sun going down behind the Statue of Liberty.

Finally, I could believe I was *really* there.

When I got back to the hotel room, I expected Jack to be at least a little bit curious. But he didn't ask me a single question about what I'd done all day. His self-control – for surely he must have been dying to know – was almost superhuman. He took the brown paper bag of hip groceries I'd bought for us, pulled out the pack of Lucky Strikes and didn't even say *Thank you*. For myself, I had nothing like his restraint. After half an hour's tongue-biting, I splurged the whole thing out.

He gave no sign of interest or even attention. He just lay there on the bed, staring up at the fly-blown ceiling.

If I asked *Are you listening*? he would grunt and maybe twitch a little.

An argument was bound to come – and it only took until the evening of the second day.

It had been gallery day for me – two Guggenheims and two Whitneys. My head was full of lazy white spirals and huge white cubes, African and Conceptual Art. Jack, as far as I could tell, hadn't moved since I left him that morning.

'Aren't you even curious about what it's like?' I began, sitting down and easing off my shoes.

'What?' he asked.

'America. New York. Anything outside this fucking room.'

'No,' he said. 'I'm not even curious about this room.'

'Then what are you here for?'

'You,' he said.

This jammed the brakes on.

'Then why don't you speak to me?'

'I'm waiting.'

'You're *waiting*.'

'For the right moment.'

'Which will be?'

'When we blow New York. When we hit the road.'

'We'll go tomorrow,' I said. 'Like we planned.'

'Cool,' said Jack.

I almost slapped him.

To calm myself down, I took a shower.

There was lichen growing on the wall up above where the tiles finished – that, I remember quite clearly.

Jack came in while I was washing my hair.

He hadn't seen me naked since Brighton: the night before, I'd slept in a long T-shirt and knickers.

Definitely no sex.

'I'll be okay once we're on the road.'

'You better be,' I said. 'And you'll have to go out tomorrow. We have to get rid of half of Koko before we pick up the car.'

The two urns had been sitting on top of the TV ever since we arrived. It somehow seemed wrong to leave them packed inside my suitcase. The TV was turned into something of an altar by their presence.

6

We took a cab to the Brooklyn Bridge and walked halfway out across its much-described span. (To me it looked like the ruler-and-pencil drawings I used to do during a double Maths period.)

It was a crispish morning, a little hazy. Our suitcases were waiting for us behind the check-in counter of the hotel. I had already phoned ahead (again) to check that our car would be ready for collection. There was nothing left for us to do in New York except dispose of Koko.

But there was a problem: Brooklyn Bridge had no edge. Instead, there was a sort of raised boardwalk with three lanes of traffic going by on either side. Through the narrow gaps between the boardwalk planks I could see the water glittering dully. These gaps seemed to be our only option.

We stood there for a minute or so, cars thrumming the bridge as they sped by. Jack had been holding the urn in one hand, like a can of soda, throughout the journey.

I'd been worried that our cab driver might notice the urn and start a conversation. But, if he said anything, it was in Russian.

There was a fresh breeze blowing, and I wanted to avoid getting Koko's ashes blown farcically back all over us.

Jack was looking at me the way he had since we went through check-in at Heathrow – like *I* was in charge, like he could leave *everything* up to me, like I would make *all* the decisions.

'What?' I said.

'We could always climb out along that.' Jack indicated one of the many narrow iron beams that caged over the three-lane roadway.

'Are you mad?'

If we'd made it to the end, we'd have been able to drop Koko's ashes straight down into the water. If we hadn't made it, we'd have been run over by a dozen cars and caused a major pile-up.

I knelt down.

A class of schoolkids walked past, following their teacher.

'We'll have to drop the ashes through here.'

'Great,' said Jack, but knelt beside me.

'Say something,' I said.

'Why me?'

'You were his best friend.'

'Koko was a she.'

'And she was Neal's cat and you were Neal's best friend.'

'She was just a cat. I never dug her all that much. She was okay, as cats go. But nothing special.'

'God, I hope you don't speak at my funeral.'

'Do you think Lang wants the urns back?'

'He didn't mention it.'

'They'd make cool ashtrays.'

'I think we have to scatter the ashes. That's part of it. According to Neal's mother, anyway. And I don't care what you do with the urns once we're finished. I don't want either of them.'

'You say something,' he said. 'Go on. Say something for the dead cat.'

I wasn't sure if Jack was being serious. He'd been smiling

ever since we got up that morning, and I didn't know why. Did he think the whole trip was for his amusement? But when he said this, I seemed to detect a new sadness in his tone – like he really wished he *could* come up with something adequate to say. I took this as a hopeful sign. Maybe Jack, at long last, was growing up.

I took the urn from Jack's hand – surprised, as always, at how small and heavy it was.

Deep breath.

'What we have here, today, are the mortal remains of Koko the cat, formerly known as Godot the cat. She was the much-beloved pet of Neal. It can safely be said that she went everywhere with him. It can also safely be said that, if she had been able to talk, she could probably have told us where Neal disappeared to and why he disappeared there. Neal used to talk to Koko like a person; and he used to talk about her like a person. She was, he said, *one hep cat*.'

I looked at Jack, but he was squinting down into the grey waters beneath us.

'I remember one day, a very special day, when I went to Bedford Park with Neal.'

What was I doing? I hadn't meant to mention this. Jack had looked up.

'Neal insisted that Koko come with us. She walked in front of us the whole way through the park. She wasn't scared of dogs or of people. She was one brave cat.'

Got out of that pretty well, I thought.

'And now we have come over to America to dispose of Koko's mortal remains in what was, in a way, her spiritual home. Neal told me several times about how Koko used to love to listen to bebop – and in particular to Charlie Parker. Well, here we are in the first city of jazz. Part of you, Koko, will remain here. The other part will travel with us the whole way across America. But the best part of you will always remain with us and with Neal, wherever he is – and that part of you is your memory. You were the most loved and the most intelligent and the coolest cat I ever knew. I hope you don't mind the water too much.'

With that I knelt down and unscrewed the lid off the urn, poured about half the ashes into my palm and then let them drop down through one of the narrow gaps beneath my feet.

I gave the urn to Jack and he did the same.

'Goodbye, Koko,' he said.

So far, I'd managed not to start crying, but something about Jack being so simple in copying what I'd done just set me off.

We walked back off the bridge and caught a cab uptown.

I was still blowing my nose and drying my eyes when we walked into the driveaway office to collect our car.

As we were stowing our little luggage in the driveaway car's huge trunk, I noticed that Jack was setting aside a book: *On the Road*. He also had a crumbly hip-looking map of the States. I knew, from that moment, *exactly* what was coming; and I also knew that *this* time Jack wasn't going to have his way.

We got into the front seats.

'Right,' he said, opening up the book. 'First we head up to the Bear Mountain Bridge.'

'Then what?'

'Then we turn round, come back and take off through the Holland Tunnel towards Pittsburgh.'

He leafed through a couple more pages.

'Yes,' he said, his finger hitting a line. 'The Holland Tunnel.'

For a second or two, I struggled to find the automatic seat-adjust. When I located the controls, I moved myself closer to the pedals. The rear-view mirror needed tilting down and to the left – again automatically. I was calm; I was perfectly calm.

'Mary?' said Jack. 'Are you listening to me?'

'No, I'm ignoring you.'

'But I'm planning our route.'

'*Is* that our route?'

'It is.'

'You think.'

'We *have* to go that way.'

'Astound me, Jack.'

'Because that's the way Sal goes in the book. You see, he wants to hitch to Denver using only one road – one long red line – Route 6. So, he goes north, out of Manhattan, up through Yonkers and Newburgh. He gets as far as the Bear Mountain Bridge. Then he finds that's a stupid way of doing it. There's no one to hitch a ride from. The rain is falling and he's stuck at an abandoned filling station on an empty road. Finally, some people drive him *back* to New-burgh. The guy in the car tells him to go out through the Holland Tunnel and head for Pittsburgh. So, Sal gets a bus back to New York and then takes another bus the whole way to Chicago.'

Having waited for him to finish, I now paused for a moment before replying.

(He was still adorable, even though he infuriated me.)

'In other words, you want us to do something *deliberately* stupid just because – forty years ago – a fictional character did something you want to copy, something that was *equally* stupid but at least wasn't stupid *in advance*?'

'We've got to follow Sal's route across America. That's what we're here for.'

'No, Jack – we are here to deliver an intact automobile and the ashes of a dead cat. If you want to follow in Sal's mythical footsteps, then I suggest you step out of the car and start walking. Otherwise, let the designated driver decide what route we're going to take. Okay? Because she's the one who'll be driving you *every single mile of the way* between here and San Francisco.'

All of this I said very calmly and with a big smile, just to let him know I was fucking serious.

He sat there for a long moment, knocking the spine of *On the Road* back and forth against his knuckles.

I didn't know what I'd do if he got out of the car and walked away. But, somehow, I felt totally sure that he wouldn't.

'What are we waiting for?' he said, finally. 'Let's go.'

I started the engine, checked the mirrors, indicated and pulled out.

We were on the road.

7

Our vehicle – a 1994 Honda Accord Coupe – was almost completely characterless. The interior was beige; the exterior was the metallic equivalent of beige. Everything about it was smooth and inoffensive: the lines, the trim, the steering wheel, the gear changes. In front and back, the wide seats were padded for big suburban buttocks. To begin with, I didn't mind all this – the car felt very *comfortable*. But I soon became frustrated that I couldn't hear the engine or road noise or anything. Before we were too far out of New York, I opened my window so sounds could come in off the streets: horns, engines, shouts, rhythms. Other people, around us, were setting off on their great mythical pan-American journeys – or merely returning from the mall to the suburb. Other people were *really* driving; I was just sitting there trying to guess from which direction the catastrophe was going to arrive. I was starting to panic. The car felt *too* safe. I didn't trust it. It was lying to me. The catastrophe was screaming down towards us, heat-seeking, jet-propelled. What the catastrophe was going to be, I had no idea. But that America had one in store for us, I was absolutely sure.

For the first hundred miles, I was too terrified to take any notice of anything other than the green and white signs, the pale concrete highway, the beige sedans, coupes and station wagons, the chrome supertrucks. In fact, it was only when we'd been going for several days that I felt at all able to look away from the road and towards the trees and distances.

But Jack, on that first day, was as happy and relaxed as I'd ever seen him. He was humming jazz phrases, plunging back and forth through *On the Road*, scatting nonsense words, running his fingers along hundreds of miles of already-crumpled highway.

The only interruption to his bliss came when, after four hours or so, I suggested we try and find a decent station on the radio.

He immediately became upset and defensive.

'Don't blow the whole scene, please,' he said.

And because I'd seen him sitting there in the middle of all his joy, I didn't ask again.

We pulled in to a motel late in the evening. Out front was an illuminated VACANCIES sign with a sunrise or sunset motif – I couldn't tell which. The sky was peach coloured and the cars heading west trailed long blue shadows behind them.

'Mr and Mrs,' said Jack. 'Remember.'

As it turned out, we didn't have to be married here, either.

I clicked my wedding band on the counter-top while signing the register, but the check-in guy didn't take his eyes from the television.

'Over past the palm tree,' he said, pointing to the far corner of the forecourt.

'Thank you,' I said.

'Where you from?' he asked, almost looking at me.

'England,' I said.

'You, too?' he asked Jack.

'Yep,' said Jack.

'Hmm,' said the man, as if this required some thought. 'There's a television in your room.'

'Do you have a room without a television?' asked Jack.

For the first time, the man looked at us both directly.

'What?' he said.

'We don't want a television,' said Jack

'All our rooms have televisions,' the man said.

I parked the car out front.

Jack showered first, then me.

I wasn't too tired or stiff from the driving. The car had power steering and cruise control, so my arms and legs were okay. My eyes were feeling the strain, a little.

We dumped our stuff in the room and set off on foot to find somewhere to eat.

After ten minutes, we hadn't passed anything likely-looking and the streetlights were getting further apart.

We walked back and got the Accord.

For half an hour we drove around, getting hungry and tetchy. All we could see were chains: McDonald's, Burger King, Pizza Hut, Taco Bell. Occasionally there was a low, glamorously neon but dangerous-looking bar. Jack kept saying *No*.

New York had been different, chockful of little-places-round-the-corner where you could get a Danish and coffee. In my two days there I had already discovered the joys of the refill. With my bright-eyed bushy-tailedness, I saw the refill as a symbol of the New World – different from and better than England; generous, excessive, perilous. Two days running I'd gifted myself with caffeine-Parkinson's, extreme hyperness, a sklooshy stomach and a bladder that needed emptying every couple of blocks.

But here, west of Pittsburgh, just short of a town called Bellefonte, we had nothing to choose from but chains.

'We have to eat and we have to eat *somewhere*,' I said to Jack.

'Do you know how long it is since I made one of those gimpy joints?'

'When were McDonald's formed? Aren't they at *all* hip?'

'I was about sixteen years old, for krissakes.'

'And did you enjoy it?'

'I can't remember. Probably. I didn't know any better.'

'Shall we starve or shall we compromise?'

'The big pizza one looked the coolest – or the least uncool.'

We drove the couple of miles back to Pizza Hut.

It was just like any of their franchises in England. It had the usual bare brick walls, the framed corporate posters, the lush corporate pot plants, the brick-coloured floor tiles. The only difference was they expected you to eat the pizza with your fingers.

Jack hid behind his dark glasses and whispered in my ear.

'Do they have cherry pie and ice-cream?' he asked.

Our waitress said *No*.

'What about apple pie?' whispered Jack.

I passed the question on.

No again.

'Can we cut out of here?'

'*Jack.*'

We ordered.

When I got up to go to the restroom, our waitress beckoned me aside.

'Is your friend blind?' she asked.

I looked back at Jack, sitting alone in the wooden booth.

'Yes,' I said. 'And he's not my friend, he's my brother.'

This was the second of my American lies. (The first had

been about Jack and me being married – and I hadn't even had to use that one, yet.)

'Gee,' said our waitress.

Hurriedly, I went to the loo. *What if she delivers our order while I'm in here?* I thought. *Will Jack give me away?* But I got back in plenty of time.

The lie was a good idea – it made the meal much more exciting. If Jack started to reach for the salt, I grabbed it before he could get there, said *Oh, you want the salt?* and placed it in his palm. If I saw the waitress looking over, I pretended to wipe up around his messy plate. Jack didn't seem to notice anything unusual, which made me wonder.

I only told him about the lie once we got into the parking lot outside.

'Why?' he asked. 'What kind of trip is that?'

'Because it doesn't matter,' I said. 'She'll never know. She can't check. I can say what I want –'

'But I don't even look like you at all. Are you okay?'

' – and I can *be* who I want. I'm not responsible for myself any more.'

This thought, which only came to me as I said it, made me feel incredibly light-headed.

I stepped up, pulled Jack's dark glasses off and kissed him, hard.

Let the waitress see – I could care less.

Back at the motel, Jack undressed and jumped into bed while I closed the blinds.

'Come *on*,' he said.

'Wait.'

I switched the bedside lamp on and switched off the overhead light.

253

'I'm waiting,' he said.

'Good.'

'*Impatiently.*'

I went into the bathroom for a quick pee.

All of a sudden, I felt vulnerable.

The only people in the bedroom when I went back in would be Jack and me: Neal wouldn't be with us; Lang wouldn't be watching. But it was more than that – everyone we knew was thousands of miles away, in another country, across an ocean. We were really alone. No one could stop us or watch us or have anything to do with us. Jack could beat me up or murder me – though he wouldn't, I knew. But, in theory, he could.

'Mary?' he said. 'What are you doing?'

Of *course* he wouldn't murder me. He couldn't drive.

When I eventually came to bed, I got in without taking my clothes off – except for my shoes. Jack didn't seem to think this was at all unusual. Gently, he persuaded me out of my jeans, my T-shirt, my bra, my pants.

Cars whizzed and trucks boomed past, only a few yards away from us.

Jack's body lay close by my side. The mattress dipped in the middle, tilting me towards him. We were almost face to face. A single sheet covered us, and I didn't want it to slip. I looked towards the door to make sure no one was standing there.

The fingers of Jack's right hand were toying with my nipples, moving back and forth from one breast to the other. I wanted to look into his eyes, but his eyes were closed. There was a slight smile on his face.

With my free hand, I reached across and took hold of his chin. Then I brought our mouths together.

We had hardly kissed at all, since getting out of the car.

His face was sharp with stubble.

When I kissed him, I did it intensely – to let him know I wanted him, wanted him totally, but that I wanted something else as well.

Without saying a word, I was asking him all the questions I had but was too scared to ask. And all these questions were really just one question: *how can we do this?*

From this one question other questions flew off like sparks: *have you really forgotten? Where is he now? Where is he? Aren't you scared? Isn't this wrong? Are you secretly glad? Did you plan all this? What do you think of me? Am I doing the right thing?*

Jack's answer, if it was an answer, was to move his fingers down over my belly and down between my legs.

I missed Neal – I missed his gentler hands. I wondered if Jack had clipped his nails or if he was going to cut me, like he always used to.

When the first of his fingers went inside of me, it felt okay – it didn't feel like he was doing any major damage.

I reached down anyway and pulled his hand back and up. Lacing my fingers in between his, I started to circle my clitoris.

Just like I knew he would, Jack took over after about fifteen seconds. I didn't mind. It was what I'd wanted.

In a moment, everything changed. My cunt had just gone cherry bomb, but the rest of me felt sub-zero.

This was wrong. I wanted to say Neal's name. I wanted to bring him out of my thoughts and into the room. This whole thing – this journey, but especially this night – this should all be for Neal.

How Jack would have reacted if I *had* called out Neal's

name, I'm not sure. He'd probably have thought I was making some kind of sex-addled mistake.

I couldn't believe he was capable even of looking at me without thinking of Neal.

As Jack kept on, not particularly expertly – sometimes losing me altogether, sometimes bringing me up too fast – I began slowly to thaw out.

Half of me wanted to tell him to stop and half wanted to tell him how to do it better.

Then I remembered lying to the waitress, and how good it had felt not having to be me, and how excited I'd been when I told Jack, and how he hadn't really seen what it meant.

I tried to remember what the waitress looked like, whether she was Jack's type, but I couldn't picture her.

Then, two things happened. First, I started to forget who I was. Not completely, but enough for me to stop thinking about my past, my problems. Second, I heard myself telling myself, in my head, *This is Jack. This is the one you wanted. This is the reason the whole thing started.* And because I wasn't so clear about who I was any more, but could have been just anyone – the waitress, a girl he picked up in a bar, some prostitute, Maggie; and because I knew exactly who he was, and knew his selfishness and all his other faults, but loved him anyway; and because Neal was still there with us, even though he wasn't; because of *all* this, I brought myself up onto my elbows and whispered something in Jack's ear, something I'd never said to anyone before: 'Just fuck me.'

8

The second day, we drove on from Bellefonte, staying on Interstate 80, aiming towards Chicago. We undershot by a long way and finished up in Sylvania, Ohio.

Looking over the map, shortly before we set off, Jack had noticed a town called Bedford about seventy-five miles to the south of us.

'We could go there,' he said. 'See what it's like.'

'We don't have time, Jack,' I said, breaking the peace we'd established the night before. 'The car has to be delivered from New York to San Francisco in ten days. We have to average over three hundred miles a day. More, if we want any time with the car in California. Yesterday we only managed two hundred. We can't afford detours.'

About fifty miles later, we made up.

It was only on the third day that Jack and I started to get into the distances – or the distances started to get into us. Jack might ask me a question, about whether I wanted to stop for lunch yet or if I remembered some minor detail from *On the Road*, and I might not answer him until another mile or five had gone by, another town had disappeared behind us. And Jack wouldn't be at all anxious while waiting for me to reply. It didn't matter how long I took: there was always another mile in which I could answer, another town where we could stop. Actions and their consequences, just like questions and replies, seemed to drift further and further apart. We were into a different, more languorous rhythm: the rhythm of the rising and falling, curving and tilting road. Billboards went by, the same ones, again and again, until we were almost hypnotised by them. For a hundred miles at a time, the same bumper sticker would get a little ahead of us, then drift back, then start to move ahead again. After a while, we started not to really care about anything – anything except keeping going, keeping moving.

Finally, we made it past Chicago.

Jack got very excited as we started to go through places that Sal had been: Joliet, Davenport, Iowa City, Des Moines, Adel.

He would read long passages out from the book on his lap. 'This is where Sal is riding in a dynamite truck,' he would say, or, 'Sal is driving the middle-aged lady's car down this very stretch of highway.'

Whenever he made a connection between the map, the book and the road, he became very happy.

In between times, he tended to sit staring ahead. I wasn't sure if he was gazing into some mythic West or trying not to get carsick. On a couple of occasions he'd asked me to stop so he could get out and breathe some fresh air. Once, he had the dry heaves and had to lie down in the back seat for an hour before we could carry on. Jack's requests that we stop always came at the worst possible moment: *Pisscall!* he'd shout, just when we'd passed an intersection and had nothing but fences and horizon ahead for fifty miles.

That day saw us leave Ohio, skim the top off Indiana,

traverse Illinois and get halfway across Iowa. We eventually came to rest just past Des Moines. We bought some groceries and checked in at a motel. We'd covered just over a third of the total distance.

I fell asleep before I even took my shoes off. I didn't dream and Jack didn't wake me up until after eleven the next day. We were meant to vacate the room by nine-thirty, but he'd pleaded successfully with the owner. Although I tried hard, I couldn't think of anything he'd done before that was so unobtrusively kind.

Over breakfast in a diner a couple of miles down the road, we decided that Cheyenne was the obvious place to aim for. That would get Nebraska out of the way, at least. We weren't expecting Nebraska to be particularly fun.

It was a mad day's journey, over six hundred miles, but I was becoming obsessed with covering huge distances. I'd started to break the speed limit whenever I could.

So far, after the excitement of New York, I'd found the rest of America pretty boring. The towns were often indistinguishable: low-roofed commercial buildings, white wooden churches, huge playing fields, dusty filling stations. It sometimes seemed to me that every house in America was trying to be a mini White House. They all had front porches flanked by white columns; they all had Old Glory on a flagpole in the yard. I almost expected to see miniature reporters and camera crews standing out front, filing reports on the latest Something-gate.

Of course, there were huge stretches of nothing. But these spaces depressed me even more. The further west of the Mississippi we got, the dryer and less Englandy it became. Trees thinned out, then disappeared. There were more crops, fewer houses.

I started to think we were filming some ultra-low-budget

movie with a stationary car but a wind-around painted back-drop – the same silo, farm, cloud, McDonald's went by again and again and again and again. Sometimes, I'd stop at one of the McDonald's and go to the loo – but this was even more *déjà-vuish*: on the inside, the restaurants were indistinguishable from each other. In England, McDonald's mostly have to fit themselves in to odd-shaped buildings on the high street – so they acquire some character almost by default. Here, they seemed to have been injection-moulded, spray-painted and then just dumped wherever there was a free space by the roadside. The only thing that ever changed, from one to the next, were the accents of the employees. But though their way of talking might be different, giving each restaurant *some* personality, their sullen, glazed expressions when salting the French fries, and their Happy Team Member smiles (ow!) when trapped behind the till, were as universally unvarying as the tills and French fries themselves.

Jack, of course, preferred to use the facilities of the filling stations and truckstops where we stopped for gas and cigarettes.

We hardly spoke to anyone but each other the whole way across – and the further we went, the more comfortable we became with not talking at all.

Now and again, Jack would start to sulk when I suggested we turn the radio on. Once every couple of hundred miles, Jack would suggest some stupid detour and I would shout at him for a bit. But generally, we got on much better than I'd expected.

By the time we stopped on the outskirts of Cheyenne, it was very late in the evening of the fourth day.

I was completely mad. I'd driven over six hundred miles and was all for keeping going.

From here on, things started to go a lot worse, then a lot better, then a lot, lot worse.

We'd been heading for trouble from the moment we got on the plane to America. And not just *any* trouble – this *particular* trouble.

If I had been a little more careful about checking my route against Jack's, I could have seen it coming: I'm not sure if I could have avoided it, but I might have made it pass a little more smoothly.

On the evening of my Mad Day, we picnicked in our motel room. Neither of us mentioned where we should aim to reach by the following evening, though this was one of our usual topics of conversation. Jack, I think, was holding back.

9

We had just got in the car and were settling ourselves for the fifth day, when he said it – a single word.

'Denver.'

I looked over at him.

We were heading west. Denver was one hundred miles due south. If we went to Denver we'd have to drive a two-hundred-mile round-trip just to get back to where we were now.

'Salt Lake City, Jack,' I said, in control, in *control*.

'Sal hitches along Route 6. Sal gets out at Cheyenne. Sal goes down to Denver. Sal catches a bus to San Francisco. The bus comes back through Cheyenne.'

'Are you Sal? Am I Sal?' Losing it.

'Sal stays in Denver. It's a very important place to him. Dean Moriarty's father is there, on Larimer Street – and a bunch of other crazy cats: Dean Moriarty himself, Carlo Marx, Chad King, Tim Gray –'

'Hey!' Losing it completely.

' – Roland Major, Ray Rawlins.'

'Did we follow that stupid detour in New York?'

'This is different. That was Sal's stupid mistake. But Denver is what Sal has been thinking of all the weary way from New York. Denver is where he's been headed for all along.'

'And *we're* heading for San Francisco.'

'So is Sal.'

'We have six days left.'

'Plenty of time. We can afford a day hanging out in Denver.'

'With all the crazy cats who died twenty years ago.'

'From Denver, Sal takes a bus straight to San Francisco. No detours, no hitchhiking.'

'Have you *ever* hitchhiked anywhere?' I was shouting, now.

What made me *most* angry was that Jack was right – we did have a day to spare, at least: my Mad Day had gained us that. Salt Lake City to San Francisco could be done in a couple of reasonably sane days. But every atom of my body was for heading west, west, west – and as fast as possible. I was secretly hoping to arrive on the coast two whole days early.

Jack didn't answer for a moment.

'Have you ever hitchhiked?' I pressed.

He opened the door and got out of the car.

We were still in our parking space out front of our low-roofed motel room. I had driven straight into it the night before, so I sat facing carpet-pattern curtains and the car's reflections in the window.

Jack went to the trunk, opened it and got his suitcase out.

'Now is *not* a good time to start,' I shouted back to him.

'See you in San Francisco.'

'Get in, Jack.'

'I'll be at the YMCA in four days.'

'San Francisco has *four* YMCAs.' This may even have been true, but I didn't know for sure.

'The one nearest the bridge.'

'The Golden Gate Bridge or the Bay Bridge?'

He stared at me, deadpan. The suitcase in his hand was enough.

'Get in, Jack.'

'I'm going with Sal.'

'Get in the car!'

The man in the room next to ours had come to the door in his boxers.

I felt like my next line was *What you looking at, buddy?* But I didn't say it. Instead, I jumped out of the car.

'Where are you going?' asked Jack, putting his suitcase down on the asphalt.

I didn't reply. I was doing some serious stomping around.

'I'm not leaving Sal here,' he said.

'When did you finally go mad? I mean, get relevant, Jack.'

'Denver,' he repeated.

'I'm going for a walk,' I said. 'Stay here with the car.'

What was I doing? Here we were, in a motel forecourt in Cheyenne, arguing, with an audience, about our route, about literature.

For a moment or two, I had definitely felt as if I was in a movie – not a very well-scripted or edited one; one of those ones where the sound-boom keeps dipping in at the top of the picture.

All we'd needed to really complete the scene were a couple of handguns. I'm sure our next-door neighbour would have enjoyed a Mexican standoff before breakfast.

There was nowhere to walk – not even a sidewalk or a grass verge. The motel was one of about eight, all in a line. Jack stood there, watching me; I had to get out of his sight.

There was a gap of about five feet between the side wall of the last motel room and a row of bushes next to the highway. I went through it, crossing over a patch of weeds, broken glass, litter and stones. Luckily, the bushes joined up with a wall at the front of the neighbouring motel: I wouldn't have to climb over or through anything. Instead, I turned left and walked along between the two rows of motel room

264

windows. Most of the curtains were drawn and most of the rooms were empty, except for one which had a single suitcase on the bed. It was in the other motel, not ours. I stopped to gaze at the suitcase, brown, ordinary, lying on its side on the bedspread. The yellow light from outside cut the room in diagonal half.

Whose is it? Where are they? What's inside it? The fact that I would never know made me suddenly very depressed.

America was a very big and scary country.

I didn't want to be alone.

Jack was going mad.

I was going mad.

There were still over five hundred miles to go to San Francisco.

I sat down in the dusty shadow of our motel and started to cry.

10

Halfway to Denver, Jack looked across at me and said: 'Why did you change your mind?'

Although I'd been expecting the question ever since I got back in the car, I still didn't have a proper answer. I wanted to have one – I *badly* wanted to have one, because I didn't like to feel that I was behaving like some irrational cow.

'Was it because I said I'd hitchhike?'

There are two roads from Cheyenne to Denver, just as Sal says – and one of them passes closer to the mountains than the other. That was the route Sal chose, so we'd chosen it as well. I could see the mountains to the right, behind Jack's profile. He had been looking out in that direction most of the way down. For once, he could be fairly certain that what he was seeing was what Sal saw.

'For Neal,' I said. 'And because we *do* have some time spare.'

'I thought so,' said Jack.

'What? About Neal?'

'The time.'

'You don't want to talk about Neal, do you?'

Having cried once that day already, I was far less wary than usual of heading into emotional zones.

'There's not that much to say.'

266

'Lang disagrees. He said the reason we were taking this journey was so we could sort things out.'

'When did you talk to him?'

'I went down to pick up the ashes, remember?'

Jack had gone back to looking at the mountains.

'He said that?' he said.

Now we'd started talking about it, I thought we'd better continue.

'Who do *you* think is most responsible for what Neal did?' I asked.

'We don't know what Neal did.'

'He disappeared.'

'No, he cut out for somewhere. I don't know what his intended destination was. It wasn't off of a cliff. That wasn't his scene. He was going after some new kick.'

'Do you blame yourself or do you blame me?'

'Well, Neal's a wild and crazy cat –'

'Tell me!' I shouted.

Jack readjusted his dark glasses. He scratched the back of his neck. He reached onto the dashboard for his cigarettes, then put them back, then picked them up again.

'I blame myself,' he said, very simply.

'Because of the way we behaved?'

Jack tapped a cigarette against his knuckles.

The mountains looked very blue.

'Because I let a chick get in the way.'

'What?'

'Neal should have known that he was the most important thing to me.'

Jack lit his cigarette.

'I really don't think,' he said, 'that you had all that much to do with it.'

'Don't be stupid.'

'It was me and Neal, just us.'

'But Neal was in love with me.'

Jack took a long drag on his cigarette before answering.

'He was in love with me, too.'

'He slept with me.'

This made him think for a moment.

'With me, too,' he said.

'On our own, apart from you.'

'That as well,' he said.

'Without Maggie?'

'Without *her*, without *you*.'

'When?'

'All the time – before Maggie came along – after – that time when you waited in the car, outside Lang's – upstairs, while you thought we were working – all the time.'

'So you were lovers?'

I remembered their kiss on the beach – the kiss I had forced them into. At the time I'd seen it as something unusual. But what if it hadn't been? What if the only unusual thing about it was me being there?

'That's one way of putting it. *We made out* is another.'

'What are you saying?'

'Neal was jealous of you and me together. He didn't want you to interfere between us. I told him that he was the most important one, that you were just a chick, that I loved him – but it didn't seem to be enough. He wanted me to send you away, so we could just be together like before.'

At this point I don't know how I was capable of driving in a straight line.

'But he wanted Maggie to come to Brighton with us. He even wanted her to stay when she came down that time.'

'Neal wanted everyone to be friends – but we were *more*

than friends. He thought if Maggie came down it would even things up, keep things simple.'

'How would it be simple?'

'No one would have to choose. Everyone would be divided three ways, not split in two. You would even sleep with Maggie, on your own. Neal's a very generous cat.'

I was wild, now – asking any question that occurred to me.

'Why didn't you invite Lang to join in when she didn't come?'

'Neal wanted to, but I said *no*. He's a disgusting old man.'

Jack was lying, I was sure of that. At some point, he'd started lying. When, though? Which had been the first lie? Was he lying to me as I'd lied to the waitress? But she was just a stranger to be left behind – none the wiser, none the poorer. I was with him the whole way. I was driving. Why was he lying to me?

'Did you sleep with Otto?'

'No.'

'Did Neal?'

'Maybe.'

'But Neal said he was a virgin, the first time.'

Jack turned to look at me.

'He meant with a woman.'

'What about Maggie?'

'She never let him. She was too uptight about that kind of shit. I think she just wanted to be my "girlfriend". Maggie was one dumb chick.'

I had to ask him.

'Why are you lying?'

'This is the truth.'

'You don't know anything about where Neal went, do

you? You're not lying about that as well? Has he got in touch with you?'

'All I know is what you know. Neal took off in your car. The car was found at Beachy Head. Neal wasn't in the car. Neal hadn't jumped.'

I remembered what Lang had said, about his final conversation with Neal. They had sat in the car, he'd said, talking about me and talking about Jack. But that still didn't prove that Jack wasn't lying. They could have been having the exact opposite conversation to the one Jack was implying: Neal could have been saying how Jack was coming between him and me.

'We should have talked about this before,' I said.

'Heading for Denver was a smart move,' said Jack.

'I don't think I'd have come if I'd have known.'

'You're gonna dig Denver,' said Jack.

There wasn't much in Denver *to* dig, as far as I could see. There was a ring of empty lots and parking lots, derelict and semi-derelict buildings. There were a few businesses: a laundromat, a drug store, a car repair shop. It didn't look as if there were any crazy cats here. But even worse than this desolation was the centre which shone before us: a bunch of medium-tall mirror-glassed skyscrapers – unhip as hell.

We parked the car and walked into the city's vacuous heart.

At the foot of the skyscrapers were wide, pale, pedestrian zones. The sidewalks were litter free and the shopfronts looked like they'd just been washed.

Jack walked through it all, clutching his *On the Road* and trying not to take it in – trying not to realise how hollow his victory had been and how hollow his dream was.

A bit further on, we came to a green bit. Office workers were sitting on lawns, eating things out of brown paper bags. There was a big white-domed building which must have had something to do with state government.

Jack sloped onto one of the lawns and lay down on his back.

It was only now I noticed how scruffy we looked in comparison to all the suited and skirt-suited Denverites. They looked like they'd stepped out of a brochure for high-class office furnishings.

The city itself looked like an architectural drawing come to life. We were the happy citizens who would be depicted as little stick figures, spending our leisure time in the pleasant public spaces and recreation zones.

Jack was groaning, loudly. It was about lunchtime and we hadn't eaten yet.

'Are you hungry?' I asked, sitting down. This was about the first thing I'd said to him since our conversation in the car.

He rolled to and fro on the grass. Every so often, he threw his arms out to the side and let off a particularly loud groan.

'Is this really America?' he asked, and then continued rolling.

Jack put his hands over his dark glasses and rolled a few metres away from me. He stopped and lay flat on his back. His copy of *On the Road* was still in his hand. He played dead for about half a minute, then started twitching.

'Is he okay?' asked a woman sitting nearby.

'He's fine,' I lied. 'He does this when he's happy.'

She didn't look convinced.

Jack rolled all the way back to me, groaning.

'How can anyone *live* here?' he said.

The woman looked over again. I wasn't at all worried if

she heard. In fact, I wanted her to. We'd be gone soon, anyway. It didn't matter. It wasn't really us.

'I don't know,' I said. But then I thought of my friends on the secretarial course and their small ambitions. I *did* know. 'They probably have nice homes to go back to.'

'It's got no *soul*.'

I looked around.

The lawns were pristine, the buildings sparkled, the sky was icy blue, the people were young and healthy.

'You're right,' I said.

'I don't even want to go to Larimer Street. I'll just be disappointed.'

'You seem to have been noticing rather a lot, recently.'

'I've been looking for Sal, but he's not here.'

'We could explore a bit more.'

'No, this is it, Mary. This is all there is.'

He turned onto his front and pushed his forehead against the grass. *On the Road* fell out of his grasp. He pulled his hands up to cover his face.

'Are you sure he's alright?' asked the woman.

'Please don't interfere with his treatment programme,' I said. 'He only gets days out like this every so often.'

That shut her up.

I was finding it very difficult to be angry with Jack. He was the only person in the country I knew and the only one in about two thousand miles that I'd fancied. Whether we liked it or not, we were in this together.

He started laughing, then looked out peekaboo-style between his hands.

'Hey,' he whispered, 'let's go shoplifting.'

I I

First, we decided to have lunch.

We walked back between the skyscrapers and found a deli-style café with a few tables outside. It was about one-thirty, so most of the office workers had already eaten.

We sat down and a girl came out and took our orders. She was about sixteen. When she asked, I told her we were *from Portugal*. When she asked *Where's that?* I said, *Canada*. She went back inside without comment.

Jack leaned over and whispered: 'We're not going to pay for this.'

'Of course not,' I said.

Something crazy had come over both of us. We hated America for disappointing us so badly and were out for whatever revenge we could accomplish.

The girl brought us a couple of triple-decker sandwiches and cream sodas. She took the check off her round silver tray and placed it under the sugar shaker.

We took our time.

As we ate, I looked out for cops. I hadn't seen any the whole time we were in Denver, but I still didn't want to take chances.

The streets became even emptier as the late-lunchers went back to their workspaces and terminals.

'Ready?' said Jack, who had been keeping an eye on the waitress.

'Yes,' I said, checking once again for cops.

Jack stood up, still looking into the deli. I tried not to make a scrapy noise as I pushed back my aluminium chair. Jack walked past me, heading towards the corner of the block. My heart was banging so loudly inside me that I thought I was going to be sick and snot up and shit myself and die, all at the same time.

'Okay,' said Jack.

We walked away – not too slowly, not too fast.

For about five paces, we were okay. Then Jack sped up a little, then I did, then he did, then I did – and by the time we reached the corner, we were racing each other.

I looked back quickly but didn't see the waitress.

'Is she after us?' Jack asked.

'No,' I said.

Jack opened his hand. He was holding the sugar shaker.

We slowed to an out-of-breath faster-than-usual walk. The only other people running, that day in Denver, were joggers.

We didn't want to be suspicious, but of course we were. Compared to the people around us we appeared dark, scruffy, fizzing with discontent, foreign. Anyone who looked at us could see that we didn't work for a corporation. In this city of lawyers, we were obviously criminals.

So, we realised, we had to be a little bit careful. We gave ourselves an hour's shoplifting before we left.

By the time we got back to the car, I had acquired a swag bag full of goodies: some postcards of mountains, a pack of tissues, plenty of chocolate, a tin of anchovies, some bright red lipstick, two pairs of silk panties and a book about diabetes. Jack had been more daring and more discerning. When he sat down in the back seat and unloaded his pockets, including one on the inside of his jacket that I'd never seen before, he had two Denver Broncos baseball caps, some blank cassettes, a bottle of hair conditioner, a pair of black silk stockings, a fluorescent marker pen, a pack of cards, some Oreos, a copy of *USA Today*, a ball of green wool, a giant avocado and a book of Larson cartoons.

We drove out of Denver as if we had conquered it.

I didn't even have to ask, Jack put the radio on of his own free will. He had surprisingly little trouble tuning it in, for someone supposedly unfamiliar with all modern technology. After fuzzing over a couple of country and some religious stations, he hit pop and stopped dead. The bass boomed from behind the back seats. I didn't know the song – a woman was singing it in a waily, insincere voice. It was perfect.

The music kept thumping us forward all the way back up to Cheyenne.

Here, we turned left, zooming into the West again – back onto I-80, already miles and miles away from our crimes and our victims.

We stopped at a diner for a second lunch, burgers followed by Belgian waffles. There was no way we could eat anything more, so soon after the triple-deckers. Instead, we just sat there, laughing at how stupidly huge the portions were – then ran off without paying.

(This was the first time in our trip that Jack hadn't ordered apple pie and ice-cream for afters.)

Life had suddenly simplified. Jack seemed to have had some sort of Denver epiphany. All the self-imposed rules he'd lived by for so long had suddenly gone. He no longer cared about unhipness.

For a couple of miles, in the afternoon, he held his copy of *On the Road* out the window as I drove along.

'Should I drop it?' he said.

'You might regret it.'

'Never.'

'Give it to someone,' I said. 'We should give all of this stuff away.'

'Not *all* of it, most of it – otherwise we won't really have stolen anything.'

The next time we stopped for gas, I left the sugar shaker on the counter – hidden by the till, where the assistant couldn't see it.

When I got outside, Jack was giving the baseball caps away to a couple driving a mobile home.

'I told them we were eccentric Irish millionaires,' he said, as I pulled onto the freeway again.

'What did they say?'

'They got really excited and asked had I been to County Cork?'

'Really?'

'I said I was the Count of County Cork.'

He turned the radio back on. We were giggling like idiots.

'We're not good people!' I shouted.

'We're bad people!'

'We steal!'

'We tell lies!'

'We leave without paying!'

'We don't love America!'

'Oh, we're terrible,' I said, trying to calm down.

'We commit un-American activities!'

'We're Bonnie and Clyde.'

Jack leaned out the passenger window and shouted: 'I am a communist! I love Stalin! I am Karl Marx's biggest fan! I am Lenin's fire engine! I am Che Guevara's motorbike! I am Fidel Castro's beard!'

And I leant out of my window and shouted: 'I'm a fucking whore! I'm just a fucking English whore! You want your cock sucked, you fucking fuckers? I'll suck it for fucking free!'

I pulled the car over to the side of the road and started to kiss Jack.

Between kisses, I said: 'Did you hear what I said?'

'No,' he said. Lying, I think.

'Good,' I said, and reached down and unzipped his fly.

He looked so shocked!

I took out my chewing gum and stuck it on top of the steering wheel.

'Watch out for cops,' I said, my head moving down into his lap.

We checked into a motel just past Sinclair at five in the afternoon. We weren't even halfway from Cheyenne to Salt Lake City, but I didn't give a shit.

Jack gave our names as Mr and Mrs Cork from Denver. He also requested that the porn channels be put through to our cable TV.

We'd stolen a load of junk food in a convenience store on our way through Laramie. The chocolate ice-cream was completely melted, so we dripped it over each other in the shower.

'It's a shame we don't have any drugs,' said Jack, as he moulded a semi-solid bit onto my nipple.

'We could always try sniffing Koko,' I suggested. 'Ow!'

'Maybe we'll get some in Salt Lake City,' he said.

'It's a Mormon town,' I said. 'There's not even alcohol allowed.'

Jack faked a heart attack on the bathroom floor.

'Jack!' I squealed.

After we'd washed the chocolate out of each other's hair, we got into bed and watched the Playboy Channel.

We started out laughing at all the women and trying to guess which of their bits were false; but that got boring, so pretty soon we ended up trying to guess which bits were real.

The programmes weren't very sexy, but we got turned on anyway – more by the idea of watching it together than by the thing itself.

The rest of the evening was a total slob-out.

One a.m. Just before I fell asleep, I said to Jack, 'I enjoyed today.'

The lights were out, but headlights passing over the blinds kept the room a muzzy slow-motion yellow.

'So did I.'

'Before today, I just felt the whole thing was slipping by without me getting anywhere near it.'

'Yeah.'

'Okay, you're tired. I'll shut up.'

'What?'

'Sleep well.'

12

When I woke up the next day, I'd come down a bit from the initial high – and my period had started.

I had started to worry about being a criminal, about being caught. I didn't want to spend the best years of my life in an American jail, getting raped by tattooed bull-dykes.

But as soon as Jack turned the radio on in the car, I became hyper again.

In his hands Jack held the Gideon Bible. It was the copy that had been in the bedside table of our room. He'd stolen it, but not really. He said that he'd swap it for the one in the next motel room we stayed in – and so on, until we left America.

'But you left a gap to start with,' I said.

'I left *On the Road*.'

We were about two miles from the motel.

'Do you want me to go back?'

'Never! It's only my travel copy. I have three more back in England.'

This surprised me. I mock-gasped.

'In your famous house, where no one can go?'

Jack laughed, more at himself than me.

'I'm a man of mystery.'

'Where *do* you live?'

He laughed again.

'I can't tell you that.'

'But Jane knows.'

'Who told you that?'

'A friend.'

'Uh-huh?'

'Won't you invite me round for tea?'

'Maybe,' he said. 'One day.'

'I think I know what it's like. It's full of books, so you can check all your facts and catch people out.'

'You mean the Library of Ultimate Hipness?'

'So there is one?'

'It's massive. The work of years.'

'You live with your parents, though.'

Jack stopped laughing.

'We're going to California, aren't we?' Jack asked.

'Salt Lake City is in Utah.'

'But we'll be in California the next day.'

'Nevada is pretty big. We might only make Reno.'

'But one day soon, we'll be in California?'

'Without doubt.'

Jack was getting bad-tempered, so I shut up.

We'd already got sick of the Hot 100, so Jack had tuned in to an oldies station. It was very strange to have him there beside me and be listening to Carole King, The Carpenters, Steely Dan, Eric Clapton. They did play one Dylan song, but it was from when he was with the Travelling Wilburys.

The land we were now passing through seemed like one huge cornfield. It fell away, yellowy-green and widescreen, to the bluffs in the blue distance. The road signs were further and further apart. The only buildings were farms, down lanes a couple of miles off the highway. Always, there seemed to be another tall silver grain silo appearing on the horizon. It didn't seem possible that people could survive out here. For the first time I started to really worry about what would happen to us if we broke down. Only the music kept me from having a panic attack.

'My head feels funny. I think I'm going to have a head-ache,' said Jack, as we drove into Rock Springs.

'I've got some Nurofen in my bag.'

'Let's stop at a pharmacy, if we see one.'

I didn't argue.

We came across one pretty soon. I drew up in front of it, parking between two pick-up trucks.

Jack went in on his own, and came out five minutes later carrying a large white paper bag.

'You actually bought something!' I gasped.

Jack smiled and said: 'I'll show you when we stop for lunch.'

We found a restaurant a couple of blocks further along. Jack and I sat in a window seat, keeping an eye on the car. I had a salad. I wasn't feeling very hungry. Jack decided on chicken.

'Go on,' I said. 'What did you get?'

The white paper bag stood between us on the table.

Jack leant into his big shoplifting pocket and pulled out two packs of outrageously blonde hair dye. The featured model looked like she'd stepped right out of the Playboy Channel.

For the first time since we left Sinclair, Jack's face cracked into a proper smile. The headache seemed to have gone – if there had ever been one in the first place.

'They have more fun,' he said.

I started to laugh.

'I want to have fun,' he said.

'You want me to do it for you?' I asked.

'You as well,' he said. 'But not before we get to California.'

'Okay,' I said. 'What's in the bag?'

'Open it.'

It was a bottle of suntan lotion.

We were taking no chances for that evening. It seemed our patriotic duty to get pissed out of our heads while we were staying in Salt Lake City. In Rock Springs, we stocked up on cigarettes and alcohol. God Bless America.

So much had happened in the last twenty-four hours, I couldn't quite believe how much. What I'd been trying very hard not to think about was the argument which had started it off. I knew that, at some point, the subject had to come up again – and it might as well be before we got to San Francisco. There was plenty of recovery time between now and then, I thought. Jack would have to speak to me about the hair-dying. I would be pushing it, but it was worth the risk.

'Is Neal gay?' I asked.

Asking the question felt liked driving into a wall of fog after the miles and miles of wide open spaces.

'He wanted to fuck Maggie, if that's what you mean.'

Jack didn't seem too pissed off. His tone hadn't implied *Shut up*.

'I was thinking more about me.'

I told Jack about what happened when Neal and me had gone to Bedford Park that day. How he'd told me he loved me and how I'd kissed him. I left out the part about him showing me his driving licence – that was private.

'You mentioned that while we were on the bridge. I didn't know what you were talking about. I was thinking, when did they go sneaking around behind my back?'

'Do you mind?'

'Of course I mind.'

'What do you think about Neal? Why did he say he loved me?'

'If he said it, he meant it.'

Here we go. Off the deep end.

'And if you had to choose between me and him, who would *you* choose?'

'Who did I choose, you mean.'

I thought about this for a moment.

'Then why didn't you phone me for six months?'

'You told me not to.'

But I didn't mean it, you stupid idiot!

'You still went out with Jane,' I said.

Jack looked down at his shoes.

'Nobody's perfect,' he said.

This made me laugh.

'She asked me so nicely.'

'Right. You had nothing to do with it.'

'As little as possible, honestly.' He was laughing.

'Don't you want to ask if I saw anyone else?'

'Yes.'

'Well, I didn't.'

All through our journey, we'd been driving at the end of the day towards some amazing sunsets. But the one that evening, over Salt Lake City, was the most gorgeous so far. The sky went from fluorescent white on the horizon to halogen yellow, Belisha orange, light-bulb red and, over our heads, phosphorescent blue. We had the sun-flaps down and our dark glasses on. The vision before us was dangerously beautiful. We could quite easily have crashed.

The lights in the skyscrapers were on, but the sun was still reflecting up off the surface of the lake and down off the clouds.

I remembered watching the sun setting from the World Trade Center – how the streets were already dark while up at the top we had minutes of daylight left.

I didn't like the look of any of the hotels in the city, so we carried on a little further.

We checked in as Mr and Mrs Lang from Ampthill, New Jersey.

Jack and I took it in turns to be first in the shower at the end of each day. In Salt Lake City, I was first. The water jet was strong and scorchy. I showered for a long time, changed my tampon. Jack showered and then we got pissed.

13

In six days we had come over two thousand miles.

The morning's hangover only added to my general feeling of disembodiedness. I'd never before been half so light-headed. Gravity was thinning out. At every step I threatened to float off into the air. The spaces between things and around things were particularly clear. Every object seemed to have a clarity of construction that I hadn't noticed before. Overnight, the earth had turned into the moon. This isn't how my period usually makes me feel at all. (It usually makes me feel like a hot-water bottle full of boiled puke.) The whole experience was very trippy.

I wasn't at all clumsy moving about – I didn't knock things over, like I usually do.

At breakfast, reaching for the salt, I watched my hand plunging through what seemed like infinite space.

By the time I grasped the shaker, I'd forgotten what it was for.

I wasn't sure if Jack was feeling the same way – and I didn't want to ask him in case he thought I was going mental. But he did seem pretty spaced as we got into the car.

We hadn't spoken much since getting up.

Perhaps he was still annoyed that I'd told him the night before that sex would be too grunky; perhaps he was just privately negotiating terms with his hangover.

That day, I probably wasn't the best person to be behind the wheel of a car. Strange things kept happening to my spatial awareness. At one moment, I felt as if we weren't driving forwards but plunging down. All the cars on our side of the highway were falling westwards; while all the cars on the other side, even though they were headed in the opposite direction, which should have been *up*, were also falling. A bit further along and I started to think that the car was upside down, stuck onto the road by some force I didn't understand, but that − if I lost concentration for an instant − the force would fail, causing us to plunge down into the sky beneath us.

When we made our first stop for gas, I bought us some candy bars and a couple of fat Cokes. I'd hoped they would get my blood sugar back to normal, but that didn't seem to be the problem. If anything, I felt more spaced out than ever.

At the next stop, I went into the rest room and dunked my head into a sink full of cold water.

We'd been planning to make the Reno state line by the end of the day − then we could take our time through California.

I felt like a complete wuss, but I knew I couldn't keep going for very much longer.

All we'd done so far was about seventy-five dangerous miles.

'Let me drive,' said Jack, when I told him.

'I really don't feel very well.'

'I've been wanting to have a go the whole way along. I'm sure I'd be okay for a couple of hours.'

'We're stopping at the next place we see. I need to sleep.'

'Why not?'

Speaking was a real effort.

'Because I want to drive the whole way. How would you feel if you'd driven the whole way across America except for just fifteen shitty miles in the middle of nowhere? You'd want to go back and drive them. But you couldn't. They'd be gone for ever. *I'm* driving.'

'Okay,' said Jack. 'We can always drive back to here and start from this exact spot.'

'We'll carry on tomorrow,' I said. 'I need to sleep for a while.'

We found a motel. Jack booked us in and put me to bed. I slept for twenty-four hours straight. I'm not sure what Jack did. I think he watched TV with the sound down low.

When I woke up, there were candy wrappers and fat Coke cans on the bedspread. Jack hadn't been able to get any decent food in.

I was glad he hadn't driven off in the car on his own.

He was still asleep.

We'd lost a day, but as soon as I stood up, I knew the world was back to something like normal. My legs still felt like stilts, but only very short ones.

I ran into the bathroom and was sick. It felt strangely great.

I knew we'd be in Reno by the end of the day.

Nevada, as promised, was big and grey and dull and empty.

There was nothing to look at and nothing to talk about. Nothing we could find on the radio fitted in with the nothing we saw around us – and nothing we could find was strong enough to beat it.

After a hundred miles or so, we realised that there was nothing we could do but wait for the horizon ahead of us to become the road underneath us and for the road underneath us to become the horizon behind us.

'What did you think of me, when you first saw me?' I asked.

'At the poetry reading?'

'No, Neal's party. I must have made a big impression!'

'I was trying very hard not to look at you – in case Maggie saw and got jealous.'

'She didn't get jealous till the reading,' I said.

From this distance, even the idea of Bedford Central Lending Library was ludicrous. Could such a place really exist?

I told Jack about when Maggie had spookily warned me off.

'Sounds a lot like her,' he said.

'You still haven't answered.'

'I liked you, but I didn't think you were my kind.'

Our eyes were flirting like fuck while our mouths played hard to get.

'Which is?'

'Like Maggie – blonde and a bit more obvious, statuesque . . .'

'You mean she had big tits?'

I looked down at my boyish chest.

'Maggie did have huge tits,' Jack said.

'And a huge arse to go with them.'

'Oh, yes,' said Jack, smiling.

'So I was a bit skinny for you?'

'But I've changed my type. My type has changed. You're my type, now.'

'What else?'

Jack looked out the passenger window. A flat muddy landscape scrolled by.

'You didn't wait. You started a fight straight away.'

'That's a good thing?'

'I like scary women.'

'*Women*, not *chicks*.'

Jack looked embarrassed at this. He turned slightly, as if to check there was no one in the back seat.

'Mmm,' he said. 'Women.'

'Do you think of *me* as a woman?' This, I think, was the most important question I'd ever asked Jack.

'Well, you're the designated driver.'

I was spluttering out a reply when he said: 'Yes, okay. Yes. Yes, I do.'

That was enough: I didn't say another word – I didn't want to give him the chance to muck it up.

I wanted to enjoy my little moment of glow.

'Do you miss Bedford?' Jack asked.

It was after lunch. We'd decided it was too risky not to pay: most of the other customers drank beer and drove trucks. Inconspicuous, we were not.

Nevada filled the windscreen again, from the far left to the far right. If I looked in the rear-view mirror, Nevada was there as well – and most of the time it didn't even look back-to-front.

'I don't live in Bedford, I live in Ampthill.'

'Okay, England.'

'I've been thinking quite a lot about my mum and dad. I have to phone them when we arrive.'

'What else?'

'Well, this place makes you miss Planet Earth.'

'I'm missing it.'

'I'd like a decent cup of tea,' I said. 'And some toast and Marmite.'

'You can't believe in this place; it isn't solid enough.'

'Do you shoplift in Bedford?'

'Not much. But there it feels like I might get caught and something might happen to me. Here –' The sentence wasn't one you could complete.

'I know how you feel.'

'Have you shoplifted before?'

'No. Never.'

'We can talk here, though. We can say anything we like. I think we'll forgive each other, whatever we say.'

'Perhaps,' I said, not sure at all about that.

But Jack hadn't quite finished.

Just before he said it, I guessed what he was going to say. *No!* I wanted to shout. *Jack!*

I wished I could freeze-frame him and rewind the conversation, start it again, make it go differently.

But he said it, and he was looking straight at me when he did.

Three fatal words.

'Oh, Jack,' I said, trying not to drive off the road.

This was bad.

'Do *you* love *me*?'

This was awful.

Until he'd said it, I'd thought I had.

Back in England, I'd really resented that I did. There wasn't anyone I wanted *less* to be in love with. I didn't even want to *see* him again. I hated him. Hated, hated, hated. But then, after being with him all this way, talking to him and sleeping with him, I'd started to like him more and love him less.

If only he'd asked me that evening after Denver – I could easily have answered, then.

But I had to answer *now*. There had already been enough of a delay. Jack was probably already interpreting.

I decided to tell the biggest lie of all.

Jack seemed to believe it.

He told me to pull over and we kissed for a while.

This wasn't what was meant to happen. I'd expected us to be not speaking by two days out of New York. What had gone wrong?

14

In the outskirts of Reno that evening, in a cramped motel bathroom, laughing our heads off, we became blondes – Jack first, then me.

I didn't dare think what Mum would say when she found out. (Part of me suspected that Dad would secretly be pleased. He'd always had a soft spot for Betty Grable.)

Jack got peroxide all over his black T-shirt, which he then insisted on wearing.

'Hey,' he said, 'tie-dye, man.'

We stood there, staring at each other in the mirror.

The sink was completely trashed.

We looked so tarty. Jack's hair, starting off dark brown, not black, had gone a couple of shades lighter than mine. I was wearing non-matching bra and panties, which made me look even more of a slut. Jack passed me a cigarette.

'Are we flammable?' he said.

'Highly,' I said, and kissed him.

He took the cigarette off me.

'Do you think I look like Maggie?' I asked, worried.

Jack stood behind me and looked at me over my shoulder.

'Not at all,' he said. 'You look lovely.'

'Are you sure?'

Blondes had always been such easy hate-objects. They said such stupid things. They were so immoral.

But, if that was the case, I'd been a blonde in spirit ever since Denver – if not New York. If not Brighton. In fact, now I thought about it, if not since the moment I first met Jack.

'I still think we should have done our pubes,' Jack said.

'Let's go out,' I said.

Maybe I was still in love with him after all. It was a possibility.

We were walking down a long Reno street. I wasn't sure we'd ever be able to find our way back to the hotel. Jack was holding my hand. We kept giggling when we caught sight of ourselves in store windows. A competition had started over who could say the most completely blonde thing.

'Aren't the streetlamps pretty?' said Jack. Where had that crispy wispy lisp come from?

'Like a lovely line of sparkly stars,' I said.

'Or a necklace of pearls.'

'Streetlamps are so *cool*, aren't they?' I said.

'I really *dig* them.'

'There wouldn't be any light without them.'

'Except in the daytime.'

'Oh, yeah,' I said, all candyflossy. 'I forgot.'

Giggle, giggle. Etcetera.

I kept thinking about us walking along the street to the poetry reading. Although there were only two of us here, people were still looking at us, we were still a gang – and we were still the fucking coolest thing out.

We found a bar, went in and ordered a couple of Buds.

Everything in the place was very familiar from the beer ads we'd been catching on TV: the green pool table, the wall memorabilia, the jukebox music, the rubbernecking rednecks.

None of the booths were free, so we climbed onto a couple of bar stools. This was a bad idea, as we were now facing our reflections in a large mirror.

'Which one's me?' said Jack, pouting.

'I don't know.'

'Toss you for it.'

'Okay.'

'I want the one on the right.'

'Which is right again? I can never remember.'

The waitress brought our beers. She was about thirty, with a lot of corkscrew curls and surprisingly little make-up.

'You two ain't from Reno, right?' she asked.

'No, ma'am,' said Jack.

'So where you from?'

'California,' I said.

She smiled, not sure who the joke was on, or if there was one, or if it was worth giving a fuck about.

'You don't sound like you're from California.'

'Oh, we're not from there originally,' I said.

'We're from New York,' said Jack.

The waitress decided to let this go.

'I like your hair,' she said.

'Thanks,' I said, and gave her a smile.

One of my minor regrets about the trip was that we hadn't met enough Americans. Jack seemed to think this was a good thing – and whenever we did start talking to one, he always tried to put them on. But I found myself liking this woman. There was something sad about her – and she wasn't stupid.

'I'm Mary and this is Jack.'

'Hi, I'm Nancy.'

We shook hands. She took in our rings.

'You here on honeymoon?'

'No,' said Jack. 'This is my assistant. We're scouting locations for a beer commercial.'

'You are?' said Nancy.

Just then a group of four men walked up to the bar and she went over to serve them.

'Why did you tell her our names?' said Jack.

'I didn't want to lie to her.'

'She's just the same as the others. Why not?'

'It's a bad thing to lie,' I said, dropping back into my blonde persona.

'Lying gets you into trouble,' said Jack, joining in.

'I like your hair.'

'Let's go.'

'Why? I'd like to talk to her some more. She has nice nail polish.'

When I looked over, Nancy was leaning across the bar and whispering in the ear of one of the four men. We made eye contact and she pointed us out to him.

He came over.

He was very tall.

'Hi, I'm Len,' he said. 'This is my bar. Nancy says you're thinking of doing some filming in here.'

He was English.

'Well, are you?' he said, when Jack and me didn't reply.

'We're here on honeymoon,' said Jack. 'We were just having a little joke.'

'You're English, right?' said Len.

'Yes,' I said.

Was Len going to have us killed?

'Where from?'

I could smell his cologne.

'Bedford,' said Jack.

'Well,' said Len. 'Enjoy yourselves. The last thing we want is a beer commercial shot in here.'

He went back to the other three men. Nancy was still with them. I saw him lean over and whisper in her ear.

'Jack,' I said. 'Shall we go?'

Nancy was reaching under the bar for something: a gun, perhaps.

We knocked back our beers and started to stand up.

Nancy slammed a bottle of bourbon and two glasses down on the counter.

'From Len,' she said. 'On the house.' She looked extremely pissed off. 'Happy honeymoon.'

She poured us out a couple of double shots, then left with the bottle.

Len raised his beer bottle to us.

'Cheers,' we said.

Jack leaned over and whispered: 'Lying is bad and gets you into trouble.'

We stayed in the bar till one o'clock.

Len left soon after standing us the bourbons. He didn't come over to shake hands, just waved goodbye as he went out. Nancy continued to serve us, reluctantly – working for an English boss obviously had its drawbacks as far as she was concerned.

Jack kept trying to persuade me that we had several hundred dollars to spare from what we'd saved by sleeping the whole way across in one room instead of two. He was trying to decide what we should spend them on. Our conversation was pretty stupid – the parts of it that I can remember. At one point, Jack started saying that he wanted us to get hold of a gun and start holding up gas stations.

'It's the only way to travel,' he kept saying.

As we walked back to the hotel the moon was huge overhead; only a slice off full, I think – and the stars were in different places to usual, places I was having trouble getting used to. The clouds were the black and white mottles that always remind me of firework displays at Ampthill Fire Station. When I was a kid, I used to prefer the clouds to the fireworks.

I told Jack this and he said he felt the same.

Somehow, we found our motel.

15

The car was due to be delivered some time the following day, before six in the afternoon.

Over a bleary breakfast of scrambled eggs and home fries we decided to aim for San Francisco by sundown. That would leave us plenty of time to deal with Koko. We were going to take her either to Big Sur or to the Golden Gate Bridge.

Everything seemed pretty clear. We set off.

Nevada was behind us in a blink.

Actually, despite my opposition to Jack's plan of following in Sal's footsteps, we had been on the same road that he'd taken – Interstate 80, previously Route 6 – for almost the whole journey.

California looked orangey-golden and flowery and futuristic and like some kind of home – especially after the badlands and mediocrelands we'd just come through.

What excited me most was how temporary and whimsical everything looked. After all those po-faced White Houses and folksy farmsteads, California – like New York – was starting to look like America *should* look.

Everything was improvised, without a huge amount of planning. There was no real reason for this building to be over here rather than over there. There was no real reason why it should even be that sort of building rather than another sort. Everything was arbitrary. I liked the effect. This wasn't how places in England were – no, this was irresponsible. It was like driving through a cartoon.

I was glad we'd dyed our hair blonde.

A couple of hours into the drive, we were approaching Sacramento. Up ahead, standing a few yards on from a minor-looking turn-off, was a guy hitchhiking.

I hadn't thought about it before, but – in the whole of our cross-country journey – this was the first hitchhiker we'd seen. There didn't seem to be much cause for debate: I indicated right and started to slow up.

Jack looked over and saw the hitchhiker.

'Keep going,' he said.

'What?'

'Don't stop.'

'Why?'

'He could be anyone.'

'He could be *you*.'

We were coming to a stop about twenty yards on from where the guy had been standing.

He was jogging along towards us, carrying a couple of big soft bags.

I couldn't tell much about him. He was wearing a baseball cap and his face was in shadow. He was in jeans and a T-shirt.

'What if he's got a gun?' said Jack.

'I can't believe this is even a question.'

I turned the radio off.

'We'll just take him to Sacramento.'

'We'll talk about this later,' I said.

I looked in the rear-view mirror, again. The hitcher was about five yards away. He was black. The engine hadn't stopped running.

'You still have time to save us,' said Jack.

I admit, I felt pretty scared.

Was this the catastrophe?

'Go!' shouted Jack.

I put my foot on the accelerator, hard. There was some wheelspin. The hitchhiker dropped his bags and threw his hands up in frustration. I could hear him shouting something.

When I looked over at Jack, he was smiling.

It was several minutes before I felt calm enough to speak.

'I can't believe you made me do that.'

'He might have killed us.'

'Or he might just have needed a lift.'

'I didn't want to take any chances.'

That was that.

I sat behind the wheel, still unable to believe how totally hypocritical Jack was being — and he didn't even seem to care. All that poor guy had been doing was trying to hitch a ride. I wasn't sure how I knew he *wasn't* a murderer — probably the style of his disappointment: he hadn't looked like a man who has been cheated out of torture and bloodshed, more like a guy with very sore feet. But, of course, I hadn't seen that until we'd driven off: I'd seen a black man. This was what really worried me — had Jack not wanted us to stop because the hitchhiker was black? And had that made any difference to how easily I'd given in to Jack? There was that guy, probably still standing by the side of the road with his thumb out, thinking he'd just been taunted by a couple of racists. And there was nothing we could do to prove we weren't — except go back and pick him up, apologise and take him anywhere he wanted to go.

I waited for the next opportunity to turn round, which came after about five miles.

'What are you doing?' asked Jack, who knew.

'We can't just leave him there,' I said.

'Keep going.'

But I drove us off the highway and over the overpass and back onto the opposite lane.

We were heading east. It was a very strange feeling.

Jack tried persuading me to forget it.

'We'll just sneak past. He won't even see us.'

Already, I was looking over the central barrier to see if the guy was still there.

'Why didn't you stop the first time? He's just going to be mad at us. It's much more likely that he'll kill us now.'

'We're going to apologise to him.'

'That'll do a lot of good.'

'Not *all* Americans are serial killers.'

'Only the nice-looking ones.'

'You thought he was nice-looking? Is that why we didn't stop? Or was it because he was black?'

'Was he?' said Jack.

'Don't tell me you didn't notice.'

'Really, I was too scared.'

'Oh, shut up.'

We passed the spot where I thought he'd been.

I didn't see him, but there were lots of trucks that might have been getting in the way.

It was another two miles back before there was anywhere to turn round. But that was pretty good: it could easily have been fifty, if this were Nevada.

I took us back, slowly, in the outside lane.

There was the small intersection.

Another five hundred yards. Another five hundred yards.

'He's not here any more,' said Jack.

'I can see that.'

'Let's get to Sacramento. I'm hungry.'

301

O

Over lunch, I didn't even ask Jack to pass the salt.

He was trying very hard to calm me down – telling me he might have got panicked and done the wrong thing. The guy, he said, was probably okay. Maybe we should have stopped. But I'd been the one driving, he said. It was my foot on the accelerator.

And all the way through lunch, I was just sitting there thinking *You fucking hypocrite!* The hypocrisy of it seemed endless.

This was Jack, his whole way of life supposedly based on Kerouac's writings; Jack, who had three more copies of *On the Road* at home; Jack, who worshipped black culture – jazz musicians, in particular; Jack, who had always said how great America would be, if only he could get there.

But he'd changed. He'd dumped his copy of *On the Road*. He'd dumped his hipster vocabulary. He'd dumped the whole concept of hipness. He'd dumped his reverence for America. And these were all things I'd wanted him to dump and encouraged him to dump, from the first moment I met him. But now it turned out that these were some of the things about him that I really loved: his blindness, which it had taken me such a long time to understand; his consistency, which was often so mad-making; his style, which was out-of-date and contemporary all at the same time; his charisma, which seemed to be wearing off.

I was sliding the sugar shaker from one hand to the other, clearing a fat path through the sugar I'd already spilt on the table.

I felt very stupid.

It seemed as if I would only fall in love with people completely wrong for me – and then that I would only love them for their annoying faults – and so I would constantly be trying to change them – but then, when they did change, becoming closer to what I thought I really wanted, I would find I didn't love them any more.

God, if that was true I was going to be *so* miserable for the entire rest of my life. I made three big circles in the sugar. I felt like the stupidest person in the world.

Jack was still saying things, occasionally.

What he'd just done was much worse than when Neal and I had caught him in the Pleasuredome. There, he'd been betraying a set of false principles; here, he'd betrayed himself – and he had also made *me* betray *myself*. What we'd just done was even worse than the way we'd treated Maggie when she found us in bed together. Then, we'd just been nasty; this time, we'd been cruel and racist and disgusting and unforgivable.

I'll take you to San Francisco, I thought. We'll do what we came to do. We'll lay Koko's spirit to rest. But after that I don't know. I'll have to decide if I can bear to spend any more time with you – or with the person you make me into.

I went to the rest room and had a good kick and a swear.

16

San Francisco cheered me up, though I still wasn't talking to Jack.

I saw the water coming up over the smooth crest of a hill and wanted to shout for joy. I felt triumphant. I'd done something undeniable.

San Francisco had more skyscrapers than I expected.

The sea sequinny-sparkled to our right as we drove over the Golden Gate Bridge.

I was praying that Jack wouldn't say anything crap, but the only words he said were: 'We're here.'

Here, for him, probably meant something different now that he'd given up on hipness. It used to mean the city where it all started – where Allen Ginsberg read 'Howl for Carl Solomon' at the Six Gallery – where Jack Kerouac was in the audience, pissed out of his tiny mind, annoying people by shouting *Go! Go! Go!* – where Neal Cassady, also in the audience, was checking out the chicks – where, afterwards, they all went off and had an orgy.

This – including the orgy – was probably what Jack had been hoping for when he organised his own little reading in Bedford.

But that original reading had started something massive off – the Beatnik craze. Men could write bad poetry and grow beards and play bongos and expect chicks to dig them for it. Chicks could wear black and cut their hair short and wear trousers and sleep with bad bearded bongo-playing poets. And a few years later they could all go off together and become fucking hippies.

(God, was I getting cynical?)

Just the sight of the skyline made Jack's ambitions appear ridiculous.

He wasn't going to start any crazes.

This was San Francisco, California, America. You could make grand gestures here, because here they just might mean something. In Bedford, Bedfordshire, England there was nothing you could do except edge out a little irony.

Neal, perhaps, had tried the grand gesture – but no one knew what his gesture was meant to mean.

The trip would have been completely different with him sitting in the back seat. In fact, there probably wouldn't ever have *been* a trip.

The sun had started to go down and all the buildings in the city were soaked in pinky-orange light. A long line of brightly etched clouds ran along the coastline, forming a sort of mad plume.

I didn't know where I was driving. I was becoming dis-orientated. All the way across there had been one thing to do – head further west. Now all that was left in that direction was the sea, then a few small islands, then Japan and China. But we were heading south, now – which meant Los Angeles, Mexico, Patagonia, Antarctica.

The world seemed to have shrunk, but also to have become in compensation far more intricately detailed – and so my place in it, going by sight alone, didn't appear to have changed. Inside, though, I felt a kind of quadruple vertigo: I was falling in every possible direction at once, into the future and the past.

In North Beach we found a hotel with vacancies that wasn't too expensive, checked in, showered.

The usual routine.

I wanted to be able to speak to Jack as if he were my friend, but I was pretty sure he'd stopped being that back before Sacramento.

Against my will, I still fancied him – even liked him. But I didn't look up to him any more. Only now could I admit to myself how much I once had.

'If you don't mind, I'd like to be on my own for a while.' That seemed the simplest way to say it.

'We're not going out?'

'I'll see you back here,' I said. 'Whenever.'

He didn't try to follow me.

I walked to somewhere with a view of the Golden Gate Bridge and watched the shadows climb it.

My parents were expecting a phone call the moment I arrived, but I was having trouble working out the time difference.

The sun rises in the east, I thought. So I have to count back – no, forwards. It's nine hours' difference, about. They're ahead. Nine hours. I couldn't manage it: I was completely zombified.

In a nice-looking deli, I bought some groceries. The guy behind the counter packed them into the usual brown paper bag. I'd miss those bags when I got back home. I thanked him.

'I'm from England,' I said. 'I've just arrived. My name's Mary.'

I wished I was up to starting a proper conversation.

'Be seeing you,' said the guy, then turned to the next customer.

Comments about the weather, I thought, probably don't go down a bundle in California.

When I got back to the hotel, Jack was sitting on the sidewalk with his brown paper bag beside him.

'You have the room key,' he said.

I really hoped that we hadn't bought *exactly* the same groceries – that would have been too soul-destroying.

'What time is it in England?' I asked.

He checked his watch.

'It's four in the morning.'

I couldn't stay awake another four hours before phoning.

'What time will it be at ten o'clock tomorrow morning?'

We were still out on the street.

'Six in the evening. Can we go in, now?'

'I still hate you,' I said.

Jack took this as a hopeful sign.

Not *one* of our food items was the same. (Unless you count the Cokes – but I got Diet and he got fat.)

No sex, but not a lot of sleep, either.

17

'Mum?'

'Mary! Where are you? Are you alright?'

'I'm in San Francisco.'

'Oh, well done. (It's Mary.)'

'How are you?'

'Your father wants to know if you're alright.'

'I'm fine. How are you?'

My dad came on the line.

'How was the car, Mary?'

'It was fine. No breakdowns.'

I covered the mouthpiece and took a sly drag from my cigarette.

'Are you alright?'

'Dad, I'm fine.' I tried not to cough.

'Here's your mother. She's got some news for you.'

'Mum?'

'Your voice sounds rather strange. Are you sure you're alright?'

'Dad said you've got some news.'

'Oh, yes. Your friend turned up.'

'Who?' I asked. 'Claire?'

'The one with the cat.'

'Neal,' I heard my dad whisper.

308

'Neal!' I shouted, and dropped my cigarette. 'Where? Is he alright? Where's he been?'

'He's got long hair, now. Hang on.'

She must have put her hand over the receiver.

I stamped out the cigarette.

'I'll pass you back to your father. He's got something to say.'

'Mum!'

'It's your friend, Neal,' said my dad. 'He's turned into one of those hippie-types, you know.'

'Was he alright?'

'He had a ring through his nose, can you believe it?'

'But did he look alright?'

'To tell the truth, he was a bit smelly. We invited him in for a cup of tea, anyhow.'

'Where had he been?'

'He'd just come from Bedford. He wanted to know if we'd heard from you. We've got a number to give you.'

He read out Neal's parents' number.

'We said that we were expecting you to call when you arrived in San Francisco, if everything went according to plan. That was about ten days ago.'

'Is he in Bedford?' I asked.

'Here's your mother for you.'

I stamped on the cigarette butt again, even though it was definitely out.

'We didn't say anything about the smell.'

'Is Neal in Bedford, Mum?'

'He smelt like old compost. It was very odd.'

'I've got to go,' I said.

'You'll ring that number, won't you?'

'I will. Goodbye.'

'Are you sure you're alright?'

'I'm great,' I said. 'The weather's lovely.'

As I put the phone down, I heard my mum saying *She says the weather's lovely.*

I'd forgotten to tell them I loved them. They always made me do that.

Jack was sitting at a table, having coffee and toast.

The diner we had silently chosen for breakfast was long and narrow and filled with golden light.

'The bread in California is crap,' he said, as I approached. 'It's full of seeds and stuff.'

I sat down, picked a slice off his plate and took a bite.

'Mmm,' I said. 'You're right.' And then, ever-so-casually: 'Oh, Neal's turned up.'

Jack looked at me, astonished. He hadn't been lying about not knowing.

'What? Here?'

'Don't be silly. He's in Bedford. Let's go and phone.'

Luckily, no one had taken over the booth.

Jack dialled, I called the number out and we both held the receiver. We were close enough to kiss, which had already become a strange idea. Neal's mother answered.

'Hello, Emily,' said Jack. 'It's us.'

'Is Mary there, as well?' she asked.

'I am, yes. Hello.'

'You see?' she said. 'I told you he'd turn up when you took Koko away.'

'Can I speak to him?' asked Jack.

'Oh, he's not here. He's with you.'

'No, he isn't,' said Jack.

'He took the plane a couple of days ago. He's in San Francisco. You still have Koko, don't you? He'll be terribly upset if you haven't. When we phoned up Lang, he told us your schedule.'

'His schedule, really,' I said.

'It's a bit complicated. Neal is going to phone me to get your address.'

'Don't you have his number here?' asked Jack.

'I suppose I do,' she said. 'Perhaps he didn't want me to give it to you. I have his address, as well.'

'Why don't you give it to me?' said Jack.

'Hang on,' I said, into the phone.

'What?' said Jack.

I put my hand over the receiver.

'We don't want to scare him off, do we? If we get his address, we still can't use it. We have to wait for him to come to us.'

Jack looked a bit dubious but passed the idea on to Neal's mother.

'It's getting too complicated for me. But he did turn up, just like the I-Ching said he would. Mary? Are you still there? You didn't believe me, did you? You thought I was just a mad old woman.'

Jack gave her the details of our hotel and took down the details of Neal's. They were within walking distance. We might even have bumped into him the night before.

'When were you expecting Neal to phone?' I asked.

'Oh, very soon. He's phoned twice today already. Don't do anything about Koko. He's very anxious about that.'

'We won't,' I said. 'I promise.'

Neal's mother sounded as if her life had come back to her. I thought of the desperately hopeful woman I'd sat opposite in the Tavistock Café. I wanted to say something to make her remember everything differently – as if I'd been her great support, as if I'd never let her give up hope. But it was Jack, actually, who'd always been convinced that Neal was okay and that he'd come back. I'd been less help (and less astute) than the I-Ching – which made me feel pretty useless and stupid.

'We better get off the phone,' she said. 'He's probably trying to get through now. Oh, I'm so glad he's going to say goodbye to Koko. You will go and wait for him at your address, won't you?'

'We will,' I said.

'Good luck,' she said, and put the phone down.

18

When Neal walked into sight, I was sitting out on the front steps of our hotel.

Jack had just popped back to our room to use the loo. What should I do? Hiding seemed silly. But Jack would want to be there for the reunion, as well. I stood up. He shouldn't have had so many refills or he should have gone at the diner. Neal saw me. His hair was shoulder length, matted into greyish dreads. I jumped down onto the sidewalk. He was wearing Army surplus boots, combat trousers and a home-made vest. I shouted something which wasn't his name. The vest was tie-dye, the trousers had felt-tip squiggles all over them and the boots were painted yellow. Neal smiled to see my reaction. He *did* have a nose ring. We were about five yards apart, now.

'Mary,' he said, very tenderly.

'Neal!' shouted Jack, running out of the hotel and down the stairs.

Neal gave me a big hug.

'When did you bleach your hair?' he asked.

'You're a fucking Crustie,' I said.

'Hello, Jack,' he said, over my shoulder.

'Where the fuck have you been?' Jack asked, putting his arms round both of us.

'Well . . .' said Neal. 'You know.'

He did smell of damp earth, a little. It wasn't unpleasant.

First of all, Neal wanted to see Koko's ashes.

We took him into our hotel room, where they rested in their usual place. He held the urns for a couple of minutes, sitting on the edge of the double bed. Then he came alive and wanted to hear all about New York, Koko's first burial, America, our hair. We tried again and again to get him to tell us something about where he'd been, but he just kept asking questions.

'Are you going to keep Koko?' I asked, when things had calmed down a little.

'Oh, no,' said Neal. 'She's going to finish her journey here.'

'Well,' I said, 'we're meant to deliver our car to the drive-away people by ten tonight. We were going to decide this morning whether to take her to the Golden Gate Bridge or to Big Sur. Jack was saying the Bridge –'

'Big Sur,' said Neal. 'Definitely.'

I expected some resistance from Jack, but none came.

'Let's go,' he said.

We took the coastal road, driving down through Santa Cruz. As before, Jack sat in the front and Neal in the back. The journey took about four hours. Neal was very impressed by how comfortable the Accord's beige seats were. I drove especially carefully. Some of the views were terrifying – huge cartoonish drops down to crashy-mashy waves. I still wasn't sure whether I wanted Neal to be hanging around on clifftops. Jack sat, quietly smoking. As we drove along, Neal began to tell us about everything that had happened – starting with recently.

It seems he had turned up at his parents' house in Bedford exactly ten days before.

We told him that was the very day we'd been saying goodbye to Koko on the Brooklyn Bridge. He didn't seem at all surprised – or even much interested.

'It's the I-Ching,' he said. 'That's what my mum says, anyway.'

After that, he'd gone round to my parents to find out what our plans were.

He'd also phoned Lang a couple of times.

When it seemed likely that he could catch us in San Francisco, he'd decided to fly out. His parents paid. They understood.

'But where have you *been*?' I asked.

'Around.'

For a while he seemed reluctant to say anything more.

I changed the subject but kept it the same.

'Why did you leave the car where you did?'

'I don't know. I mean, I don't know why I left the car. When I took it, I hadn't decided what I was going to do. I knew about Beachy Head, where it was. I'm sorry about stealing your parents' car, by the way. When I got to Beachy Head, I wanted to take the handbrake off and push it off the cliff and into the sea. That seemed the most logical thing to do. But I couldn't forget that it belonged to your parents. It was their car, not mine – however much I wanted to destroy it.'

'Actually, it's my car – they gave it to me. Don't you remember?'

Neal thought about this.

'Would that have made any difference?' I asked.

315

'I don't think so. Maybe.'

'I still don't understand.'

'I was trying to explain it in the car on the way down to Brighton: I wished we could just keep going, keep driving. But there wasn't anywhere to go. England ends too soon. There's just the cliff and the drop and the sea and bam! I thought that if I was by myself I'd be brave enough to go over the edge. It's this whole Kerouac road thing, this America myth stuff. You can't live by it in England. I was only just coming to see that, then. It'll drive you mad. It was driving me mad. It's so destructive. I was up at Beachy Head, sitting in that car, in the middle of the night, crying my eyes out. I kept taking the handbrake off and putting it back on. Just for a second. Daring myself. The car got closer and closer to the edge. But then I stopped. I sat for a long time, thinking. Something very important happened inside me. What it was – I'm not exactly sure what it was. It was about being English, really – it was about turning back, finding a way to live, accepting. I decided to leave the car there. I wasn't sure where I'd go. I knew Koko couldn't come with me. When I got out, I saw where the car was – how close to the edge I'd come. I couldn't believe it. I could easily be dead.'

'We saw,' I said.

'Did you?' said Neal.

'The police let us see it.'

'Oh,' he said. 'The police. Yeah.' This made him smile.

'There's a phone box up there. Why didn't you just phone us?'

'I couldn't explain, you see. It was an argument I'd been following in my head for such a long time. Life's okay if you just spend it all staying still and trying to imagine what moving would be like. But once you start moving, it's very hard to stop. I wasn't brave enough to take the road to its end, I wasn't far enough into the myth – I know that now. Something stopped me a few inches away. Some kind of gravity. I didn't want to go back to you, a failure. I wasn't one of you any more. I didn't know where I could go.'

I was very aware of the sea to our right. We were just north of Santa Cruz.

'I saw the sign with the Samaritans' number on it. I even thought about calling them – I suppose you could say I'd made a failed suicide attempt, almost. But if *you* couldn't understand, they had no chance. It was three or four in the morning. Very dark. I walked back to the main road, heading for Eastbourne. I was crying so much I couldn't really see anything. I thought I could see the lights from Eastbourne pier. When I got to the road, all I knew was to head away from Brighton. A few cars went past but nothing was going the other way. I was hitchhiking, you see.'

I looked over at Jack, just to make sure he'd got this.

'Then this manky old Bedford van came along, heading towards Brighton. Even though I was going in the other direction, they stopped and asked if I was okay. They must have known the road was near Beachy Head. Ruth – she's my girlfriend, now – she says I just collapsed. I didn't lose consciousness or anything, I was just crying and screaming and rolling about in the road. So, they put me in the back of the van. I was completely out of it. Ruth tried her best to calm me down. I lay there, with my head in her lap – falling in love with her. I found out later they were on their way from Eastbourne to Brighton. There was someone they had arranged to pick up in Brighton. They were travelling at night to avoid hassle from the police. When I woke up, we were outside Newbury. The others went off to join the demo, but Ruth stayed with me. They were protesting against the bypass, you know. Climbing trees and stuff. Trying to stop it getting built.'

Jack looked over at me with an expression that went: *What?*

'So that's where you've been?' Jack asked. 'Up a fucking tree?'

'Yes,' said Neal, getting excited. 'Don't you see? They were the answer I was looking for. They have a vision of England. They have a way of living. It's very real.'

'So, you're a road protestor?' I said.

'That's what the media calls us.'

Jack started laughing.

'What's so funny?' I said.

But he just kept laughing.

'I think it's great, Neal.' I looked at him in the rear-view mirror. 'Are you happy?'

'Yes,' he said. 'I am.'

Jack was still chuckling.

'So, you going off had nothing to do with Jack or me?'

'It's not that simple.'

'But it wasn't because you were in love with one of us and were jealous of the other one?'

Jack had shut up.

'No, nothing like that. I thought it would be better to leave you two alone.'

'You don't want to get rid of me and have Jack all to yourself?'

'No way.'

'Well,' I said to Jack, 'you were lying, weren't you?'

'It was just what I thought.'

'The other day, Neal, we were driving along and we saw this hitchhiker and Jack told me not to stop.'

'Hey,' said Jack. 'I *asked* you.'

'And he's thrown out his copy of *On the Road*.'

'Is that right, Jack?' Neal asked.

'I hate America,' said Jack.

'Maybe you've come to the end of the road, as well,' said Neal.

'Yeah, but at least I'm not a fucking hippy.'

'What about you, Mary?' Neal asked.

'I still quite like the road,' I said.

And I did, it was very smooth and curvy and spectacularly exciting. The sea was sparkly, just as it had been that morning at Beachy Head – but now I could enjoy its sparkliness. Neal was back. Neal was safe. Neal was okay.

'You're just like your mother,' said Jack. 'Another fucking hippy.'

'I dig my mum,' said Neal.

'She was very worried about you,' I said. 'You should at least have phoned.'

'I needed to get my shit together, you know. Hey, Mary, do you remember how I told you my mum was so anti-car that she didn't even want me to have *driving lessons*? She's so cool.'

'And Jack's the only one here who can't drive,' I said. 'How ironic.'

At last I had someone to gang up against him with.

'I spoke to Lang a couple of times,' said Neal. 'He sounded okay. Is he, do you think?'

'He blamed himself, as well,' I said. 'He thinks he should have seen it coming, from that last conversation you had with him in the car.'

'But it had nothing to do with him.'

'What did you talk about?'

'Anything, really. I just didn't want to talk about myself.'

'You didn't particularly mention either of us?'

'We talked about you two, yeah. Lang fancied you.'

I told Neal about the pass Lang made at me. This was the first Jack had heard of it, as well.

'Why didn't you say anything?' asked Neal.

'There wasn't an opportunity – not with you going mad all over the place.'

'I'd never have left if I'd have known.'

'Don't worry.'

We drove through Santa Cruz in silence. We all had plenty to think about. I was relieved. Jack, on the other hand, seemed to be sulking. He put the radio on, too loud for anyone to speak.

Through Watsonville and Monterey. We kept going.

The freeway came to an end and we followed a smaller coastal road.

I turned the music down, so we could pay some respect to the views we were getting.

'Do you remember what happens in Kerouac's book?' Neal asked, meaning *Big Sur*.

'Of course,' said Jack.

Whoa, was he in a bad mood.

We were a couple of hundred feet above sea level, huge rocky cliffs tumbling down to our right.

'I don't understand how you could leave Koko behind,' I said.

'Oh, don't,' Neal said. 'I feel so bad about it. She made such a noise as I was walking away. She knew she wouldn't see me again.'

'I'll bet you missed her more than us.'

'I wanted to come and collect her. It was devastating to hear she'd died. All I could think about was getting to see her again.'

I remembered Jack's grudging words on the Brooklyn

Bridge. *Just a cat.* Neal's mother may have been overdoing the psychic-connection business, but Koko and Neal had definitely been soul mates of some kind. Neal had once shown me a photo of himself as a kid, holding Koko in that way kids do – just putting his arms round her tummy and letting her legs dangle down. And the funny thing is, cats don't seem to mind when kids do this to them.

We hadn't mentioned what Neal was going to do after we'd finished with Koko. I couldn't envisage him joining us in bed. But I wasn't sure if I'd ever sleep with Jack again. There were still another two weeks on our plane tickets, though we could always change them. It seemed unlikely he'd want to go back straight away, now that he'd made it out here.

Big Sur was little more than a provisions store and a gas station. We made a pisscall.

There were huge pine trees all around, and the smell of them was incredible.

I went in to pay for the gas.

There were some postcards on sale, but none of Kerouac.

The gas station man looked very bored. I asked him where the best views were and he gave me directions.

I waited for Jack and Neal in the car. They seemed to take longer than necessary. I wondered if, perhaps, they were having a big fistfight in the toilets. Or maybe fucking.

Just as I was about to go over and check, they emerged into the sunlight. They didn't look in any way ruffled. Neal was still carrying Koko's urn.

I drove us back towards San Francisco, back up to Point Sur.

We parked at the roadside and got out.

There was a bit of a walk, through the pine trees, over smooth muddy paths, to the clifftop.

I couldn't find anything to say and neither, it seemed, could the others.

When we got to the clifftop, we stood there for a moment. A brisk breeze was blowing. I wished we could all be happy.

Neal asked if he could be alone for a moment.

As Jack and I walked further along the cliff, I looked back and saw Neal sitting cross-legged. It seemed as if he was going to meditate.

We walked on for a while.

Suddenly, Jack grabbed my arm.

'What have I done that's so wrong? Why aren't you speaking to me any more?'

We were too close to the clifftop for this sort of gesture to be completely safe.

'Come on, Jack. You know exactly what you did and what it meant.'

'But why do you have a problem with that? You always hated what I was. You thought it was all fake.'

'No, I didn't. Let go of me.'

'You thought it was stupid. But you never had to live by it in order to survive. It gave us a way of living. There wasn't anything else. You thought we were just cartoons. We *knew* we were cartoons. It was our way of avoiding pain, you see? Cartoons don't feel pain. Don't think we didn't know what we were doing. No one does anything by accident. Whatever we were was deliberate.'

'Why are you telling me this now?'

'Because, can't you see, I've given it up for you. I had to try really hard –'

'Oh, rubbish.'

'You're what I've got to live by, now. There's nothing else left. Maggie's gone. Neal's gone.'

'Jack, why are you being like this? Just grow up, will you?'

Even though there was only the Pacific Ocean to see us, I was still aware that we were creating a scene.

Finally, he let go of me.

'You're with me and not Neal, alright?'

'I don't know who I'm with.'

'But I love you.'

'Oh, don't get so melodramatic.'

'No?' said Jack. 'No?'

'Calm down,' I said.

'So you don't love me?'

By now, I really had decided.

'No, Jack. I don't think I do.'

'But you said you did.'

'Yes, I did.'

'Fuck you.'

'Can we talk about this later?'

'No!'

I was sure Neal would have heard that.

'We're trying to have a quiet –' I didn't know what to call it – 'a ceremony, here. Can't you wait till that's over?'

Jack stood for a moment, looking at me intensely. Then he started marching back to where Neal was. I tried to calm him down, but he wouldn't listen.

Neal was no longer sitting cross-legged.

He lay, propped up on one elbow. He seemed to be waiting for us to come back. Maybe he had heard.

Jack ran up to him and grabbed the urn.

'Hey,' said Neal.

Jack wound his arm up and hurled the urn as far as he could out towards the sea.

Neal was too stunned even to stand up.

For a moment, Jack was off balance and I thought he was going to fall.

I shot out a hand to grab him.

'The ceremony is over,' he said. 'Bye-bye, cat.'

Far below us, the urn hit the water.

This seemed to bring Neal back. He jumped up and grabbed Jack's neck.

'Why did you do that?' he said.

Jack pointed at me.

'Ask her,' he said.

Neal quickly glanced at me, then looked back at Jack again.

'Why?' he asked.

They were very near the cliff edge. Neal could push Jack off if he wanted.

I'd always thought that Jack would win any physical fight between the two, but obviously I'd been wrong.

'Let's go back to the car,' I said. 'I don't feel very safe here.'

'She likes to feel safe!' shouted Jack.

'I'm going to stay here for a while,' said Neal, letting Jack go.

'I'm going back to the car,' I said.

Jack stood for a moment between us.

Stay with Neal, I thought.

'I'm coming with you,' he said.

'We'll wait for you in the car,' I said.

Neal sat down again on the clifftop.

I walked back to the car, Jack following me.

When we got there he said: 'I'm driving. Give me the keys.'

I had already put them in the door on the driver's side.

'No, Jack,' I said. 'We're not driving anywhere.'

He pushed me onto the ground and held me there as he unlocked the door.

'You can't drive, Jack.'

I lay back, acting calm.

'Jack, stop being so mad.'

The driver's door slammed.

'Come on,' I said.

I heard the central-locking engage.

'Jack?' I said.

He wasn't listening. He was starting the car.

I was surprised how easily and quickly he did this. He must have been watching me, learning.

'Hey,' I said.

I took a step forward and banged on the window.

He didn't look up.

The car went into drive and pulled out onto the road.

I saw the side of Jack's face and his bleached blonde hair as he checked to see nothing was coming.

I banged my fists on the roof.

'Jack,' I shouted.

I don't know if he heard.

The car drove off, accelerating.

There didn't seem to be anything I could do except go back and join Neal.

I walked through the pines, alone this time.

'He'll be alright,' said Neal, when I told him.

'Are you okay?' I asked.

We sat for a while and talked about Jack, hoping he'd come back for us.

It was only when we arrived back in San Francisco, after hitchhiking for over six hours, that we found out what had happened.